T0347393

'A POLITICAL DICTIONARY EXPLAINING THE TRUE MEANING OF WORDS'
BY CHARLES PIGOTT

Considering the fact that Charles Pigott's satirical *A Political Dictionary* (1795) is regularly quoted and referred to in analyses of late eighteenth-century radical culture, it is surprising that until now it has remained unavailable to readers outside of a few specialized research libraries. Until his death on 24 June 1794, Pigott was one of England's most prolific satirists in the decade of revolutionary unrest following the French Revolution, writing a number of pamphlets and plays of which only a small part has survived.

Pigott finished *A Political Dictionary* in prison, where he served a sentence for sedition. He died before his release and the book was published posthumously. The dictionary was a brilliant satire on the 'language of Aristocracy' and combined radical politics with a high entertainment value. Indeed, part of what he wrote was considered so scurrilous that the printer left out certain lines in the printed version.

Modern scholars will find Pigott's work an unrivalled resource for mapping the rhetorical landscape of political debate in the 1790s, and one that yields a unique insight into the sentiments and rhetoric of radical discourse. The text stands as a convenient handbook providing some of the wittiest and most acidic turns on familiar satirical conventions of the time, such as for instance the 'swinish multitude' metaphor and the comparison of King George III to the mad King Nebuchadnezzar. It will be an invaluable aid to students and researchers of the period – both as a highly amusing source of illustrative quotations and as an encyclopaedia over the central sites of ideological struggle at the time.

'A Political Dictionary Explaining the True Meaning of Words' by Charles Pigott

A Facsimile of the 1795 Edition

Edited by

ROBERT RIX
Clare Hall, Cambridge, UK

Routledge
Taylor & Francis Group

LONDON AND NEW YORK

First published 2004 by Ashgate Publishing

Published 2016 by Routledge
2 Park Square, Milton Park, Abingdon, Oxon OX14 4RN
711 Third Avenue, New York, NY 10017, USA

Routledge is an imprint of the Taylor & Francis Group, an informa business

British Library Cataloguing in Publication Data
Pigott, Charles
    A political dictionary explaining the true meaning of words: a facsimile of the 1975 edition
    1. Great Britain – Politics and government – 1760–1820
    I. Title. II. Rix, Robert
    941'.073

Library of Congress Cataloging-in-Publication Data
Pigott, Charles, d. 1794.
    A political dictionary explaining the true meaning of words / by Charles Pigott; edited by Robert Rix.
        p. cm.
    'A facsimile of the 1975 edition'
    Includes bibliographical references (alk. paper).
    1. Great Britain – Politics and government – 1760–1820 – Pamphlets.
    I. Rix, Robert, 1970. II. Title.
    DA5071796.P5 2003
    941.07'3–dc21

                                                                    2003057858

ISBN 9780754636908 (hbk)

Typeset by Bournemouth Colour Press, Parkstone, Poole, Dorset

Contents

v

Acknowledgements

The preparation for a modern edition of Pigott's *A Political Dictionary* with extensive annotations was made possible with a grant from the Carlsberg Foundation to a Visiting Fellowship at Clare Hall, University of Cambridge. I am grateful for the help I have received from Paul Snyder, Emma Buckley, David Worrall and not least Jon Mee. This study would have been poorer without them. Also thanks to you, Line, for your continued support. The work is dedicated to Kai Rix (1912–2002).

Details of all primary sources are quoted in the text. The place of publication is London if not otherwise stated. Full publication details for secondary sources and editions of eighteenth-century material cited in shortened form in the text will be found in the bibliography.

The facsimile of Charles Pigott's *A Political Dictionary Explaining the True Meaning of Words* reproduced in this volume is taken from a volume held by the Bodleian Library, University of Oxford (shelf mark Johnson e.1141) and is reproduced with permission of the Bodleian Library.

Abbreviations

AR   (1781–97) *Annual Register, or a View of History, Politics and Literature*, London: G. Robinson.

BMC   (1949–52) *Political and Personal Satire: Preserved in the Prints and Drawings in the British Museum*, ed. Mary Dorothy George, 11 vols, London: British Museum.

DNB   (1996) *Dictionary of National Biography*, CD-ROM, Oxford University Press.

Grose   (1994) Francis Grose, *The 1811 Dictionary of the Vulgar Tongue: Buckish Slang, University Wit and Pickpocket Eloquence*, London: Senate.

Jordan   (1792–96) *Jordan's Political State of Europe*, 10 vols, London: J. S. Jordan.

OED   (2000) *Oxford English Dictionary*, 3rd edn, on-line version, Oxford University Press.

PH   (1806–20) *The Parliamentary History of England from the Earliest Period to the Year 1803*, ed. William Cobbett, London: T. C. Hansard.

PR   (1775–1813) *Parliamentary Register: or History of the Proceedings and debates of the House of Commons (and House of Lords), containing the most Interesting Speeches, etc.*, 112 vols, London.

State Trials (1809–26) *Complete Collection of State Trials from the Earliest Period ... and continued from the Year 1783 to the Present Time*, ed. T. B. Howell and T. J. Howell, 33 vols, London: Longman.

Editions of Pigott's Works Cited

Pigott, Charles (1791), *Strictures on the New Political Tenets of the Rt. Hon. Edmund Burke illustrated by Analogy between his different Sentiments on the American and French Revolutions; together with Observations on particular parts of his last Letter to a Member of the National Assembly and an Appeal from the Old to the New Whigs*, London: James Ridgway.

—— (1792), *The Jockey Club; or a Sketch of the Manners of the Age, Part the First*, 12th edn, London: H. D. Symonds.

—— (1792), *The Jockey Club; or a Sketch of the Manners of the Age, Part the Second*, 9th edn, London, H. D. Symonds.

—— (1793), *Treachery no Crime, or the System of Courts exemplified in the Life, Character, and Late Desertion of General Dumourier in the Virtue of Implicit Confidence in Kings and Ministers and in the Present Concert of Princes against the French Republic*, London: James Ridgway.

—— (1793), *Persecution: The Case of Charles Pigott*, London: Daniel Isaac Eaton.

—— (1793), *The Jockey Club; or a Sketch of the Manners of the Age, Part the Third*, 4th edn, London, H. D. Symonds.

—— (1794), *The Whig Club; or a Sketch of the Manners of the Age, Part the Third*, printed for the author.

—— (1794), *The Female Jockey Club or a Sketch of the Manners of the Age … with corrections and material additions*, 4th edn, London: Daniel Isaac Eaton.

—— (1794), *New Hoyle; or the General Repository of Games. To which is added, an Epitome of the Statute Laws on Gaming, with the Different Cases of Contested Betts, Bonds, and Other Securities, which have been Legally Argued and Determined*, London: James Ridgway.

Introduction

Charles Pigott was born into a landed Shropshire family. His father, a baronet, was a staunch Jacobite who had entered Parliament for Chetwynd Park just before the Hanoverian accession. Pigott was given the usual advantages in life for a young man of his class, receiving his education at Eton, and later Trinity College at Cambridge.[1] He is known to have immersed himself in the fashionable world of betting and carousing, and became a well-known face with the Jockey Club, the governing body of the horse racing society, who met at Tattersal's on Hyde Park Corner to gamble on the horses they had competing at Newmarket racing course.[2] Unlike other racing events, which were for the general public, Newmarket was an exclusively upper-class affair. The Prince of Wales and his brothers were connected with Newmarket, and to be seen with the coterie here was the very mark of class and distinction.[3]

At Newmarket, Pigott mixed especially with a coterie of young Whig gentlemen who squandered their fortunes on gambling and betting. One prominent Jockey Club member was the Whig leader Charles James Fox, whose addiction to gambling and revelry was notorious. It appears that Pigott and Fox were acquainted, and rumour had it that Fox had helped Pigott by raising a subscription among the members of the Jockey Club to relieve him of his debts.[4] Pigott was certainly known as a seasoned gambler, and he is credited with having edited a translation of Edmond Hoyle's famous guide on how to bet, play cards and be successful at the faro table (published in early 1794 as *New Hoyle; or the General Repository of Games*). When this was advertised in the Whig paper the *Morning Chronicle* in January, it was with a warning not to buy any editions of the book that were not Pigott's.

Pigott took up journalism and wrote occasionally for the *Morning Post*, which had close connections with the racing world at Newmarket.[5] The paper was later to employ notable men of letters, such as Samuel Taylor Coleridge, William Wordsworth, Robert Southey and Charles Lamb, but at the time when Pigott contributed to its columns, it specialized in gossipy 'anecdotes' and slanderous 'personalities' of the rich and famous.[6] The paper appeared, after all, at a period that has been dubbed 'the Age of Scandal', due to increased public appetite for rumour and sensation.[7] Pigott's 'journalistic' experience primed him for his later career as a scandalmonger.

Pigott established himself with a work entitled *The Jockey Club: or, A Sketch of the Manners of the Age*, first published in February 1792. This was a series of vignettes, in the form of character assassinations, of the coterie at Newmarket. Pigott lifted the veil on the moral, sexual and political shortcomings of an aristocracy that included the Prince of Wales and his younger brother, the Duke of York, as well as several politicians. The work attained immediate popularity, running into five editions within three months of its publication and at least twelve editions before the end of the year. There is no indication that Pigott had originally intended a sequel, but the overnight success compelled him to write both a second and a third part before the end of 1792. Over the next couple of years, the pamphlets were republished and he kept adding extra material to the new editions – as (to his annoyance) did his publishers.[8] Using 'Jockey Club' as a trademark on a title-page became a way of shifting copies of works unrelated to Pigott's publications.[9]

Pigott may have betrayed his old friends at Newmarket, but it was a betrayal with ideological motives. His censure of the gay butterflies who strutted their fancy clothes at Newmarket was an innovation compared with the jibes at fashionable society that had dominated satire earlier in the century. Pigott was among the first to pitch scandal-mongering as a criticism of social inequality; for, with the notable exception of Hogarth, satirists of the *haute bourgeoisie* were often satisfied with mocking the foppery of the upper classes, leaving the weightier issues of politics aside.

Before part one of *The Jockey Club* was published, Pigott had already shown himself as a political commentator. In 1791, he came out against Edmund Burke in *Strictures on the New Political Tenets of the Rt. Hon. Edmund Burke illustrated by Analogy between his different Sentiments on the American and French Revolutions*. Pigott lamented how Burke had betrayed his former libertarian views in *Reflections of the Revolution in France* (1990). At this point, Pigott still subscribed to the opinion that the Whigs could change things for the better, and he would confess 'the utmost respect for the personal and political character of Mr. Fox'.[10] Yet, during the course of 1792, Pigott would turn against Fox and the sphere of Whig politics he dominated. The development is recorded in the instalments of *The Jockey Club*, which became progressively more radical and uncompromising.

In the second and third part of *The Jockey Club*, Pigott not only sharpened the incendiary tone but also extended his shooting range to include people beyond the Newmarket Jockey Club. Yet he kept the original title, which was possible because 'to jockey' had a number of connotations that could be put to new use; one of them being 'to cheat, trick or outwit'. Pigott could therefore now include the 'Jockeys and Jugglers in Courts, in Politics and the Law', as well as describe Prime Minister William Pitt as an 'able driver'.[11]

In the third part of *The Jockey Club*, Pigott was no longer willing to stick with his old friend Charles Fox ('on whom we have heretofore been lavish in our praises') and now took sides with Thomas Paine, whose radical reorganization of society outlined in the second part of *Rights of Man* (1792) was much more than the Foxite Whigs could stomach. Pigott inveighs against Fox for his 'folly and impudence to call Mr. Paine's work a libel, a work, every page of which breathes the purest philanthropy, – whose only object is to meliorate the sad condition of humanity: – to take away the superflux from luxury and plunder, and apply it to the relief of indigence and misfortune'.[12] Pigott had come to regard his former boon companions of the metropolitan Whig aristocracy as unfit to improve the corruption that permeated the system of government. He could now clarify to his audience as well as to himself that the 'principle' behind all the *Jockey Club* pamphlets was 'spurning the barbarous injustice, which grants to wealth and titles the infernal privilege of sanctioning every species of infamy and corruption'; this along with 'all the bitterest evils mankind endure, originate from a blind adherence to ancient customs'.[13]

Pigott's alienation from Fox and the Whig circles is further cemented in *The Whig Club, or a Sketch of the Manners of the Age*. The Whig parliamentarians were here described as a society of men 'who possess as great talents, and as corrupt principles ever were kown [sic] to elevate or debase the human character'.[14] Pigott would later continue his onslaught in several of the entries of the *Political Dictionary*.

Pigott's radicalism may have been helped along by his older brother, Robert (1736–1794), who had moved to the Continent in 1776, and was directly involved in the republican clubs in Paris.[15] But the formation of opinion domestically undoubtedly played a significant role. In 1792, reformism in Britain was fundamentally re-structured. The Government adopted a new alarmist stance out of fear that revolutionary terror might be exported to Britain. This, in turn, forced supporters of libertarian principles to take on more extremist positions. Pigott joined the London Corresponding Society, which was founded in January 1792 by the shoemaker Thomas Hardy, who was later to be charged with treason. This was the first of many radical corresponding societies and democratic clubs, about which the Government was alarmed because their low weekly subscription fee invited artisan and plebeian membership.[16] Pigott also became a member of the revived Society for Constitutional Information, which consisted primarily of aristocratic Whigs. The presence of the notable gentleman radicals John Horne Tooke and John Thelwall meant that ideas were in circulation here that the Government would not take lightly (as their indictments for treason in 1794 would later prove).

Having established a reputation as a notable radical writer, Pigott began mixing within the circle of other radical men of letters and publishers in London. Two prints by the caricaturist Richard Newton (published 20 August and 5 October 1793) show Pigott visiting radicals on the gentleman side of Newgate prison. In the first, he is seen relaxing at a dinner in Lord George Gordon's rooms; in the second, he is promenading inside Newgate's walls with radicals who were sentenced for sedition.[17] Pigott is also recorded to have dined with prominent radicals in John Frost's room on 7 August 1793, as William Godwin notes in his diary.[18]

Although Pigott's new Painite radicalism begged for a politically more focused framework, he was not entirely willing to give up the recipe that had proved so successful. In 1794, Pigott further published *The Female Jockey Club*. Apologizing for having left out the ladies the first time around, this was yet another stint at milking the market for gossip and scandal. In fact, the politics of this pamphlet are less palpable than what had gone before. The publication was somehow redeemed by the interjections of commentary on how forced marriages socially enslaved young women. In one place, Pigott derides the 'policy of her Ladyship's papa, always bent on what he deems the main chance [of financial benefit]', and expressed the hope that a woman can be 'guided by her own choice' rather than 'miserably sacrifice affection either to wealth or power'.[19] The injunction against matrimony as a ruinous institution was a theme taken up by several radicals, most notably William Godwin in *Political Justice* (1793). But William Blake's *Visions of the Daughters of Albion* (1793) also resonates with similar sentiments.

It is hard not to be struck by the strange ambiguity inherent in Pigott's pamphlets. There is clearly a sensationalist strain in Pigott' exhibition of the aristocracy's dirty linens. What added to the marketing value was, as he lets on, that he had 'the misfortune to have acquaintance with' many of those he named and shamed.[20] The exposés tapped a lucrative market of scandalmongering that also flourished in periodicals such as the *Town and Country Magazine* and the *Bon Ton Magazine; or Microscope of Fashion and Folly*. The former was published by the printer H. D. Symonds, who was also the publisher of Pigott's *The Jockey Club*, and the latter extracted Pigott's vignettes in 1792. Yet, as Pigott carefully explains to us, his exposés serve a nobler purpose. The snipes at individuals are documentary evidence to illuminate how the 'manners of the age' are sapping the strength of the nation. Pigott explained that he was holding a 'mirror up to Nature, to shew Vice its own image' with the mission to turn 'the bias of popular admiration'. In exposing the extravagances of individuals, he hoped to show up the whole 'unnatural system', which 'continues the custom to annex such servile awe and prostituted reverence to those who are virtually the most undeserving of it, and whose sole merit consists in their birth or titles'. Only 'a revolution in government' can bring about a 'revolution in morals'.[21] For Pigott, the 'Age of Scandal' and the age of political enlightenment went hand in hand.

In *A Political Dictionary*, Pigott justifies his exposure of the vices and follies of the ruling elite on the grounds that the customs prevailing 'amongst the great ... no matter how contemptible, mischievous, or unnatural' will naturally be adopted and practised by the rest of society. This is because, at the time, their conduct had 'a vast influence ... over the morals of society and how much its welfare consequently depends on the examples of the superior orders'.[22] It is relevant here to assess Pigott's invectives with the well-known movement for moral reformation at the time.

In 1787, George III had issued a *Proclamation for the Encouragement of Piety and Virtue and for the Prevention and Punishment of Vice, Profaneness, and Immorality*.[23] The same year, the prominent Evangelical William Wilberforce established the Proclamation Society, which revived the efforts of the much older Society for the

Reformation of Manners (1692). The emphasis was on the upper classes to set a good example. Drunkenness, illicit behaviour and flamboyance in dress were clamped down on, and orderliness, discipline and moral rectitude were expected. Another prominent Evangelical, Hannah More, would in *Thoughts on the Importance of the Manners of the Great to General Society* (1787) make it an imperative that the upper classes were exemplars of good behaviour so that it might trickle down and reform society at large. Evangelicalism was influential long into the next century, and laid the foundation for what we today recognize as Victorian middle-class prudishness.

Pigott stands at some distance from this movement. First of all, his criticism derives not from the observance of Christian piety but from the world of journalistic populism. His attacks on immorality were targeted precisely at the moral bulwarks the Evangelicals tried to buttress. After all, social tranquillity and a respect for the King and one's betters were paramount for Evangelicals. In the 1790s, both in and out of Parliament, the Evangelicals went along with Edmund Burke in interpreting the French Revolution as a loss of civilization resulting from atheism and an abandonment of traditional values, which had degenerated society in the decades leading up to the fall of the Bastille. Pigott, on the contrary, sees the Revolution as a re-establishment of the true and natural rights of man. Pigott mocked the hypocrisy of Hannah More and the coterie of Bluestocking ladies in *The Female Jockey Club*.[24] In *A Political Dictionary*, Wilberforce may be lauded for his philanthropic interest in abolishing slavery and the slave trade, and yet he is flawed by his superficiality in so far that his paternalism did not include liberties for Englishmen.

Pigott's sallies against the royals, aristocracy and gentry did not pass unnoticed. The Prince of Wales's friend and one-time manager of his racing stables, Sir John Lade, threatened Pigott with a suit for libelling his wife, who was referred to as a 'common prostitute' in the first part of *The Jockey Club*.[25] Letitia Darby (or Smith), also known as 'Nelly', had previously been enamoured with the notorious highwayman Sixteen-String Jack (Jack Rann), who was hanged at Tyburn in 1774. She was also said to have had an affair with the Prince of Wales's younger brother, the Duke of York. For *The Female Jockey Club*, Miss Elizabeth Luttrell filed a suit for libel. Pigott's publisher, the radical bookseller Daniel Isaac Eaton, was convicted of selling the work. Before the jury was given the case, Judge Lord Kenyon announced that it was a gross libel.[26] However, Eaton's attorney, John Gurney, managed to arrange a settlement.

One of Pigott's old acquaintances, an anonymous 'member of the Jockey Club', launched a counter-attack in which Pigott's own morals came under scrutiny. In a pamphlet, Pigott was accused of blackmailing society ladies, 'the purchase of his silence' allegedly being worth 'upwards of five thousand pounds'.[27] This is not implausible, as the seller of *The Jockey Club* and publisher of some of his political pamphlets, James Ridgway, was certainly involved in such antics.[28] The practice was, in fact, similar to that of selling 'paragraphs', which had constituted the economic basis for several papers in the 1780s. It was said that in Pigott's old paper, the *Morning Post*, hardly a paragraph was not paid for by someone or other. Its popular 'anecdotes' and 'personalities' were an efficient way of discrediting a political opponent or rival. These sold at advertising rates, and terms such as 'suppression fees', 'insertion fees' and 'contradiction fees' became part of newspaper lingo. As Lucyle Werkmeister has noted, the noble principle of 'the Liberty of the Press' came 'to mean a newspaper's freedom to decide which faction's money it would accept'.[29]

But Pigott's venomous pen was not only a nuisance to individuals; it was also deemed a threat to society at large. With a letter to the Queen of 24 September 1792, the Prince of Wales enclosed a copy of *The Jockey Club* with pencil tracings (underlining passages such as 'If the American Revolution operated as an example upon France, it is natural to imagine, from the vicinity, that the French Revolution will operate at least with equal effect upon us. The people will soon revolt against the influence of corruption'). The Prince described it as 'the most infamous & shocking libellous production y[e]t ever disgrac'd the pen of man', and linked it directly to 'those damnable doctrines of the hell-begotten Jacobines' and their 'Republican principles', which he urged the Queen should be 'taken up in a very serious manner by Government & prosecuted as a libel upon the King, yourself, & the constitution'.[30] The Queen sent it to Home Secretary Henry Dundas, who passed it on to the Attorney-General. A week later, Dundas assured the King that steps were being taken to prosecute the responsible parties. On 28 November, indictments were ready against the booksellers James Ridgway and Henry Symonds for selling Pigott's work with Paine's *Rights of Man* and his *Address to the Addressers*. In May 1793, Ridgway was sentenced to two years in Newgate and Symonds to three years, and they both incurred large fines. The booksellers William Belcher in Birmingham and Richard Philips in Leicester were also prosecuted.[31] Pigott himself was probably not indicted because his name did not appear on the title-page. In cases where authorship was judged hard to establish, sellers were often targeted rather than the writers whose works they sold.

However, Pigott did not escape the net of Government spies. On 30 September 1793, he was arrested for an incident unrelated to his publishing career. On that day he had been drinking and carousing in the London Coffee House in Ludgate Hill with William Hodgson (a surgeon who was enlisted in Division 2 of the London Corresponding Society). They had allegedly toasted the French Republic and 'an overthrow to the different governments of Europe', as well as having spoken sedition against the King and his Coalition partner in the war with France, the Landgrave of Hesse Cassel. Pigott and Hodgson were taken into custody. As they were transported away, they were said to have 'called from the coach-windows to the people, "The French Republic!" and "Liberty while you live!"'[32]

The charge against Pigott for sedition was never tried, as it was thrown out of court on 2 November. Three days later, he was set free. As a man with a nose for publicity, Pigott was well aware of the public interest in court cases against radicals, and published in pamphlet form *Persecution: The Case of Charles Pigott: Contained in the Defence He had Prepared and Which Would Have Been Delivered by Him on His Trial if the Grand Jury Had Not Thrown Out the Bill Preferred Against Him* (1793). Hodgson, on the other hand, was prosecuted in December and given a two-year jail sentence with an added fine of £200. Without the money available to a man of Pigott's background, he had to remain in prison after the expiry of his sentence for not being able to pay the fine. To help raise money to relieve this debt, Eaton and other booksellers sold the pamphlet *The Case of William Hodgson now Confined in Newgate, for the Payment of two hundred pound, after having suffered two years' imprisonment on a charge of sedition, considered and compared with the existing laws of the country by himself* in 1796.

Before the prosecution against Pigott was dropped, he was held in custody in Compter Dungeon, which was situated to the north of Newgate, immediately across the street. His time here proved fatal. In a four-page 'Introduction', included in some copies of *A Political Dictionary*, Pigott complains that Compter Dungeon has brought him ill health, and that he anticipates an imminent death. This was perhaps a result of catching 'gaol fever' (typhus), which killed several other radicals who suffered imprisonment. His health did not recover, and the *Gentlemen's Magazine* could, in an entry for 24 June 1794, announce that Pigott had died at his apartments in Westminster, and that his remains were interred in the family vault at Chetwynd, Shropshire.[33]

A Political Dictionary

A 'Preface' included in some copies of *A Political Dictionary, Explaining the True Meaning of Words* is Pigott's short address to the reader, written while interred in Compter Dungeon. He writes that the 'work' he had 'begun some years ago' is now 'finished'. However, as *A Political Dictionary* contains numerous references to events of early 1794, this statement seems inaccurate. We know that Pigott changed publishers in 1794. *The Female Jockey Club* was published in 1794 by Daniel Isaac Eaton, who was in prison at the same time as Pigott on charges of publishing seditious material. Apparently, Pigott left his papers to Eaton, who published *A Political Dictionary* in 1795, after Pigott's death. Jon Mee has suggested that the possible reason why Pigott abandoned Ridgway, who had published some of his earlier political pamphlets, may be because Ridgway had authorized his attorney to give up Pigott as the author of the work for which he was sentenced to the Solicitor of the Treasury.[34]

It is not clear to what extent Eaton tampered with Pigott's original manuscript papers, but it seems most likely that Eaton may simply have published more or less what Pigott left, leaving the organization of the work sloppy in places. There is alphabetical disorder for example (pages 56–8), several of the quotations are inaccurate, and keywords in the text direct us to definitions which turn out not to be there. This was typical. As a contemporary reviewer had earlier noted, Pigott's pamphlets bore the marks of 'hasty composition'.[35]

Pigott's work is not a dictionary in any regular sense. The alphabetical listing is only a *trompe l'oeil*. He gives us an 'ideological index' to the large body of unjust laws, policies and corruption of British society. The systematization of his observations into dictionary form is only a way of emphasizing the range and scale of political oppression at the time. It is quite clear that the *Political Dictionary* was composed in sections, as entries juxtaposed to each other often address the same or similar issues. For example, *Placeman*, *Pluralist* and *Poet Laureate* follow each other on page 104. What they have in common is a critique of the system of patronage, by which offices – in the civil service, ecclesiastical and as 'court' poet, respectively – were given as rewards for political support to the Government. The third in the series, one may note, is actually redundant, as Pigott has already defined *Laureat* [*sic*] on page 64.

In the 'Preface' (not included in this facsimile edition), Pigott writes that *A Political Dictionary* was written over a number of years, for which reason the 'reader will easily perceive the inequality of its style, and the capricious and fluctuating temper of mind of the author'. The extended time-span it took to compose the work accounts for the unevenness of the material included. What in some passages is the nurturing of a hope for mankind standing on the threshold of a new age of revolution sits uneasily with other passages that reflect a deep scepticism of human nature as inherently corrupt.

In terms of method, Pigott's attacks on what he calls the 'language of Aristocracy' vary between straightforward strikes (that is, simply and candidly revealing to the reader the 'true meaning' of a concept or practice) and a more playful satirical method by which he puts on an aristocratic voice in order to satirize the absurdity of a concept through irony, exaggeration and hyperbole. The latter method, by which the language of oppression is gleefully 'accepted' only to show up its shortcomings and defective nature, was a common strategy in radical satire at the time and thrived in the periodicals *Politics for the People, or a Salmagundy for Swine*, published by Eaton, and *Hog's Wash*, published by Thomas Spence.[36]

There is also variance in the way the push for radical reform is argued. In some places, Pigott weighs the failings of the modern Whigs against the glorious examples of seventeenth-century rebels against monarchical encroachments on liberty, such as Sidney, Hampden and Russell. This sort of argument was often used, and fell on the safe side of calling for political action. In other places, however, Pigott incites to a revolution by which George III, Pitt and the horde of political sycophants would be executed (see for instance *Scaffold*, *Rapier* and *Unhanged*), which could very well have been subject to prosecution. But in all cases, it is clear that Pigott had lost faith in moderate Whig reform and sees radical change as the only possible solution for any real change.

At the time Pigott compiled the material for *A Political Dictionary*, Samuel Johnson's *Dictionary of the English Language* (1755) had long been established as a normative work and a cultural benchmark for Britain as a nation. The references to Johnson in Pigott's definitions reflect this fact. But, more importantly, Pigott adapts Johnson's method for linguistic definition: exemplification by citation. Johnson specified on the frontispiece of his *Dictionary* that the words included are 'illustrated in their different significations by examples from the best writers'. All in all, this amounts to about 116 000 quotations. It has long been known that Johnson chose his quotations for their fitness as moral, social and political exempla over their helpfulness for clarifying linguistic usage. Johnson himself writes in the explanation he gives for *philology* that one must 'temper all discourse of philology with interspersions of morality'.[37] The way Johnson's citations can be pieced together to form a consistent (albeit disorganized) moral treatise has since been clarified by modern historians.[38] In *A Political Dictionary*, Pigott chooses appropriate citations from the Bible, classical historians, contemporary satires and a host of political writers from Cicero to Thomas Paine to lend authority to his invectives against tyranny and injustice. The quotations are not, however, chosen at random. There is a conspicuous presence of writers who were at one time or another associated with the Opposition at the time Walpole was prime minister. Bolingbroke, Pope, Gay and especially Swift were all critics of Walpole's abuse of public funds.[39] Walpole was infamous for the wealth he built on the profits of his office, including the Palladian country house, Houghton Hall. As First Minister of the State, appointed by the King, Walpole managed the royal influence through the corrupt use of places, pensions, sinecures and straightforward bribes. As one reads through *A Political Dictionary*, one realizes that allegations of corruption are central to Pigott's condemnation of the Government under George III and Pitt. In this, the tirades of the anti-Walpolean writers are put to new use.

That Johnson wrote the *Dictionary* with the bias of a self-confessed Tory and supporter of the Church of England was famously pointed out by his biographer James Boswell in 1791.[40] It is perhaps no clearer than in Johnson's definition of *irony* as 'A mode of speech in which the meaning is contrary to the words: as Bolingbroke was a holy man'. Tory minister Henry St John Bolingbroke's deistic views and perceived political infidelity were what prompted Johnson's jibe. His definition of *pensions* as 'pay given to a state hireling for treason to his country' is quoted by Pigott, who, like his contemporaries, was well aware that politics and language were not entirely separate spheres.

In terms of generic form, Pigott seems to have been influenced by several precursors, and probably changed his mind on which template to use as he went along. In the longer entries, such as *Faith, Government* or *War*, Pigott seems to draw inspiration from Voltaire's *Dictionaire Philosophique* (1764), which was a collection of miscellaneous philosophical thoughts with an unmistakable political inflection.[41] In other places, Pigott aims at more immediate personal and topical satire. There are especially many references to events and debates in Parliament of late 1793 and the first half of 1794, which seems to indicate that Pigott, after his release from prison, abandoned the more philosophical tenets and went straight for the jugular of Pitt and his supporters.

A native precursor for Pigott's work is *Pearson's Political Dictionary* (1792). In the 'Introduction' to this book, it is explained that it is written by the recently deceased Joseph Pearson, who was 'principal door-keeper' at the House of Commons for more than thirty years. There are no philosophical pretensions here, as it is spoken by a man whose merit is to demystify political jargon and bring it down to earth. The intention to speak 'plainly' is reflected in the level of swearing the book contains. *Proclamation*, for example, is explained: 'A piece of paper pasted on walls, to frighten the people out of their rights; the same as idle cautions against p——— g-posts, and of just the same use. People will always know where they have a right to p—ss, and will p—ss when they please'.[42] But, if *Pearson's Political Dictionary* surpasses Pigott in the coarseness of its idiom, it was far more moderate in terms of politics. The editor describes Pearson as 'a stickler for the privileges of the people' but 'no violent republican'.[43] There is nothing like Pigott's revolutionary and regicidal principles.

Pigott wrote at a time when language came under attack from radical quarters.[44] The most erudite sally was launched by John Horne Tooke, who was active in the reform movement of the 1790s.[45] The first part of Tooke's linguistic examination *ΕΠΕΑ ΠΤΕΡΟΕΝΤΑ or the Diversions of Purley* was published in 1786. Although this was a serious scientific study intent on showing the philological errors of 'universal grammar' as propagated by James Harris (see Pigott's entry on *Nominative case*), its political intentions were clear, and many sentences were deleted by his publisher, the radical bookseller Joseph Johnson, who apparently feared charges of sedition. Tooke pointed out that words such as *Monarchy* and *Constitution* sustain the institutions they name only because they hold a certain status as ideas. He was sceptical of all abstract ideas, which he believed were only made 'true' on basis of their accepted usage. Through numerous tracings of words back to their etymological roots, Tooke attempted to reveal the abuses of language, as these abuses authorized a political system. Although Pigott gestures towards using etymology and grammar to do the same (see, for example, *King*, *Potentate* and *Uproar*), *A Political Dictionary* remains a satire, not an attempt at scientific investigation. If many of Tooke's etymologies have later proven to be dubious, Pigott's are always deliberately so.

Yet Pigott shares Horne Tooke's fundamental premise, that language is creative in the construction of political reality. This was a central theme in radical discourse. An attack on how Governments in Britain have used abstractions to win over the population to their side against the political bugbears that threatened their hegemony was launched by the radical writer William Fox in his pamphlet *On Jacobinism* (1794). Fox traces how a language of delusion has 'been peculiarly resorted to in that state of this country, in which those who govern have found themselves necessitated, in some degree, to resort to artifice to obtain or maintain dominion, no longer deeming it expedient to rely totally on force'. He describes how 'words have been successively adopted without any definite import, merely to enable the ambitious and the crafty to carry on their design'. According to Fox, British history can be mapped linguistically as an account of the abstract terms Governments have 'invented to deceive', and with which they continue to confound 'the ignorant multitude'. 'From the commencement of the last century,' Fox writes, 'a few cant words have been the powerful means of producing all the revolutions and events we have experienced.' For example, 'Papist ... produced our glorious Revolution, and in connection with the Pretender, generated the Hanover succession.' The royal House of Hanover was then 'triumphant until the present moment, when threatened, with danger by the dreadful words Rights of Man'. To combat this, it has been 'deemed expedient to resort to the word Jacobin for support'. In the present situation, Fox therefore urges his readers that 'it will become us to be cautious and suspicious when new terms and additional cant phrases are introduced into our political vocabulary'.[46]

It is precisely the new 'cant' invented by the establishment that Pigott sets out to undermine in *A Political Dictionary*. For instance, he notes that when the 'people, vexed and goaded by oppression, express discontent' then it is construed with an entirely different meaning in 'the aristocratic dictionary', where it receives the name of 'sedition'.[47] But if the redefinition of constitutional rights was one way of silencing the Opposition, the propagation of new catchphrases, such as calling the war against republican France 'just and necessary', was another. In Parliament, this exact phrase was the subject of a heated debate, as the Opposition saw it to be a species of particularly manipulative rhetoric and objected to its use in official documents.[48]

The need to 'Explain the True Meaning of Words' can be seen as a response to the redefinition of moral duties, virtue and vice in the volatile political climate of the early 1790s. The Government's first significant preventive step against radical activities was taken on 21 May 1792 with the issue of a Royal Proclamation 'for the preventing of tumultuous meetings and seditious writings'.[49] As it was noted at the time, there were obvious parallels to be drawn between this and the Royal Proclamation against vice issued in 1787. The 1792 Proclamation sought to redefine 'sedition' as the new moral enemy. Radical publications and practices were described as 'wicked and seditious', whereas virtue was defined as respect for 'the Laws, and happy Constitution of Governments, Civil and Religious, established in this kingdom'. The continuity between the two papers signed by the King was picked up by the caricaturist James Gillray in his print *Vices overlookd'd in the New Proclamation* (1792).[50] The satire bore the inscription: 'To the Commons of Great

Britain, this representation of Vices which remain unforbidden by Proclamation, is dedicated, as proper for imitation, and in place of the more dangerous Ones of Thinking, Speaking & Writing, now forbidden by Authority'. It is a design divided into four panels displaying vices associated with members of the royal family. The King and Queen are hoarding bags of State money in reference to their alleged avarice; the Prince of Wales is drunk and in bad company; George III's second son, the Duke of York, is pursuing his passion for gambling; and the third son, the Duke of Clarence, is in the arms of the comedy actress Mrs Jordan.

Accusations against royal vice are also levelled by Pigott, but an even more prominent theme in *A Political Dictionary* is the redefinition of political virtue. On page 4, under *Association*, Pigott writes:

> The meaning of this word has lately undergone a *revolution*. In former times it was deemed legal for Englishmen to associate, for the purpose of discussing political principles and their own rights. Such meetings were once held constitutional and meritorious; Pitt and the Duke of Richmond, and other *Friends of the People*, were the chief supporters of them. Now government deems them unconstitutional and seditious ...

Pigott's criticism of how the right to associate had changed from being defined as 'meritorious' to being 'seditious' was aimed at those politicians who had themselves once affiliated with reform associations, but in the wake of the French Revolution had embraced alarmist measures and supported the Government's prosecution and imprisonment of members of reform societies. The most obvious example of this political apostasy was William Pitt. As a young MP, he had on 7 May 1782 proposed reforms to Parliament for fairer representation. After a reform bill was defeated for the second time, Pitt had met with other reformers on 16 May 1783 under the auspices of the Society for Constitutional Information (Pitt was not member) in the Thatched House Tavern, St James's Street, to organize a petition. The meeting was also attended by the Duke of Richmond, who in 1780 had proposed a plan for universal manhood suffrage and annual Parliaments. However, after becoming Privy Councillor in 1782 and joining Pitt's Cabinet, Richmond did not speak of reform again.

In all fairness, it must be said that the radicalism nurtured in the plebeian reform organizations of the 1790s, such as the London Corresponding Society, went far beyond the constitutional changes for which Pitt and Richmond had originally petitioned. In 1783 Pitt had told the House that his proposal for parliamentary reform was 'not to innovate, but rather to renew and invigorate the spirit of the constitution, without deviating materially from its present form'. Yet both Pitt and Richmond[51] also showed themselves as enemies to the kind of moderate reforms they had once supported. This irony was pointed out in Parliament on 25 May 1792 in the debate on the Royal Proclamation against seditious correspondence, when the reformist Whig Charles Grey drew attention to Pitt's and Richmond's signatures on the resolution of the Thatched House Tavern, which he then presented to the Commons.[52] Pigott's disbelief at the two politicians' apostasy was shared by the satirical poet Peter Pindar, who wrote that what is now sedition 'in the mouths of PITT and RICHMOND'S LORD' had once been 'a sweet and inoffensive word!'[53] They were brought to shame for their hypocrisy when Richmond was called upon to testify in the Treason Trials of the radicals Thomas Hardy, John Horne Tooke and John Thelwall, which began on 28 October 1794 in the Old Bailey. In court, Richmond was forced to admit that the accused were charged with little more than supporting the very same measures he had proposed in 1780. Two months after the radicals had been acquitted, Richmond was sacked from the Cabinet.

The introduction into the political debate of linguistic representation as a major theme owes much to the influence of Paine's *Rights of Man* (1791–92), the most notorious radical tract of the time. In this, the aristocracy's deceitful twists and turns of language are exposed and dissected. The royalists, Paine writes, 'hold out a language which they do not themselves believe, for the fraudulent purpose of making others believe it'. Throughout he reveals the arbitrary relationship between substance and its names. One example is the titles of nobility by which the people have been duped into believing that some men are better than others by birth: 'Titles are like circles drawn by the magician's wand, to contract the sphere of man's felicity. He lives immured within the Bastille of a word.'[54] Language has become a mental prison for the people, and to break the false illusion of power that keeps the existent order in place, the improper use of language must be stormed like the revolutionaries had stormed the Bastille on 14 July 1789.

Pigott concurs with this idea, and virulently attacks the hollowness of titles at several junctions in *A Political Dictionary*. But if the more acute linguistic awareness that emerges in *A Political Dictionary* is a departure from his earlier work, it is important to see that it develops themes already present in the *Jockey Club* pamphlets. In exposing the extravagances of nobility, he had expressed the hope to topple the 'unnatural system', which 'continues the custom to annex such servile awe and prostituted reverence to those who are virtually the most undeserving of it, and whose sole merit consists in their birth or titles'.[55] In fact, *A Political Dictionary* is best understood as a continuation of the *Jockey Club* series. According to the title-page, his definitions are 'Illustrated and Exemplified in the Lives, Morals and Conduct of the ... Most Illustrious Personages'. Pigott sets out to expose the vices of a self-indulgent *beau monde* and turn the moral climate against this culture. In *Jockey Club* III, he had written that there prevails 'in England at the present juncture a scandalous revolting profusion, – vulgar abortive attempts at elegance and grandeur, – a degree of gluttony, selfishness, and universal depravity, with an apathy and indifference to public concerns ... a treacherous display of luxury and partial wealth, which have always eventually proved the bane of empires'.[56]

The attacks Pigott launches on everyone from King George III down are personal, but not because the objects of his virulent attacks are unusually evil men. They are seen as products of a hierarchical system that inherently perpetuates corruption. To secure his own power base, the monarch employed the money from his Civil List to create places and pensions for his supporters in Parliament, also secret pensions and bribery were practised. This jeopardized the independence of civil government. As Pigott asks of those individuals in receipt of the royal bounty (under *placeman*): 'Is it the king that has made them rogues, or they who have made the king a — [tyrant?]'.[57] Replacing one individual with another will be of little avail, as vice is endemic in the system. Pigott's entries in *A Political Dictionary* document a British society in a state of absolute decadence and decline. The moral fibre of the nation is seen to have been corroded by apostasy, effeminacy, mystifying religion and, above all, corruption. Many contemporaries accepted the theory that if corruption was allowed to spread in a society, the liberty of the citizens in the nation would founder and tyranny take its place.[58] Pigott's observation men of politics have lost the will to rule (the Opposition just wanting to share the spoils of the plunder) makes one think of Edward Gibbon's analysis in *The History of Decline and Fall of the Roman Empire* (1776–87). This analogy is to some extent helped along by Pigott's use of quotations from Sallust, Horace, Cicero and Shakespeare's *Julius Caesar*.

A Political Dictionary was published in a number of editions, both in Britain and America, though it never reached the popularity of the more gossipy *Jockey Club* pamphlets. During 1795, the printer Richard 'Citizen' Lee published a series of nine pamphlets extracting definitions from *A Political Dictionary*, which he mixed with passages from other radical writers, such as Joseph Gerrald and Joel Barlow. These were cheap 'one-penny trash', which brought Pigott's writing within reach of the lower orders. Lee is perhaps best known for his regicidal broadsheet *King-Killing*, for which he was prosecuted and convicted.[59] Around the same time, Lee also published (at the price of three pence) a fifteen-page *Political Dictionary for the Guinea-less Pigs, or a Glossary of Emphatical Words made Use of by that Jewel of a Man Deep Will* [William Pitt] *in his Administration and his Plans for Yoking and putting Rings in the Snouts of those Grumbling Swine, who raise such Horrid Grunting, when Tyrannical Winds blow high*. In the Preface, Lee makes the observation that 'The prostitution of language has lately, been so glaring, and notorious that in my opinion, it requires a nice discrimination, to distinguish, even in our own Language, the true intent, and signification, of many Phrases, now in general use.'[60]

Although Pigott has received remarkably little attention on his own in modern histories and criticism, *A Political Dictionary* has continued to be cited, not least because it lends itself to illustrative and often enjoyable quotation. For students of the period, at whatever level, *A Political Dictionary* is an indispensable record of political rhetoric at the time, a kaleidoscope of state corruption as seen through the lens of a radical. This remarkable historical document is here made available for the first time since the 1790s.

On the Annotations

Whereas Pigott in the *Jockey Club* pamphlets claimed to have a privileged insight into the lives of the people he discussed – having known some of them personally or otherwise been part of the same circles – practically all the references in *A Political Dictionary* tap what was already public knowledge. He picks up on both rumours and facts that occupied the Opposition press, and repeats many of the charges habitually levelled at Pitt's Ministry, Church and King. Pigott's ambition is not cool objectivity but the incitement of outrage at the many abuses of power. It follows that the interpretations of his victims' motives further a political argument. Therefore, I believe that the best way of explaining Pigott's references is by means of parallel examples from contemporary satires. Much of what was common coin can be gleaned from the satirical prints and drawings published during the time. Many of these have magisterially been described by Mary Dorothy George in *Political and Personal Satire: Preserved in the Prints and Drawings in the British Museum*; especially volumes six and seven are invaluable resources.

There are also other sources to be considered. An important clue to the world of radicalism which Pigott inhabited is the material printed and sold by his publisher Daniel Isaac Eaton from his print-shop the Cock and Swine at 14 Newgate Street, London. In 1794, Eaton set about a publication programme for bringing out inexpensive re-prints of 'Political Classics' in weekly 48-page numbers. These included many of the theoreticians and ideologues – Harrington, Locke, Sidney, Paine, Rousseau and others – whom Pigott cites or refers to in the pages below. Eaton included many satirical pieces in his journal *Politics for the People*, and these, along with the other pamphlets that left his press, provide a useful context for understanding Pigott's brand of radicalism.

At the time the bulk of the entries for *A Political Dictionary* was written, Pigott had abandoned his trust in the Whigs, and much of the ideological content derives from Thomas Paine, whose two parts of *Rights of Man* achieved a phenomenal circulation and therefore served as an easy and immediate frame of reference that would strike a chord with most radical readers. Paine wrote this work as a response to Edmund Burke's *Reflections on the Revolution in France*, notably focusing on his opponent's ornate and manipulative rhetoric. Pigott himself had responded to Burke's views in *Strictures on the New Political Tenets of the Rt. Hon. Edmund Burke*, and throughout *A Political Dictionary* Burkean rhetoric features as the epitome of the 'language of Aristocracy'. The 'languages' spoken by Paine and Burke basically structured the ensuing debate in Britain. I have attempted to point out Pigott's references to this sphere of rhetorical combat when the references are most direct.

In his jibes at politicians, Pigott draws much information from contemporary reports of proceedings in Parliament. Journalists gained access to Parliament in 1778, and reporting of the debates became common in newspapers from 1783 onwards. Radicals naturally took an interest in the proceedings. An objective account of the speeches was, for instance, published by H. D. Symonds (who was also the publisher of *The Jockey Club* I–III) in *The Senator: or, Clarendon's Parliamentary Chronicle*. For each individual discussion Pigott takes up, I have attempted to refer to the record which gives the best or most easily accessible background for understanding the satirical digs. For the biographies of Pigott's gallery of commoners, peers and nobility, the two most important reference works are the *Dictionary of National Biography* and *The House of Commons 1790–1820*. Information on contemporary radicals can be found in the *Biographical Dictionary of Modern Radicals*, which, as an indication of Pigott's hitherto marginalized position, does not include an entry on him (!) There is a limit to which it is desirable to go into depth with the accuracy of Pigott's citation of economic figures. Figures published at the time were often based on not entirely unbiased calculations, and at least need the kind of careful interpretation that is beyond the scope of the present edition.

From the world of politics there is only a short step to the world of law and judicial practice, which also occupies Pigott throughout. The standard work for information on these issues was William Blackstone's *Commentaries on the Laws of England*, which went through numerous editions in the latter half of the eighteenth century. A useful guide to the specialized jargon Pigott refers to is *A Classical Dictionary of the Vulgar Tongue* (first published in 1785). This was a popular work compiled by Francis Grose, who writes in the Preface that he includes well-known cant from such varied places as 'Newmarket, Exchange-alley, the City, the Parade, Wapping and Newgate'.[61]

For the sake of economy, I comment on an event, issue or person as fully as possible in one place and then refer to this commentary elsewhere. This is usually at its first occurrence, or else where commentary will seem most logical. Cross-references in the annotations are marked by small capitals. For the personages that frequently make their appearance in the annotations, there are short introductions to be found in the appendix 'Cast of Characters', in which biographical aspects specifically relevant to Pigott's text are summarized. Finally, a word on spelling – Pigott often differs in the spelling of a name from the standard adopted in modern histories. In the annotations, I have chosen to opt for the generally accepted spelling in order to facilitate the reader's further pursuit of information in works of reference such as those mentioned above.

Notes

1   Pigott was admitted at Cambridge on 25 April, 1769; see *Alumni Cantabrigienses*, Part II. Biographical information on Pigott can be found in Rogers, 'Pigott's Private Eye'; Frow, 'Charles Pigott and Richard Lee'; Black, *Jockey Club*, pp. 126–7, 228–30, and Harriet Pigott, *Private Correspondence*, 1, pp. 5–12. Forthcoming essays of much value are Jon Mee's articles: 'A bold and free-spoken man' and 'Libertines and Radicals in the 1790s'. I am grateful to Dr Mee for letting me see copies of his essays before publication.

2   For Pigott's connection, see Robert Black, *Jockey Club*, pp. 228–31.

3   This racing course had a significant presence in the public consciousness and spawned a number of comments, such as G. Downing's comedy *Newmarket; or, The Humours of the Turf* performed at the Theatre Royal in Drury Lane (London: George Robinson, 1774). For a recent history; see Thompson, *Newmarket*, esp. pp. 81–123.

4   *An Answer to three Scurrilous Pamphlets entitled The Jockey Club by a member of the Jockey Club*, 2nd edn (London: J. S. Jordan, 1792), p. 13.

5   Richard Tattersal, a key figure in the Newmarket circle, was an early proprietor of the paper; see Werkmeister, *London Daily Press*, p. 28.

6   Werkmeister, *London Daily Press*, pp. 5, 61–108

7   See White, *Age of Scandal*.

8   In *The Female Jockey Club*, p. xxxviii, Pigott wrote the following 'Postscript': 'As in the last editions of the former Jockey Club, Part 1st, and Part 2d, the publisher thought proper to introduce three new characters ... the author assures the public, that he never wrote a panegyric on those men, and that their characters were inserted altogether without his knowledge or consent.'

9   See, for example, *The Minor Jockey Club, or, a Sketch of the Manners of the Greeks* (London: R. Farnham, 1792).

10   Pigott, *Strictures*, pp. vi–vii

11   Pigott, *Jockey Club* III, p. 14.

12   Pigott, *Jockey Club* III, p. 195.

13   Pigott, *Jockey Club* III, p. iv.

14   Pigott, *Whig Club*, p. 133.

15   The *DNB* has an entry on Robert Pigott, the oldest of three brothers. He is also mentioned in Alger, *Englishmen in the French Revolution*, pp. 39–45. In his history of the Newmarket Jockey Club, Robert Black reveals that Robert Pigott had been connected with the Jockey Club and was nicknamed 'Shark' after a famous horse (pp. 126–7). It thus seems likely he is the one who introduced Charles into this circle.

16   Pigott was connected to the London Corresponding Society, Division 25; see Mary Thale, *Selections*, p. 112n. The publications of and other material relating to the Society have recently been re-published in Davis (ed.), *London Corresponding Society 1792–1799*.

17   *BMC*, 8339 and 8342.

18   Jon Mee, 'A bold and free-spoken man'.

19   Pigott, *Female Jockey Club*, p. 68. See also Rogers, 'Pigott's Private Eye', 260–61.

20   Pigott, *Jockey Club* III, p. 216.

21   Pigott, *Jockey Club* I, pp. i, vi.

22   Pigott, *Jockey Club* III, p. 31.
23   Printed in the *Gentleman's Magazine* 57 (1787), p. 534.
24   Pigott, *Female Jockey Club*, pp. 192–8.
25   See Pigott's response in *Jockey Club* II, pp. 60–62.
26   Thale, *Selections*, p. 204n. For further information on Eaton, see Davis, 'Good for the Public Example'.
27   *Answer to three scurrilous Pamphlets*, pp. 13–14.
28   See Mee, 'Libertines and Radicals in the 1790s'.
29   Werkmeister, *London Daily Press*, pp. 7–8.
30   Aspinall (ed.), *Correspondence of the Prince of Wales*, 2, pp. 284–8.
31   Rogers, 'Pigott's Private Eye', p. 258.
32   The circumstances of the arrest and the initial court hearing were reported in the *Gentleman's Magazine* for October, 63 (1793), pp. 953–4.
33   *Gentleman's Magazine*, 64 (1794), p. 672.
34   Mee, 'A bold and free-spoken man'.
35   *Analytical Review* 16 (1793), p. 490.
36   For an examination of this satirical mode, see Smith, *Politics of Language*, pp. 68–109.
37   All citations are from *A Dictionary of the English Language in which the Words are deduced from their Originals and Illustrated in their Different Significations by Examples from the Best Writers*, 2 vols (London: W. Strathan, 1755).
38   For discussions of Johnson's strategy in this respect; see DeMaria, *Johnson's Dictionary*; and Allen Reddick, *Making of Johnson's Dictionary*.
39   See Urstadt, *Sir Robert Walpole's Poets*, esp. pp. 136–55, 172–230.
40   James Boswell, *Life of Johnson* (1791), ed. John Wilson Croker (London: John Murray, 1847), p. 97.
41   See Pigott's reference to Voltaire and his *Questions sur L'Encyclopédie* in *Treason no Treachery*, pp. 76–7.
42   Joseph Pearson, *Pearson's Political Dictionary, containing Remarks, Definitions, Explanations, and Customs, Political, and Parliamentary; but more particularly appertaining to the House of Commons Alphabetically arranged* (London: J. S. Jordan, 1792), p. 43.
43   Pearson, *Political Dictionary*, p. v.
44   The best overview of the subject is still Smith, *Politics of Language*. See also Mitchell, *Grammar Wars*, and Lucas, *Writing and Radicalism*.
45   Tooke was indicted for Treason in 1794 (see Pigott's definition of *Habeas Corpus*). For a full biography of Horne Tooke, see C. and D. Bewley, *Gentleman Radical*. For an analysis of Horne Tooke's methodology; see Rosenberg, 'A New Sort of Logick and Critick', and Smith, *Politics of Language*, pp. 110–53.
46   William Fox, *On Jacobinism* (London: M. Gurney), pp. 2, 3.
47   See definition of *Discontent*, p. 17.
48   See note to *Necessary War*, p. 84.
49   Printed in *PR* 33, pp. 130–32 and *PH* 31, pp. 470–71.
50   *BMC*, 8095.
51   Pitt, *Speeches*, 1, pp. 72–5.
52   *PR* 33, p. 145.

53   Peter Pindar [John Wolcot], *Pathetic Odes Pathetic Odes* (London: John Walker, 1794), p. 391.

54   Paine, *Rights of Man*, pp. 143, 287.

55   Pigott, *Jockey Club* I, p. 6.

56   Pigott, *Jockey Club* III, p. 126.

57   See below, p. 104.

58   Burtt, *Virtue Transformed: Political Argument in England 1688–1740*, pp. 15–38.

59   For information on Lee's seditious career, see Barrell, *Imagining the King's Death*, pp. 604–42.

60   Richard 'Citizen' Lee, *A Political Dictionary for the Guinea-less Pigs* (London: R. Lee, 1795?), p. 2.

61   Grose, *Dictionary*, p. 7.

A

POLITICAL
DICTIONARY:

EXPLAINING THE

TRUE MEANING OF WORDS.

ILLUSTRATED AND EXEMPLIFIED IN THE

LIVES, MORALS, CHARACTER AND CONDUCT

OF THE FOLLOWING

MOST ILLUSTRIOUS PERSONAGES,

AMONG MANY OTHERS.

The King, Queen, Prince of Wales, Duke of York, Pope Pius VI. Emperor, King of Pruffia, the Tigrefs of Ruffia, Dukes of Brunfwick, Portland, Richmond, Newcaftle, Leeds. Earls Chatham, Fitzwilliam, Darlington, Spencer, Howe, Chefterfield. Lords Grenville, Morniagton, Moira, Mountmorris, Mulgrave, Fitzgerald, Harvey, Judges Kenyon and Loughborough. Hon. Frank North. Sirs George Saville, Gilbert Elliot, Francis Molyneux, Watkin Lewes, Roger Curtis, Sydney Smythe, Francis Sykes, Richard Hill. Landgrave of Heffe Caffel, Madam Schwellenbergen. Meffrs. Pitt, Fox, Burke, Dumourier, Warren Haftings, Wyndham, Powis, Dundas, Thornton, Wilberforce, Reeves, Arthur Young, George Hanger, Charles Jenkinfon, Colonel Tarleton, Brook Watfon. Aldermen Curtis, Anderfon, Le Mefurier, Sanderfon. Bifhops and Clergy. Charles I. and Louis XVI.

BY THE LATE

CHARLES PIGOTT, Esq.

AUTHOR OF THE JOCKEY CLUBS, &c. &c.

LONDON:
PRINTED FOR D. I. EATON, NO. 74. NEWGATE-STREET.
MDCXCV.

PUBLICATIONS BY D. I. EATON,

At the *Cock and Swine*, No. 74, Newgate-ftreet, London;

THE WORKS OF CHARLES PIGOTT, ESQ. THE AUTHOR.

	£.	s.	d.
The Cafe of Charles Pigott — —	o	1	o
Treachery no Crime ; or, The Syftem of Courts	o	2	o
Strictures on Burke — — —	o	1	6

THE WORKS OF OLD HUBERT,

The Village Affociation — —	o	1	6
The Knaves-Acre Affociation —	o	o	4
An Addrefs to the Hon. E. Burke, from the Swinifh Multitude — —	o	o	6
The Budget of the People, 1ft and 2d part, each	o	o	1
Pearls caft before Swine —— ——	o	o	1
Maft and Acorns —— —	o	o	2

Thefe are the Times to try Men's Souls	o	o	6
Age of Reafon, by Thomas Paine —	o	1	6
D. I. Eaton's Three Trials—for Rights of Man—Letter to the Addreffers—Politics for the People, each	o	1	6
A Convention the only Means of Saving us from Ruin. By Jofeph Gerrald — —— —	o	2	6
The Same	o	1	6
The Addrefs of the Britifh Convention —	o	o	6
Confiderations on the French War : in a Letter to the Right Hon. W. Pitt. By a Britifh Merchant	o	1	6
Politics for the People, publifhing in Weekly Numbers	o	o	2
Evidence fummed up, or the Apparent Caufes of the prefent War —— —— —	o	o	6
Virtues of Hazel ; or, the Bleffings of Government	o	o	6
Letters to the People of Great Britain on the Prefent State of their Public Affairs — —	o	1	o
Extermination ; or, an Appeal to the People of England on the War with France — —	o	o	6
Catechifm of Man, pointing out, from found Principles, and acknowledged Facts, the Rights and Duties of every rational Being — — —	o	o	6
Conftitution of France (the New) ——	o	o	3
The True Churchman — —	o	1	o
Life of Alfred compared with the prefent Corrupt Syftem	o	o	6
Letter to the Church of Scotland, by Mark Blake, Efq.	o	o	6
Addrefs to the Public, alias the Swinifh Multitude	o	o	1
Conftitution of America, and their Declaration of Reafons for feparating from this Country ——	o	o	6
Defence of Burke — — — —	o	1	o
Meafures of Miniftry to prevent a Revolution are the certain Means of bringing it on ——	o	1	6
Monarchy no Creature of God's making —	o	2	o

In Weekly Numbers, Price 6d.

POLITICAL CLASSICS;

CONTAINING,

ALGERNON SYDNEY,* ROUSSEAU, MILTON, HAR-
RINGTON, MORE, BUCHANNAN, LOCKE, PAINE,
PRICE, BURGH, GODWIN, &c. &c.

And every thing that has been adduced by any Author of whatever Country that can convey Information, and may thereby
promote the happiness of Man.

ADDRESS TO THE PUBLIC.

A grateful fense of the many obligations, as well as my duty to the Public, has induced me to acquiefce in the folicitations of many of my friends,
to give thefe Works to the World at as eafy a rate as poffible, as a
certain means of deftroying thofe weak and partial affections which the
generality of my fellow-citizens entertain for the particular forms of
government under which they live. And I fincerely hope, that every
perfon who may perufe thofe pages, will apply difpaffionately their reafon
and underftanding, in reflecting on the beauties of a juft and equitable
form of government, in comparifon with thofe profufe, venal, and corrupt fyftems which now almoft univerfally obtain through the globe;
wherefore, as felf is the firft principle of every individual, our own
ought to be the firft under confideration and attention, where, upon a
calm enquiry will be found as much corruption and abufe of power as
in any other government in Europe; for it matters not to the peafant,
or mechanic, whether a King, a Bifhop, or a venal Parliament, robs
him of the earnings of his labour; his fufferings, and their tyranny, are
equally felt. Under impreffions fo confummate and ftrong, I fhall apply to their conviction the Works of the above judicious Philofophers,
who, to their immortal honour, have united Learning and Philanthropy
with Patriotifm; and in their Works have laid down fuch principles of
government, as muft flafh conviction on the moft defpotic mind, and
which have lived, and will live, to immortalize their names till time is
no more.

Their Works fhall be printed uniformly of one fize and letter, on fu-
perfine paper; and throughout the whole the greateft neatnefs fhall be
obferved, as it is my wifh to render it a defirable acquifition to every
library in the kingdom.

D. I. EATON.

Printed and Publifhed by DANIEL ISAAC EATON, at the Cock and
Swine, No. 74, Newgate-ftreet, London.

* Sidney's Works are now complete.

PIGOTT'S

POLITICAL DICTIONARY.

A.

ABSURDITY,—Mr. Pitt's furplus fund, his Majefty's civil-lift, and the combination of kings, to reftore priefthood, ariftocracy, and monarchy in France.

Abufe,—the different governments of Europe; privileged orders; church eftablifhments.

Adam,—the only *man* of his time, a true *Sans Culottes*, and the firft revolutionift.

Addrefs,—an echo of venal proftitution; an infidious, minifterial trap to *catch* popularity, never to be trufted.

Admiralty,—an office of the firft refponfibility, requiring the greateft talents, induftry, and experience, in the man who prefides over it; filled by an IDEOT, becaufe he happens to be brother to a PRIME MINISTER.

Advantage,—the evacuation of Toulon; the retreat from Dunkirk; the French triumphant mafters

B   of

of the fea; and Earl Moira's expedition to the coaſt of Britanny.

Alarm,—the *tocſin* of delufion; plunging En-gliſhmen into all the calamities of war, under the falfeſt pretence of their liberties and properties being endangered, to cover the real deſigns of ha-tred, jealouſy, defpotifm, and revenge. A pretext for profecutions, unconſtitutional augmentation of the army, the introduction of foreign troops, bar-racks, &c. &c. &c.

Alarmiſts,—miferable politicians, who have been dupes of the found, terrified by the downfal of ariſtocracy in France; bewildered by apprehenfions and fears for themfelves, they have loſt all fenfe of their duty towards the people, and have joined the confpiracy of courts againſt the intereſts of huma-nity. For example, Duke of Portland, Earls Fitz-william, Spencer, Meffrs. Windham, Powis, and a liſt of *et ceteras, ad infinitum.*

Alderman,—ſtupidity, gluttony, fervility, ava-rice; perfectly reprefented in the perfons of Meff. C—t-s, And—ſ-n, Le Meſ-r—r, and S—nd—ſ-n; turtle feaſting, &c. &c.

Ally (new),—George III. Pope Pius VI.

America,—a bright and immortal example to all colonies groaning under a foreign yoke, proving the invincible energy and virtue of Freedom, and enjoying a ſtate of profperity, ſince ſhe has thrown

off

off her dependence on Great Britain, hitherto un-known in the nations of Europe.

Ambaſſador,—a privileged ſpy; a genuine re-preſentative of royalty.

Ambition,—an irreſiſtible ſtimulus to *perſonal* aggrandizement; a rage for foreign conqueſts; a ſovereign contempt for *public* calamity, and an ever-laſting attachment to courts.

Ankerſtrom,—a generous TYRANNICIDE, equal if not ſuperior to BRUTUS.

Apathy,—a word characteriſtic of modern Bri-tons.

Apoſtate,—one who barters his political princi-ples for a ſum of money, for a penſion, a place, or a garter; Dumourier, Pitt, Burke, Moira, and other *great* men.

Argument,—proclamation, manifeſtos, Newgate, fine, pillory, BOTANY BAY.

Ariſtocrat,—a fool, or ſcoundrel, generally both; a monſter of rapacity, and an enemy to man-kind.

Army (ſtanding),—an engine employed in mo-narchies, by which nations are enſlaved. Dalrym-ple obſerves, that " ſlavery follows a ſtanding army, " as ſure as the ſhadow follows the body."

Aſs,—a beaſt of burthen. The celebrated natu-raliſt Buffon ſays, that an *aſs is the moſt patient of*

all

all animals; but the philofopher had never read the hiftory of JOHN BULL.

Affertion,—the king's fpeech on opening the feffions of Parliament, 1794; the account of brilliant fucceffes obtained by the combined powers; the Britifh Conftitution, the chef d'œuvre of perfection, the envy and admiration of the whole world; the inexhauftible refources, and unprecedented profperity of England; the madnefs of reform; the neceffity of carrying on the war; and, finally, the virtue of Mr. Pitt and his adminiftration.

Affociation.—The meaning of this word has lately undergone a *revolution.* In former times it was deemed legal for Englifhmen to affociate, for the purpofe of difcuffing political principles and their own rights. Such meetings were once held conftitutional and meritorious; Pitt, the Duke of Richmond, and other *Friends of the People,* were the chief fupporters of them. Now government deems them unconftitutional and *feditious,* and the affociators ftand a good chance of being confined four years in Newgate, or, if in Scotland, of being loaded with *irons,* and tranfported to Botany Bay. Neverthelefs, on the other hand, affociations are formed under the immediate fanction of this very identical Pitt, for the fuppreffion of thefe once conftitutional meetings, and *his* affociators are regarded

garded by *him* as the only true loyalifts, the beft friends to their country. Sir George Saville was a diftinguifhed member of the firft affociations; Mr. Reeves, a placeman, the *Prince* of Spies and Informers, is at the head of the latter. It remains for fober-minded men to determine, on which fide the truth lies; it is for them to judge, between a common hireling and Sir George Saville, the Pa-triot of his day. Other affociations are alfo *ftrictly legal*, and warmly countenanced by a *generous* ariftocracy; fuch, for example, as are united for the prefervation of game, and for bringing to condign punifhment the *guilty culprit*, who fhall have dared to kill a hare, or pheafant, that laid wafte his half rood of garden, and deftroyed its produce, intended for the fupport of himfelf and family.

Attornies,—a fet of mifcreants (for the moft part) in rapacity and cruelty inferior to none, but thofe who exercife a jurifdiction over them.

Author,—Duke of Leeds; Lord Mountmorres; Honorable Frank North; George Hanger.

B.

Balance of power,—a catch-word that incites nations to war; the politician's dream; a word now falling into difufe, its fallacy being detected.

Bankruptcy,—a proof of national profperity; the advantages refulting from our war with France.

France. Vide Dundas's fpeeches, Parliamentary Regifter.

Bargain,—minifterial loans; Brook Watfon's contract; 200,000l. a year fubfidized to the King of Sardinia, to enable him to defend his own dominions; fubfidies to the Elector of Hanover and the Landgrave of Heffe Caffel; a penfion of 1500l. per annum to the Jefuit of St. Omer's; the pecuniary douceur granted to Sir Gilbert Elliot, for his fervices at Toulon, &c. &c.

Baronet,—Sir Francis Molyneux.

Barrifter,—loquacity, impudence, prefumption, vanity, confequence, fophiftry, inconfiftency, and felf-intereft. Garrow.

Baftille,—Newgate; New Prifon, Cold-bathfields, finifhed under the SPECIAL DIRECTION of Mr. PITT.

Beggars,—national profperity! (Spital-fields) (ruined manufactures).

Bifhop,—a wolf in fheep's cloathing.

Blindnefs,—the Englifh nation; ' none are fo ' blind as thofe who won't fee.'

Bombaft,—Lord Grenville, and Pitt's fpeeches. Vide Parliamentary Regifter.

Boxing,—a fafhionable amufement, lately in great vogue, and chiefly patronifed by *Princes of the blood,* and *Nobles of the realm.*

Brag-

Braggadocio,—Colonel Tarleton, Sir Watkin Lewes, Sir Roger Curtis, Sir Sidney Smythe.

Brafs,—Dundas.

Bravery,—the *Royal Dunkirk Hero,* Lord Mulgrave, Earl Howe.

Briton,—flave.

Briton, (True) a minifterial newfpaper, fynonymous for *true informer,* defpotifm, lies, felf-intereft, and corruption.

Brunfwick, (Duke of) the *victorious hero* who threatened to exterminate twenty-five millions of people, if they did not fubmit to his arbitrary conditions ; and who, in lefs than a fortnight afterwards, was completely routed and put to flight, by a few volunteers of the above people.

Brutality,—thief-takers ; the keepers and turnkeys of gaols. A judge paffing fentence of DEATH againft a *youthful* convict not *fourteen* years old, for STEALING FIVE SHILLINGS. The late Earl of Lincoln, now Duke of Newcaftle, profecuting a countryman for killing a hare on his eftate, and afterwards declaring, on being told the magiftrates had *only* condemned the man to fix months imprifonment in the county-gaol, that had he known the fentence would have been fo *mild,* he would have profecuted him in the Exchequer, when he might have been able to tranfport the *culprit* to Botany-bay. The Lord Advocate of Scotland's fpeech

in

in the Englifh Houfe of Commons, on the cafe of
Muir and Palmer. The amufements of Princes
and nobles; boxing, cockfighting, hunting down
hares, fhooting partridges, woodcocks, &c. &c.
draymen abufing their draft horfes, and the Earl
of Darlington, a young NOBLEMAN, poffeffing
50,000l. a-year, riding one generous animal *fixty
miles in fix hours,* and thereby caufing the horfe's
death! Quere, Which be the greater brute, his
lordfhip or the horfe?

Budget,—new taxes; an increafe of influence to
the Crown, and of mifery to the poor.

Bully,—Lord Hervey, Lord Robert Fitzgerald,
the Britifh Envoys at Florence and Berne.

Burden,—a civil lift, a ftanding army.

Butchery,—a regiment of Englifh militia, at the
command of their officers, firing on their countrymen, the unarmed inhabitants of Briftol, when a
number of men, women, and children were killed.

C.

Calumny,—uniform abufe and exaggerated falfehoods againft the French.

Candour,—Earl Moira, on his paffage from oppofition to adminiftration; Pitt fupporting the neceffity for extending the prerogative of the Crown,
and juftifying himfelf for keeping up and enlarging
the fyftem of corruption, which he had formerly
pledged himfelf to abolifh.

Cannon,

Cannon,—the only argument of conviction to despots.

Chancery,—a tribunal which profeſſes to have no other objeĉt in view than the ſtrictĉeſt equity; an office requiring the moſt incorruptible honour and integrity, but which is generally filled by the vileſt tools and ſycophants of power, and, inſtead of being a faithful adminiſtration of ſpeedy and impartial juſtice, is proverbial for its extortion and delays. This office is generally allotted as a re-ward for apoſtacy.

Chaos,—confuſion; the Britiſh conſtitution, King, Lords, and Commons.

Charity,—enormous contributions for French rebels; an utter negleĉt of our own poor.

Chaſtity,—(*vertu unique*) Queen Charlotte.

Church,—a patent for hypocriſy; the refuge of ſloth, ignorance and ſuperſtition, the corner-ſtone of tyranny.

Citizen,—the moſt honourable of titles; the definition of a virtuous man.

Clemency,—the court of King's-bench; the court of Juſticiary in Scotland.

Client,—an unfortunate victim to ill-placed con-fidence, to the rapacity and plunder of lawyers.

Coalition,—an union of parties, when monopoly on either ſide is impoſſible, and when the principle itſelf is threatened, to defend and divide the loaves and fiſhes.

C

Cock

Cock (game),—a fanguinary, cruel tyrant. Vide the bill of indictment preferred againft D. I. Eaton; where the Attorney-General compares a game-cock to a cruel, fanguinary tyrant, and fays, that it muft mean our moft gracious Sovereign GEO. III.

Company, (Eaft India)—chartered robbers, licenfed murderers, fending out military ruffians to conquer, plunder, and defolate the remoteft countries.

Confidence,—a word employed by ftatefmen, in order to preferve their power, and enflave a nation to their yoke.

Confequence,—Pitt, *full dreffed*, furrounded by his myrmidons on the Treafury bench.

Confiftency,—Meffrs. Fox, Grattan, &c. &c.

Conftitution,—a code of laws, founded in principles of equal rights, and general happinefs, fuch as Kenyon and Afhurft define that of England, but which their practice proves directly the reverfe.

Contractors,—a fet of men who are known to live in luxury on the plunder of the ignorant, the innocent, and the helplefs ; upon that part of the community which ftands moft in need of and beft deferves the care and protection of the legiflature. In all Minifterial *contracts*, it is never a queftion of making a profitable bargain for the public ; the only object is to enrich the CONTRACTOR, who is always a *creature* of the *Minifter*. Brook Watfon, &c. &c. &c.

Contraft,

Contraſt,—the invincible ardour, the independ-ent ſpirit of a FRENCH REPUBLICAN ; the tame ſervility, the fawning ſycophancy of a *Britiſh courtier*; the RIGHTS OF MAN, by THOMAS PAINE ; *the libel on the human race*, by the *Right Honourable Edmund Burke*; the manifeſtos of ty-rants, the anſwers of freemen, the *impudent aſſer-tions* of *Grenville* or *Mansfield*; the IRRESISTIBLE TRUTHS of STANHOPE ; a convention of the peo-ple, a parliament of ariſtocracy.

Corporation,—an infamous relic of the ancient feudal ſyſtem ; a tyrannical, excluſive monopoly, generally conſiſting of gluttons, idiots, and oppreſ-ſors ; brutes in a human form.

Corruption,—" the oil which makes the wheels " of Government go well." Vide Arthur Young's Example of France, a Warning to Britain, p. 191.

Courtier,—Duke of Montroſe, Lords Cheſter-field, Elgin, Sidney, Rivers, Onſlow, &c. &c. &c. a ſycophant.

Court,—the dunghill that breeds the above ver-min ; the focus that conſumes the induſtry and la-bour of the people. Halifax, himſelf a courtier, ſtiles it a den of well fed, well dreſſed beggars.

Cowardice,—military ruffians aſſaulting the Rev. Dr. Knox, his wife and daughter, at the Bright-helmſtone theatre.

Crown,

Crown,—a jewel that dazzles the eye of the vulgar by its extensive splendor; the gewgaw and pageantry which it displays, reconciles the nation to a bauble which costs a million annually to support, drained from the virtue of industry, and the sweat of labour. Partial splendour, public calamity.

Cruelty,—Lord Hood commanding a man of war filled with helpless prisoners to be sunk; the horrors perpetrated on men and women in La Vendee by rebels fighting against the liberties of their native country; criminal laws that inflict capital punishment for trivial offences; the SLAVE TRADE.

D

Dagger,—a figure in rhetoric, unknown to ancient and modern orators, till the days of Mr. Edmund Burke, to whose *pointed* genius we are indebted for the discovery.

Damien,—a virtuous assassin, who aimed an abortive blow at the life of a tyrant (Louis XV.) who by his prodigality and brutal vices had scattered famine far and wide over his country, and corrupted the morals of a whole people. Damien underwent the most studied and excruciating tortures; his eye-balls were torn out; hot boiling lead, drop by drop, was poured into their sockets, and every refinement of cruellest invention

prac-

practifed on his mangled body ; and for what ? for an ineffectual attempt to rid the world of a monfter, who every day of his life was the caufe of mifery and death to thoufands. Damien expired on the bed of torture. The other was fuffered to die in peace on a bed of ftate ; but after death, the people could not be reftrained from venting their execration, and pointing their wrath againft his putrid Royal corpfe.

Death,—the grand leveller of human diftinctions. Armed with his dreadful fcymitar, he mows down princes and peafants indifcriminately ; but he is partial to forrow and misfortune, vifiting the wretched under their afflictions, and relieving them from all their troubles, while at the very fame inftant he will hurl a tyrant, in the plenitude of omnipotence, from his throne, and level the conqueror of worlds in the duft. He will ftand invifible at the elbow of Kings, when they are meditating the moft wafteful and unbounded fchemes of ambition and conqueft, the flavery of their own fubjects, and the extermination of diftant empires. Death in an inftant blafts their infernal projects, and fends them to their account, with all their enormities on their heads.

Debauchery,—Carlton-houfe, Kempfhot. The Dunkirk Hero in a fit of intoxication at three o'clock o'clock in the morning at a brothel, furrounded by half a dozen proftitutes, watching a favourable opportunity to pick his pocket.

Scene in W-t-n's, Berkeley-ftreet.

Debt (National).—*Politicians* defcribe the immenfity of our public debt as the fureft proof of our profperity. *Philofophers* lament it, as the caufe of unparalleled taxation and poverty to the people.

Degeneracy,—Old England.

Delufion,—the ruling principle and laft furviving hope of the Britifh Cabinet.

Democrat,—one who maintains the rights of the people; an enemy to privileged orders, and all monarchical encroachments, the advocate of peace, œconomy, and reform. Ariftotle affirms that liberty can never flourifh out of a democracy. Montefquieu calls it the nurfery of virtue.

Difcontent (popular). In the ariftocratic dictionary, fedition. When people, vexed and goaded by oppreffion, exprefs difcontent, ariftocracy deems it fedition. The judges tell them they have *no right* to complain; things cannot be better, and the *law* finally condemns them to the pillory, fine, and two years confinement in one of his Majefty's *Baftilles,* there to learn patience, refignation, and fubmiffion. The word will alfo admit of another conftruction. " When popular difcontents have " been very prevalent, it may fafely be affirmed
" that

" that there has been something amifs in the *confti-*
" *tution,* or in the conduct of Government."———
Burke's Thoughts on the Cause of the Prefent
Difcontents. Mr. Burke's opinion has fince undergone a complete revolution.

Difappointment,—Our *Royal Dunkirk Hero* raif-
ing the fiege of that place, reduced to the neceffity of leaving his artillery behind, and of faving
himfelf by a precipitate flight; the evacuation
of Toulon, and the recovery of King George III.
in the year 1789.

Difinterefiednefs,—the rapacity of courtiers, increafing with the diftreffes of their country; Lord
Grenville accepting the Auditorfhip of the Exchequer, a finecure yielding ten thoufand a year, while
the nation is almoft reduced to beggary; and
Lord Loughborough giving up the Common Pleas
for the Seals, at a time when, on an average, there
was not more than fifty commiffions of bankruptcy
figned per week, and when the profits of each commiffion to his Lordfhip *did not exceed* FIFTEEN
POUNDS.

Diffimulation,—an art in which Kings excel.
The late Louis Capet, King of France, fell a victim to the fatal fkill with which he practifed its
refinements. There are other Kings ftill greater
adepts in the art, and who continue to practife it
with incredible fuccefs, although it is not morally
im-

impoffible but a fimilar fate may finally befal them. *Fafts and prayers*, all the external *cant* of religion, are attributes of diffimulation. Halifax ftiles it " a jewel in the crown."

Divinity,—the Bench of Bifhops uniformly voting in their capacity as legiflators, againft the maxims of the gofpel, in fupport of war and extermination.

Drunkennefs,—Meffrs. Pitt and Dundas, when fo intoxicated with liquor, as not to be able to articulate their words, engaging a vaft majority in the Houfe of Commons to precipitate their country into a war with France; the feftivities of Brighton, Holwood, Wimbledon, Gordon Houfe, Downing-ftreet; the Duke of Norfolk drinking common gin with the *Royal Sovereign*, at her lodgings in Strand-lane.

Dullnefs,—Poet Jerningham's *tragedy*; the Siege of Berwick; Lady Wallace's *comedy*; Mrs. Robinfon's novels; the Houfe of Peers; fafhionable routs; Monfieur Le Texier's Readings; and their Majefties private parties.

Dunce,—Lord G--nv-lle, Tom St--le, Colonel Cawthorne, &c. &c.

E.

Effeminacy,—a word, the meaning of which was once illuftrated by the French nation, till the no-

ble

ble spirit of republicanism destroyed the ancient character, and gave birth to those prodigies of heroism and magnanimity, that at present justly rank it the first nation of the earth.. Effeminacy is now perfectly well described in Fop's Alley, at our Opera House in the Haymarket, by the descendants of Hampden, Sidney, Russell, and other British patriots. The two nations have undergone a complete revolution of character. *Regeneration* and *degeneracy*.

Emigrant (English),—one who, like Dr. Priestley or Thomas Cooper, is compelled to fly from persecution, and explore liberty in a far distant land, probably America, the states of Europe, for the most part, France excepted, being rank despotisms. The late dreadful punishments that have been inflicted under the sanction of a Government *calling itself free*; the restrictions imposed upon citizens, the intolerable and still increasing taxes, the foreign armies that have been landed, and the military barracks erected throughout the country, have produced an extraordinary effect on the public mind, and threaten such an emigration as ought to create the most serious apprehensions. When Mr. P-tt was called into power, the death-warrant of Old England's remaining liberties, and, with them, of her greatness, was signed. It were preposterous to suppose, whenever peace shall be establish-

D   ed,

ed, that Induſtry and Labour will devote their
ſervices to an old, exhauſted, worn-out ſyſtem,
working its own diſſolution, and which is only pre-
ſerved in its preſent rotten ſtate by an immenſity
of impoſt, that robs the virtues by which alone it
is kept from mortification ; while new conſtitutions,
UNTAXED, with every advantage of climate, and
all the irreſiſtible charms of Freedom, ſhall invite
them to emigration. England, thy Sun is ſet.

Emigrant (French),—one who flies his country ſtruggling for freedom, and becomes its enemy; who enliſts under a foreign banner to fight
againſt it. One who labours by treaſon and maſſacre to revive that ancient deſpotiſm, under which
ſo many millions of victims were born *without hope*,
and periſhed *through want*, but under which, he
himſelf enjoyed all the *milk* and *honey* of the
land. One who leaves his wife, his children,
and every thing that ſhould be moſt dear and ſacred to him, in the hands of his enemies, and who
hopes to deliver them by ſword, by fire, and by
famine ; who finds it unjuſt that theſe enemies (his
countrymen, whom he has abandoned) ſhould
ſeize his effects, and treat him with rigour, although
he publickly avows, that ſhould he himſelf be victorious, he will ſhew grace and indulgence to
none. One who complains alſo, that the foreigners, on whoſe ſervices he relies, have the moſt in-
tereſted

terefted and venal views, although at the fame time he confeffes that thefe foreigners owed no obligation to him, and that they all had ever been the fecret enemies of his country, &c. &c.

Enemy (natural).—*National enmities* have been always produced and encouraged by kingly and prieftly policy. The wolf is the *natural enemy* of the lamb; the vulture of the dove. *By inflinct they are fo. They muft live;* but one people can never be the *natural enemy* of another; unlefs we confider mankind in the fame favage light as the vulture and the wolf. A nation is no more than a member of that large family, the human race, and can only flourifh in proportion with the felicity and welfare of the whole. What greater abfurdity can be imagined, than that a people who owe all their profperity to commerce, that is to fay, to their connections with other people, fhould call themfelves the *natural enemy* of this or of that people, and indeed of every thing that is not confined within their own circle! Is it not evident that this abominable prejudice is kept up by a gang of *plunderers* and *monopolizers,* under protection of CHURCH and STATE, who find their advantage and emolument in it?

Enquiry,—according to the modern conftruction, fignifies Sedition. In the old Englifh dictionary, it was held a CONSTITUTIONAL PRIVI-

LEGE,

LEGE, derived from MAGNA CHARTA and the BILL OF RIGHTS, for the people to *enquire* into the conduct of Kings or Ministers, and into the errors of their government ; but all things now seem in a state of revolution, and, according to Mr. P-tt's new code, which is implicitly adopted by all the legal courts through the three kingdoms, *enquiry* implies disloyalty, sedition, or treason, and they who are *audacious* enough to claim this ancient *obsolete* privilege, expose themselves to the penalties of fine, pillory, or imprisonment, and if in Scotland, of transportation for fourteen years to BOTANY BAY. The people, however, begin to murmur at the revolution that the word has undergone, and to *think* this is not altogether a FREE country.

Enterprize.—This word implies judgement to conceive plans, with ability and skill to execute them. The *best* definition of the word may be found in the history of our last campaign against the French in the years 1793-94, and in the gallant Earl Moira's *projected œconomical* expedition to the coast of France.

Equality,—in the *Alarmist* vocabulary, signifies every thing morally and physically impossible ; equal wisdom, equal strength, equal wealth, &c. &c. but equality *truly* signifies, both in France and England, as well as every where else, "EQUAL
" RIGHTS;"

" RIGHTS ;" a RIGHT of every citizen, not dif- qualified by nature or by crime, to the protection and benefits of fociety ; a right of voting for the election of thofe who are to make laws by which he himfelf is to be bound; by which, his liberty, his property, and his life are affected, and an equal right of exerting to advantage the genius and ta- lents which he may poffefs—*the equal rights of na- ture.*

Extermination,—the principle of the war in which the combined powers are engaged againft France ;—to *deftroy* twenty-five millions of people, or otherwife to *force* on them fuch a government, as thefe combined powers, in their *clemency* and *wifdom,* fhall approve: fuch is the war in which the rulers of nations have involved their fubjects ; in which, already more than 300,000 men have been flaughtered, during the courfe of two campaigns ; neverthelefs, thefe horrible maffacres feem only to have increafed the fury, by which thefe defpots are ftimulated ; and thus myriads of innocent, ignorant victims ftill continue, without reflection, to obey the tyrants order, and to yield their willing throats to the butcher's knife. " Ye gods, what havock " does ambition make amongft your works!"

F

Faction,—in its *primitive* fenfe, fignifies mifchief, confpiracy, oppofition to good and lawful government ;

ment ; likewife, *fecret* cabals or an *open*, violent conteft between two unprincipled, reftlefs, rapacious parties, for a monopoly of the fpoils of a plundered, exhaufted people. In another, that is, in the *Minifterial* fenfe, *faction* is *virtue*; but a *virtue* liable to the heavieft penalties and punifhments. Affociations of citizens peaceably met together for difcuffing the abufes of Government, and for deliberating on the fafeft and moft effectual method of procuring their reform; an enquiry into the meafures of their fervants, (the Minifters) and an exercife of thofe privileges, which Englifhmen were taught by fome of thefe minifters themfelves to believe inherent in their *free* conftitution, are now conftrued into faction, and thus, the word is poffeffed of *two different* fignifications.

Whether Mr. P-tt's *modern* reading, or the *ancient* conftruction be the *juft* one, well deferves the ferious confideration of our *popular focieties* throughout Great Britain and Ireland, who would act wifely in affording to their *heaven-born* Minifter, a STRIKING fpecimen of *their* opinions on the fubject.

Perhaps, after all, the moft accurate definition of the word *faction*, is to be found in the coalition between alarmifts and courtiers, in defence of R-y-l prerogative, of extravagant finecures, fupernumerary places, and unmerited penfions; as

well

well as of every other species of corrupt influence, againft the rights and liberties of mankind ;—in the confederation of Kings againft the independence of the French Republic, as folemnly ratified by the people, through the organ of reprefentatives, FAIRLY and CONSTITUTIONALLY elefted by their own FREE UNBOUGHT fuffrages.

Faith,—credulity, fuperftition. An article loudly extolled and vehemently infifted on, in all ages, by PRIESTS and KINGS. Succefs has crowned their exertions. Mankind, on every occafion, have *opened a gullet* wide enough to fwallow the abfurdeft paradoxes, the moft glaring impoffibilities. Only fay, that " an army of foldiers was feen laft " night to pafs over the moon, " and you will immediately perceive a vaft legion of implicit believers making their comments and remarks on the *phenomenon,* explaining it on the authority of fcriptural prophecies. Nothing too prepofterous for popular credulity, which has been always fed and cherifhed by the great leaders in Church and State; knowing this, on that bafis only their empire depends. Thus have nations by dint of error and fuperftition, for a vaft fucceffion of ages, yielded themfelves up to the dominion of r-y-l or prieftly authority, which, in moft inftances, have formed a coalition for the purpofe, whereby

the

the community have been plunged into a fathom-
lefs abyfs of fervitude and ignorance, from which
patriotifm and philofophy have hitherto laboured
in vain to refcue them. The FAITH infpired by
prieftcraft and *ftate-craft*, is the prime caufe of
that mifery and tyranny, which, to this hour, continue to rage through the univerfe. The SCOURGES
OF THE WORLD are held out by PRIESTS, as the
VICEGERENTS OF HEAVEN, and the opinions
and confciences of men, till very lately, have been
almoft entirely directed by *priefts;* but as their
empire is terribly convulfed by the revolution in
France, which has ferved fo effentially to enlighten
the human underftanding, may it foon be totally
deftroyed, and may Wifdom, Peace and Philanthropy erect a lafting throne, on the wreck of
FAITH, Error, and Superftition! Their reign
has been too long ; they have ruled with an iron
fceptre. It is time for Peace to fix her refidence
amongft us. The Millenium, however, can never
arrive, till FAITH in *priefts* and fovereigns be annihilated. Their intereft, their ambition is war—
the grand engine of CHURCH and STATE.

Fame,—a term in general moft barbaroufly mif-
applied. Murderers have been ftiled heroes, and
conquerors gods. To immortalize *their* memory,
maufoleums have been raifed, the arts of invention
ranfacked, and the imagination of genius exhaufted;

ed; while the *real benefactor* of mankind, caſt
during his mortal pilgrimage in an humble ſphere,
may after death, continue to rot in an obſcure,
neglected grave, without any honourable memorial
to preſerve his name from obſivion.; but it is time
ſuch unnatural prejudices and unjuſt diſtinctions
ſhould ceaſe. Every generous ſpirit aſpires to
FAME. It ſhould be the virtuous ſtudy of phi-
loſophy to give to public gratitude a proper direction. Too long have genius and talents been
proſtituted at the footſtool of power, to adulate
the crimes of CONQUERORS and KINGS. A
brighter example is due. Let us *juſtly* beſtow the
meed of Fame.

Let us ſtrew choiceſt flowers o'er the tombs of
virtue; let us venerate with pious ſorrow and affectionate gratitude, the bleſſed ſhades of Hampden,
Sidney, and Milton; thoſe *true heroes*, who, during
life, had virtue to reſiſt, and fortitude to endure,
the fierceſt malice of *tyrannic* power. Let us con-
ſecrate to immortality, the memory of all thoſe patriots, who have ſuffered and bled for the ſacred
cauſe of Freedom.

Let us alſo be liberal in our praiſe and benefac-
tions towards thoſe generous martyrs for righteouſ-
neſs ſake, who are now groaning in cruel bon-
dage, baniſhed to a far diſtant, barren, and inhoſpitable ſhore, the victims of a moſt ferocious deſ-

E   potiſm.

potifm. Let us pour the balm of confolation on their wounded fouls, and enfure to them the no-bleft enjoyments to which they afpire ;—the praife of their fellow-citizens, the applaufe and admiration of pofterity.

Let 'em remember that they carry with them the regret, the efteem, the affection of their countrymen ;—of fuch, at leaft, whofe hearts are not dead to humanity and to juftice.

Let them cherifh the grateful hope, that the fyftem of delufion and tyranny is about to expire, that their fufferings will be of fhort duration, that their chains will be broken on the heads of their oppreffors, and that their return will be hailed with acclamations of joy, by an applauding and regenerated people.

Let 'em alfo reflect that the breafts of the mercilefs tyrants who torture *them*, are *themfelves* tortured ;—not by the pangs of fenfibility and remorfe, but by the fcorpion ftings of terror, anxiety and alarm, which inceffantly goad them, and that amidft the tempeftous billows of the ocean, with all the devoted victims of evil Government and misfortune before their eyes, they enjoy more ferenity of mind, more fearlefs flumbers, than the *unrighteous, hardened* J—g—s who paffed the fentence againft them, or than the INEXORABLE

M-G-T-E

M-G-T-E who confented to the execution of that fentence.

Tremble, ye cruel Potentates, who plunge your fubjects in mifery and tears, who defolate nations, and convert the fruitful earth into a fterile burying ground. Tremble for your impending fate! It requires not the fpirit of prophecy to foretel your d—f—l is at hand. Shudder at the fanguinary traits with which hiftory, incenfed, will unfold your characters to future ages;—neither your fplendid monuments, nor your impofing victories, nor your unnumbered armies will prevent pofterity from infulting over your execrable remains, and avenging their anceftors on your horrible tranfgreffions.

Such will be your inevitable doom on the approaching æra of light, which promifes to break in upon us ;—while the virtues that ye have profcribed and banifhed fhall be rewarded, and the memory of the martyrs to thofe virtues, be confecrated by the grateful voice of juft and unperifhable FAME. *They* will be remembered by remoteft ages, for having ftood forth, in a moft eventful and dangerous crifis, the intrepid champions of LIBERTY and TRUTH ;—while *you* will be only recollected as examples of horror, from the cruelties and enormities ye have committed, under the mafk of *Piety* and *Religion* : ye fhall be configned to

E 2 *eternal*

eternal INFAMY, while *they* (as we have often repeated) fhall flourifh in EVERLASTING FAME.

Famine.—For the exiftence of this word, we
are indebted to the *magnanimous* exploits of CON-
QUERORS and KINGS. It is generally applied in
an extenfive fenfe, fignifying whole nations or
provinces reduced to a want of the neceffary articles of life; a general fcarcity. Indulgent nature
had liberally provided, throughout the world,
every thing requifite for the fuftenance and ufeof
its inhabitants; and it is only by an ungrateful abufe
of her liberality, by a departure from her mild and
equal fyftem, that man is become his own tormentor. The fatal politics which European governments have either preferved, or borrowed
from the old feudal fyftem; the encouragement
granted, efpecially by kingly powers, to exclufive
charters and monopolies; an irrefiftible incentive
to avarice and peculation; the miferable diftinctions into which they have fplit fociety, and the
plans invented, under the plaufible but murderous pretexts of commerce, for the purpofes of
robbery and *plunder*, have inflicted, amongft fo
any others, this horrible fcourge on mankind.
Monarchical governments are particularly *well
fkilled* in the arts of reducing a nation to a
ftate of *famine*. When the Englifh bought
up

up all the rice at Calcutta, the natives daily expired by thousands at the doors of the houses inhabited by our countrymen, and the jackalls were tranquilly beheld in immense numbers pouring down from the mountains, to regale themselves on their carcases, and to drink their blood; yet this dreadful spectacle made little impression on British sensibility. One individual, Sir Francis Sykes, originally a shoe-black (happy for the poor inhabitants of Bengal, had he never quitted that obscure harmless station) is supposed to have acquired 200,000l by the above monopoly, by which almost as many Indians are supposed to have perished; so rigidly did they adhere to the purity of their religion, which prohibits in all cases, the use of animal flesh: nevertheless Sir Francis has been long returned to Europe with his wealth, enjoys unmolested, *otium cum dignitate;* has a seat in the British senate, boroughs at his command, and has been rewarded, by our most gracious Sovereign, with the title of *Baronet.*

Famine is one of the *gentlest* instruments employed by our *heaven-born* minister in the present *just* and *religious* war with France. All the treasons he has fomented, all the massacres he has planned and caused to be committed, having proved insufficient, he still indulges the hope of being able

able to starve twenty-five millions of people, and, thereby at last to conquer that nation.

It has been well observed by a sagacious writer, " that if there *no* KINGS, there would be " *no* WARS ;" and, certainly, if there were no wars, there could be no conquests ; of course, famine would be unknown ; for nature, seldom or never, in the worst of seasons, is herself so rigorous, even in the most barren regions, or where the inhabitants are most addicted to sloth and effeminacy, as to refuse supply of their real wants. Indeed in those countries where the heat of climate disposes the natives to indolence, nature in general yields her gifts spontaneously ; whereas, in more ungrateful climes, the people are prone to toil and labour. But war does the business effectually in all countries, however fertile or industrious. During the war previous to the peace of Ryswick, the price of corn was *double* in England, and in *Scotland* *quadruple* its ordinary rate ; and in one of the years pending that war, eighty thousand persons died of WANT in the last mentioned country. Nevertheless, while Kings, Prelates, and Nobles, are not exposed to the horrors of *famine*, it is perfectly *consistent* that the people should always, as at present, 1794, co-operate with their leaders to inflict it on themselves. When famine rages in the heart of a country, the prodigality of a court

expe-

experiences no abatement; there it is unfelt; courts are exempt from the calamities which they spread over the universe.

Fashion.—Whatever custom prevails amongst the great, whatever mode of dress, particular idiom of expression, or *cant* word, is by them employed, we stile *Fashion*; and, in general, no matter how contemptible, mischievous, or unnatural, we are eager to adopt and practise the absurdity.

Thus we perceive, what a vast influence *Fashion* must necessarily have over the morals of society, and how much its welfare consequently depends on the example of the superior orders. It is therefore to be lamented, that those to whom we look up as our *betters*, should so seldom set up VIRTUE as a *fashion*; but that, instead thereof, they should only afford us an example of the most extravagant follies, of the rankest debaucheries. If a Prince of Wales should delight in the most violent excesses of the table, it is then the *fashion* to be eternally *drunk*; if he should, on every occasion, display symptoms of heedless and unbounded prodigality, it is then the *ton* to fix no limits to our expences; or, if he should take *it in his head* to talk nonsense, it then becomes quite the fashion to do like the Prince, and talk like a fool. Hence the contagion immediately pervades every department of the community,

from

from his Royal Highnefs's LORD IN WAITING,
down to the *loweſt journeyman ſhopkeeper.*

In like manner if a Duke of York, anxious to
make a ſplendid parade of his *great military talents,*
ſhould cry out for war, the whole Britiſh nobleſſe
re-echo the found, and the nation breathes the ſame
warlike ſpirit, till after two or three unfortunate
campaigns, the treaſury drained, commerce de-
cayed, manufactures annihilated, the maſs of the
people reduced to beggary, they begin to deplore
their madnefs, and to invoke the bleſſings of peace.
Now then is arrived the ſeaſon of reflection; now
is the time for Britons to deliberate on the policy
or impolicy of implicitly ſubmitting to the doctrines, or blindly adopting the principles, of the
Great. Now is the time for them moſt ſeriouſly
to conſider whether ſociety owes any obligation to
their virtues, whether it ought to entertain any rational hope of improvement, or happinefs, either
from *their* exertions or ſacrifices; and, finally, it
becomes neceſſary now to determine, how far it will
be wiſe or prudent, any longer to abide by thoſe
FASHIONS, which, for ſo many ages, have been
impoſed on the world.

Faſt (by proclamation),—a *farce.* The people
called on to go to church and neglect their buſi-
nefs, while miniſters are celebrating their carou-
ſals, and getting drunk at each other's houſes. An
impious

impious mummery, or rather blafphemy. We
are told of our national fins, and, in expiation of
them, are inftructed to befeech the GOD OF PEACE
to blefs our exterminating principles of war; to fet
ourfelves up as a people diftinct, on whom ex-
clufively, he ought to fhower his benign protection, and to crown our efforts, in deftroying
countlefs millions of his creatures. A court jug-
gle; a flimfy jefuitical contrivance to inflame the
public mind, and to give the clergy an opportunity
of promulgating their flavifh maxims, their political
herefies from the pulpit.

Favourite (Royal).—Weak and arbitrary princes, from the firft eftablifhment of monarchy,
down to the prefent day, have always had their
favourites, their Minions, their KNIGHTS of the
BACK STAIRS; many of whom have eventually
fallen juft facrifices to the vengeance of a people
who could no longer endure their outrages and
enormities. A wife Prince has no other *favourite* than the people. He can have no right to
fquander *fuperfluities* on *favourites*,—to keep up
prodigal eftablifhments for them, while the nation
is crufhed by a weight of taxes, and a majority of
it reduced almoft to a want of *neceffaries*: but, as
nothing can be more capricious than a monarch's
fancy, the fituation of thefe gentry is not the moft
enviable or fecure; and the examples yielded by

F   hiftory

hiftory are *rather a drawback* on their tranquillity.
They may be compared to fun-dials, which, while
the fun fhines upon them, all the world are eager
to confult, but are at once forfaken, and left to their
fate, as foon as he has withdrawn his rays.

Feftival,—holiday,—a day fet apart for the com-
memoration of any honourable or profperous
event. The GREEKS and ROMANS celebrated
their triumphs by Olympic games, that trained
their youth to martial exercifes, and which have
been fo beautifully defcribed by their poets and
hiftorians.

The FRENCH REPUBLIC difplays all the fubli-
mity of fentiment, all the richnefs of imagination,
and ardour of patriotifm, in thofe civic *feftivals*
which the Convention decrees, in honour of any
fplendid victory, or important advantage, which the
arms of Liberty atchieve over the forces of Treachery and Defpotifm. Magnificent proceffions, no
longer fullied by the ignoble badges of fuperftition
and fanaticifm, but embellifhed with all the infignia
of peace, freedom, and equality, animating citizens
with an invincible hatred of tyrants, and a facred
love for the divine caufe in which they are engaged. Painting, mufic, fculpture, all the arts,
elegantly and honourably brought forth for the
common fervice of mankind. A fpectacle com-
bining the happieft affemblage of fimplicity and
grandeur,

grandeur, which it is impoſſible for a generous ſoul to contemplate without glowing with the immortal ſpirit of juſtice and philanthropy.

The Engliſh obſerve *their feſtivals* in a different manner. Of late, God knows, they have had few triumphs to celebrate; but they have ſtill their public days of rejoicing;—a Prince of Wales, or Duke of York's birth-day! when *oxen are roaſted intire;* and, as if the people were not already ſufficiently ſtupified, they are to be further lethargized by dint of BEEF and PORTER, of GLUTTONY and DRUNKENNESS. Then they are taught to ſhout " *God ſave the King,*" and to believe all human virtue and morality contained in that ſenſeleſs ſound. The *only* GENIUS which diſplays itſelf in theſe our *Engliſh feſtivals,* is the GENIUS of Brutality, the GENIUS of Deluſion, or the GENIUS of Confuſion, the whole ſyſtem of right and wrong confounded, order perverted, vice and folly exalted to the ſkies, virtue and talents ſunk in the duſt;—a profligate blockhead, whoſe ſole merit probably hangs on a *royal eſcutcheon,* held up as a PAGOD of adoration, while a man like Gerrald, with tranſcendant abilities, and moſt amiable modeſty, is *tamely* beheld, in violation of all ENGLISH law, of every principle of juſtice, languiſhing in Newgate, hourly expecting to be

ſeized

ſeized and dragged to the veſſel that is to convey his poor infirm, emaciated body to Botany Bay.

The beſt illuſtration of theſe different entertainments, is diſplayed in the civic *feſtivals*, as arranged by David, and exhibited in the Champs de Mars at Paris, an account of which may be ſeen in Jordan's Political State of Europe, and in the *ſplendid feaſts* given in honour of a royal Prince or Duke's birth-day, at Brighton and other places; an account of which may be ſeen in moſt of our periodical journals for the months of Auguſt, 1791-92. From the contraſt, Britons may, in ſome degree, be enabled to form an eſtimate of the virtues and genius peculiar to each nation. To know the difference between a

BRITISH ROYALIST, & a FRENCH REPUBLICAN

GOD SAVE THE KING. VIVE LA REPUBLIQUE.

Amen.

Financier,—a Chancellor of the Exchequer who excels in taking money from the people's pocket in the eaſieſt and *genteeleſt* manner. When it is neceſſary to raiſe a loan, or to levy taxes, the miniſter, like the frog in the fable, ready to burſt with the ſenſe of his own dignity and importance, collects around him the monied men of the city, and attends to their different propoſitions, with all the affected gravity of his ſtation. He then conſults one confidential and experienced friend, who is al-

ways employed on thefe occafions, whofe advice
he uniformly follows, and then, wrapt up in the
mantle of pride and confequence, he goes down to
the Houfe of Commons, opens his budget in an
eloquent, elaborate fpeech, in which he fhines with
borrowed feathers, and thus on the merit of another, Mr. Pitt acquires the *reputation* of a moft
accurate calculator, of an excellent *Financier*.

Flat,—a kind of *flafh* word, defcribing a perfon
eafily impofed on, unfufpecting, credulous. One
who fuffers himfelf to be cajoled by *words*, without looking to *works*. One who talks of the excellence of our conftitution, at the very moment when
the conftitution is violated in all points; one who
has implicit belief in the *parliamentary orators* who
declare " that the people do not pay enough for
" their *happy* government," while they are taxed at
the rate of *feventeen fhillings in the pound*, and who
urge as a plea againft furrendering the leaft part of
the profits arifing from their finecures and penfions,
that in fo doing, they would encourage a belief that
the government was not worth fo much as was paid
for it.* Great Britain at this day is the land of
Flats.

* Vide Mr. Montague's fpeech on Mr. Harrifon's motion
for appropriating a part of certain penfions and finecure
places to particular purpofes.——Morning Poft, Wednefday,
April 9th, 1794.

Flattery,

Flattery,—a fort of bafe money, which has a vaft circulation in *Courts.* It cannot be defcribed better than in the words of a modern author: " Reverfing all the rules of juftice and humanity, " matured in the vile arts of adulation, at the " fame time arrogant and overbearing, a *courtier* " will turn his back on tranfcendent merit, in the " garb of modefty and misfortune ; while with " fawning fmiles, he will cringe at the heel of the " moft defpicable folly or hideous defpotifm, if " invefted with the *facred* robes of r-y-l impu- " nity.

" The *trade* of courtiers is *flattery* : it has paf- " fed uniform and fyftematic in its progrefs " through a fucceffion of ages ; and, on princes " the leaft deferving, it has generally been lavifh- " ed in moft copious ftreams. Mæcénas, the " patron of Genius, degraded his high charaĉter as " the parafite of Aguftus ; and the mufe of Boi- " leau was proftituted to footh the pride, and gra- " tify the vanity and ambition of Louis XIV. " who, in his day, was the fcourge and tormentor " of Europe,

" Tyrants, whofe crimes reflect obloquy on hu- " man nature, have been deified during life, and " canonized after death ; till *flattery,* having loft " its object, Reafon refumes her empire, and the " once triumphant monfter buried in the duft, his

" infamy

" infamy revives; Truth conquers in her turn,
" and honeft Hiftory paints him in faithful co-
" lours. The *fceptered murderer,* whom the
" *Chriftian Church* hailed as the *Faith's Defender,*
" and *he alfo* was *nicknamed* the FATHER OF HIS
" PEOPLE, who received the proftituted incenfe
" of praife, even from perfons, who, in that age,
" were regarded as models of primitive fimplicity
" and virtue ; now ftripped of his gorgeous and
" royal robes, long fince reduced to the com-
" mon level of mortality, is furveyed in his *true*
" *native* light, in comparifon with whom Commo-
" dus, or Nero, were gods."——Treachery No·
Crime, p. 4, 5, 6.

Fool.—It was once the fafhion in European courts
to keep a fool for the diverfion of *kings.* A *fool* is
not at prefent fpecifically mentioned in our civil
lift although we all know that it is clogged with
many *fools,* for whofe *follies* and prodigalities,
John Bull is *foolifh* enough to pay moft extrava-
gantly, while he himfelf is hardly indulged with a
morfel of bread to allay his hunger. The old cuftom
of retaining a *fool* and *jefter* is not altogether obfolete at the Britifh court. Quick, the low comedian,
and the Earl of C—ft—f—ld, are two diftinguifhed favourites and companions of our *wife* Monarch G—ge III.

Fortune,—like the fun, makes the vileft reptiles
fhine. The houfe of a Prime Minifter is regarded

as

as the Temple of *Fortune*. No deity ever had so many *votaries*. The temple, at present, is in Downing-street, where myriads assemble to pour forth their adoration; but the WOODEN GOD is threatened to be demolished; and, whenever the danger approaches, all the *votaries* will run away, and the IDOL be dashed to pieces; so precarious, so *very* precarious, is *Fortune*.

France.—The day probably is not far distant, when *all the governments of Europe* will make *amende honorable* to the French Republic, and when *all the people of Europe* will invoke benedictions on it, as their saviour, their deliverer, in having enabled them to purge the earth of their tyrants and oppressors. A nation once of the most abject slaves; now a race of heroes! When liberty is to be the prize, what miracles may not be expected?

Fulsome,—Charles Fox eternally passing compliments in his parliamentary speeches on the infamous *B—ke*. The manner in which members of both Houses of Parliament address each other. Noble Duke, Noble Lord, Right Honorable Gentleman, Learned Friend, &c. &c. &c. This language may very properly be styled *fulsome*, since it is generally applied to the most unfeeling and corrupt beings of the human race.

G. *Gaming,*

G.

Gaming,—a vice originating in avarice, almost univerfally predominant.—The example of the great ferves to encourage it, the lower claffes being never very flow in endeavours to imitate their fuperiors. Gaming, therefore, rages through all ranks and conditions—from the tennis-court in James's-ftreet, to the fkittle-alleys in St. George's-fields;—from the fpeculating, peculating adventurer, who, at *one ftroke* with the Minifter, gains 50,000l. by the purchafe of a lottery, down to the unfortunate female fervant, who pawns to her laft rag to enfure the number of which fhe dreamt laft night. It is impoffible for a *gambler* to rifque his money fo difadvantageoufly as in lotteries; but they are dreffed up in a meretricious garb, to entrap the ignorant and inexperienced.

Nothing can betray the profligacy of a minifter more, than his everlafting recourfe to this murderous inftrument of revenue, this encouragement which he annually holds forth to the depravation of morals, and to the general injury of fociety. But what fignify the morals of the people? It is his bufinefs to corrupt them; for he knows full well, that if the people had any morals, they would foon *hurl him* from his *place;* for which reafon, *gaming* and all other enormities are encouraged

which

which *bring in grift to his mill,* and which have a tendency to preferve his authority.

Gaming is an abominable vice, and always thrives in proportion to the corruption and degeneracy of a people. It was ingeniouſly obſerved by a French moraliſt, reſpecting *gamblers,*

" On commence par être dupe, on finit par être Fripon."

" We begin by being dupes, and finiſh by being knaves."

As this is too often the caſe, an honeſt man had better be content in any ſtation, than embark on the dangerous ocean of PLAY. The *French Republic* have aboliſhed lotteries, and enacted ſevere laws againſt *gaming.* But the French are *Atheiſts,* and what is *much worſe,* they are REPUBLICANS.

Garniſh.—When a poor priſoner is committed to gaol, he fares but rudely, unleſs he *tips* the turn-keys and gaoler their *garniſh,* which is the *cant* word for money on theſe occaſions. This *garniſh* produces miraculous effects; it ſtrikes off the heavieſt irons from the leg of the MURDERER; while, for want of it, the limbs of the INNOCENT are often loaded therewith. *Garniſh* is a word per-fectly well underſtood in all our *courts* of law, and although rather in the *flaſh* vulgar ſtyle, it is not altogether unknown in more polite and *immaculate courts.*

For

For a further illuftration of this word, confult Meffrs. Haftings, Loughborough, Harry Dundas, Mad. Schwellenbergen, Charlotte, &c. &c.

Garter (order of the).—The pride of modern nations converts even the play-thing of an infant into an objeƈ of glory and emulation. The Englifh triumphantly boaft that *their Kings* never wore any *foreign* order, while many foreign Kings and eight Emperors, have been decorated with the GARTER. Virtuous exultation! But the *free* nations of antiquity were not *vain* of the *vanity* of others. The Greek and Roman commonwealths fixed their affeƈions on different objeƈs.

We have in England *right honourable* and *noble Garters* of various colours; but the *blue,* which, by way of preference, we call THE *Garter,* is reckoned the prettieft; and *my Lord* will at any time give up the *green,* or the *red,* to get at the BLUE, which makes him the *happieft* of men, and is confidered by this GREAT Nation, as the *ultimatum* of GREATNESS: if, therefore, he be not fpeedily prefented with a ribband for his neck, of a *coarfer grain,* we may expeƈ to fee our *heaven-born* Minifter invefted with the *Garter. In either cafe, he will be exalted.*

Government,—an univerfal contraƈ, the objeƈ of which is the happinefs of a ftate, for whofe benefit it was formed.

When-

Whenever the object is not attained, it is *natural*, *lawful*, and *right*, to alter the *government*, and the only competent judges in these cases are the people themselves, who, while they enjoy plenty, security, and freedom, will necessarily support the system which insures to them those blessings, and who, by a parity of reasoning, will murmur and complain, and, at length, resist, when they find themselves oppressed by sumptuary and sanguinary laws, and borne down by a weight of taxation, that renders all their industry and labour fruitless.

"That *government* is best which the people "think so, and *they* not *I*, are the *natural*, *lawful*, " and *competent* judges of this matter." Burke's Thoughts on the Cause of the present Discontents.

Economy is the wisest principle of all virtuous *governments*. Whenever we perceive a departure from this principle, and a nation providing luxuriously for myriads of pensioners and placemen, by exorbitant salaries, and when we hear those minions asserting their *well earned* claims (which consist merely in the fawning sycophancy of courtiers) to those salaries, boasting of them as a reward conferred on their *services* by the *best of princes*; (the old hackneyed language of pensioned slaves,) although it be *from the pockets of a starving people*, and not from the *overflowing treasures* of this BEST OF PRINCES, that the payment is ex-

torted

torted;—when we witnefs thefe GENTRY refufing
to yield up the fmalleft part of their finecures and
douceurs towards the expence of the war, in which
they have involved thofe who are fuffering the moft
grievoufly and innocently from it, and when we
behold the lethargy of the people, under all the
bitter calamities that have been thus wantonly and
barbaroufly inflicted on them, tamely fubmitting
to the provoking arrogance, and glaring falfehoods
with which they are infulted, we may fafely fay
that both the *government* and the people have reached the acmè of degeneracy and corruption; but
as evil governments, in the firft inftance, corrupt
the morals of the nation, fo by excefs of their cor-
ruptions, is a nation finally regenerated. So it
was in France :—fo will it be in England.

In monarchical ftates, the art of government generally confifts in taking as much money as poffible from one clafs of citizens, in order to beftow
it on another clafs ; and what *ought* to be very *extraordinary*, inftead of taking it from the rich, to improve the condition of the poor, it is extorted from
the poor, to pamper the luxuries of the rich. For proof
of this affertion, confult the hiftory of our civil lift.

There are in print many more books on government, than there are princes on the earth, yet
with three or four thoufand volumes on the fubject,
kings ftill appear mainly ignorant of their duties,

alto-

altogether unfkilled in the art of governing mankind.

The maxim in kingly governments, " that kings " can do no wrong," feems to be borrowed from the fcriptures. Puffendorf obferves that David having fworn *not* to attempt the life of Shimei his *privy counfellor*, did *not* violate his oath, when [according to Jewifh tradition,] he ordered his fon Solomon *to put Shimei to death*, becaufe David had *only fworn* that *he himfelf* would *not* kill Shimei. Puff. book IV. ch. XI. art. XIII.

Puffendorf, by approving this conduct in the *Lord's Anointed*, fanctions an example, that will not be much to the *tafte* of PRIVY COUNSELLORS.

" Let the good of the people be the fupreme " law." Such is the fundamental maxim of nations. But the good of the people is made to confift in deftroying their neighbours, and in feizing their poffeffions. THE RIGHTS OF WAR. Old as the world is, at this very day it would be impoffible to point out one *government* favourable to the art of thinking, or to the improvement and delights of fociety. The nation that attempted, and is ftill ftruggling to confer this benefit on mankind, is marked out by the reft for deftruction. *Government*, according to the prefent fyftem, being for the advantage of the few, to the detriment of the many,

the

the few having the *power* in their hands, are ſtrain-
ing every nerve to increaſe that *power*, and to
render themſelves invincible ; but the *natural*
ſtrength lies in the *people*, and whenever they are
rouſed to exert it, all factitious *unnatural powers*
will be at once deſtroyed and buried in the duſt.

Of all *governments*, hereditary monarchies are
certainly the moſt *unnatural* and prepoſterous, for,
agreeably with this ſyſtem, the chances are far more
probable, that a nation be governed by folly and
vice, than by wiſdom and virtue, ſince it will
hardly be denied, that the majority of the world is
compoſed of the former. Indeed all hiſtory con-
firms this TRUTH.

But there is a kind of ſtupid vanity in men, that
inclines them to flatter the *government* under which
they are born, " though it be the moſt ſervile and
" miſerable on the earth." Modern Romans are
proud of St. Peter's church, and of their antique
Grecian ſtatues ; yet it would be better for the
people, that theſe ſuperb monuments were a heap
of ruins, if thereby they were to be better fed, or
better cloathed ; and happier, far happier would it
be for humanity, and more honourable to its character, if all the treaſures of the churches were,
as in France, made national property, and converted to public uſe.

All governments which have hitherto exiſted
had their origin in conqueſt and terror. Their
prin-

principle " le droit du plus fort," the right of the ſtrongeſt,——we have heard triumphantly boaſted the glorious republics of Greece. But what a government muſt that be which drove Ariſtides into baniſhment, and which condemned Phocion and Socrates to death! Yet theſe republics, it muſt be confeſſed, were *comparatively* excellent ; far ſuperior to the *Government* of the neighbouring monarchies. The ancient republics did not un- derſtand the repreſentative ſyſtem.

Puffendorf, in his ſeventh book, chap. v. *pro- miſes* to examine, which is the beſt form of go- vernment. He tells us, " that ſeveral have pro- nounced in favour of monarchy, and that others, on the contrary, are furious againſt Kings; but that, for his own part, it would be foreign from his ſubject, to enter into the reaſons of the latter ;" and perhaps it would be wiſe in us to imitate the example of Puffendorf, and be ſilent ; therefore we ſhall conclude the article on the word government, with the following allegorical fable.

" An eagle ruled over all birds throughout the whole country of Oritnia ; it is true, that he had no other *right* than that of his *beak* and his *claws* ; but nevertheleſs, after having provided for his own luxuries and pleaſures, he governed as well as any other *bird of prey*.——

* * * * * * * * * * * * * * *
* * * * * * * * * * * * * * *

To

To give,—bribery and corruption. In its original fenfe, quite out of ufe.

Gown,—a robe of innocence, when applied to the church. If a parfon fhould infult a citizen in the groffeft manner, the infult muft be paffed over; his *gown* protects him. *Gown* alfo, as appertaining to lawyers, with the addition of an enormous wig, conftitutes learning, purity and patriotifm. It is this fame *gown* that gives confiftency to verfatility, makes abufe candour, makes egotifm virtue, makes vanity modefty, and gives to brutality the femblance of fpirit: in fhort, it can convert a *Rook* into a *great man ! !*

Gownfman,—at Oxford and Cambridge fignifies a dafhing young buck, who is keeping *terms* of riot, extravagance and debauchery in a college, to qualify him afterwards to appear in London with *eclat.*

Grace,—in women, generally means the extremity of affectation and unnatural contorfions. Vide Mifs Farren, the Duchefs of R————, the divine p————ff—s, and the facred C————, &c. &c. *Grace,* when in converfation applied to a duke, means *nothing.* Thus *his Grace* the Duke of Leeds, has no fignification !

Gracious,—proud, infolent, falfe, and contemptible.

Grandmother,—a term of reproach never to be forgiven, if applied to a lady of fafhion.

To

To grasp,—a never-ceasing aristocratic endeavour, and the principal object in view of the members of both houses of parliament.

Grateful,—obsolete. It is at present used for *great fool.*

Gratification,—belongs to the few, and is derived from the sufferings of the many.

Gratis,—the King of Prussia's subsidy.

Grave,—for British troops,—Flanders and the West Indies.

Greatness,—in its primitive sense, liberty, valour, honour, virtue and benevolence; at present, drunkenness, tyranny, extortion, treachery, and arrogance.

Greedy,—George Rose's moderation; sixteen thousands a year, and not satisfied.

Grimace,—Lord Lauderdale's patriotism, and Dr. Moore's candour.

Groan,—sedition.

To grumble,—high treason.

Grunt,—a hog's cry; the complaint of the Swinish multitude, or the people's lamentation.

Guess,—how Pitt will be able to get through the present war.

Guilt,—patriotism and detestation of tyranny.

Guillotine,—an instrument of most rare and humane invention, lessening and shortening the pains of death to condemned criminals; so called after

the

the name of the inventor, who is said himself to have died under its axe.

As it is the cuftom to *decapitate*, and not to *hang* KINGS, there fhould be a *guillotine* in all monarchical ftates, that in cafe of ACCIDENT, their MAJESTIES might not be expofed to fuffer long and unneceffary torture. The unfortunate Duke of Monmouth received four ftrokes from the executioner, before his head was fevered from the body. With the *guillotine* fuch *miftakes* are impoffible; the bufinefs is at once effected; as the machine falls, fo fure is the head to be that inftant taken off. But notwithftanding its eafy and immediate operation, it ftrikes terror into the coward and guilty breaft. Mr. P-wis the *Alarmift*, member for the county of N-th-mpt-n, has declared, that he had rather fee ARBITRARY POWER eftablifhed in England, than that a GUILLOTINE fhould make its appearance in the country. Neverthelefs, feveral firft-rate mechanics are reported to be at work, in order that the people may not be difappointed, fuppofing it fhould *enter into their heads, that they had occafion for one.* To the French we are indebted for this difcovery; and Europe ere long promifes to borrow all their modern political improvements from that nation.

Gun,—an engine of deftruction; fo heavy, that

a man

a man in England can't carry it for lefs than a hundred a year.

To guttle,—a minifterial and aldermanic recreation.

H

Habeas Corpus,—hitherto confidered as the palladium ·of Britifh liberty, but now, by an act of Parliament, *fufpended.* On account of this fufpenfion, Meffrs. John Horne Tooke, Hardy, Thelwall, Joyce, Richter, and others, have for many months languifhed in prifon, without any fpecific charge, and without, at their firft commitment, any profpect of being brought to trial. If Britons can thus be treated by minifters, what is liberty? what is defpotifm?

Hag,—a fury; a fhe monfter; an ugly old woman. Madame S———nb———n; Lady Cecilia J————; Mother Hannau; Mrs. M———gue, and the Emprefs of all the Ruffias.

Half-feas-over,—the moft refpectable ftate of fobriety amongft princes and minifters.

Halter,—the future recompence of many great men.

Happinefs,—" that ftate in which our defires are fatisfied. Good fortune. Happinefs cannot be pofitively afcertained, becaufe the various and contrary choices by which men are guided in their pur-

purfuits, prove that all perfons do not place their happinefs in the fame thing." *Locke.* The objeét to which we afpire for happinefs, often proves our bane and deftruétion. The only true happinefs refts in virtue.

Hard-heartednefs,—cruelty; want of compaffion. Magiftrates and judges aéting under arbitrary governments are a perfeét illuftration of the word *hard-heartednefs.*

Hard-heartednefs,—the charaéteriftic of the *beft of men !*

Harlequin,—a *buffoon.* A *particular favorite* of George III.

Harlot,—the wife of a prince, declared fo by the wife heads in Doétors' Commons, who can fet afide all religious ceremonies, and reverfe the decrees of the Almighty.

Harmony,—concord, *equality.* " The plea-
" fures and advantages derived from *harmony,* are
" merely the effeéts of *equality,* good proportion,
" correfpondence; fo that *equality,* that bugbear
" to ariftocracy and kings, and correfpondence,
" are the caufes of *harmony.*" *Lord Bacon.*

Harmony,—the majority of both Houfes of Parliament! The Combined Powers! The Court of Jufticiary in Scotland!

Har-

Harveſt,—the ſeaſon of reaping the fruits of the earth. A good or a bad *harveſt*, according to the conſtitution of monarchical governments, has very little effect on the price of proviſions. In the moſt plentiful ſeaſons, the price is ſtill kept up; prodigal landlords rack their tenants, and thus the people derive no benefit from the bounty of Heaven. The rich devour that *harveſt* which the poor man's labour procures.

Harveſt,—a plentiful crop of taxes well got in.

Haſte,—hurry; precipitation. This word cannot be better explained, than by a reference to the Dunkirk hero and his army at the ſiege of Dunkirk, and on ſundry other occaſions.

Haughtineſs,—our immaculate miniſter; Lord Mansfield; Lord Loughborough; and the devil.

Havock,—deſolation; ſlaughter.

―――――――――" KINGS cry *havock*;
" Até by their ſide repeats the found, and lets looſe
" the dogs of war."

SHAKESPEARE.

" See! with what heat thoſe DOGS OF HELL ad-
" vance,
" To waſte and *havock* yonder world, which I
" So fair and good created."

MILTON'S PARADISE LOST, Book II.

Hazard,

Hazard,—the conqueſt of France.

Heaven.—The beſt definition of this word, is the conſcience of a virtuous man.

Heaven-born,—the moſt infamous of mankind.

Heir,—one who, according to the wiſe laws of primogeniture, is to inherit all his father's poſſeſſions, to the detriment of his other relations, although he be polluted by every vice, and they endowed with every virtue. Thus, monſters have inherited dominions, and become the ſcourge of the human race; and thus mankind will continue to be tyrannized over, and to be miſerable, till they have courage and wiſdom to unite, to ſhake off the yoke, and get rid at once of all thoſe barbarous prejudices and prepoſterous cuſtoms, that have ſo long poiſoned their exiſtence. [Swift obſerves, that heirs to *titles* and large eſtates have a *weakneſs in their eyes*, and a *tenderneſs in their conſtitution*.]

Hell,—a place of torment; where there is neither liberty of ſpeech, nor liberty of thought, nor liberty of action; where men can be impriſoned at the will of a miniſter, without ever being brought to trial; where the rich exult and riot at the expence of the poor; where vice triumphs, profligacy prevails, and war, taxes, and deſolation are the *conſolations* of the people.

Hell,

Hell,—the confcience of a TYRANT., REX, TYRANNUS.

Hemp,—a plant with which they make *ropes.* Never did the cultivation of *hemp* deferve more encouragement than in the year of our Lord 1794, when the horrible crimes of ariftocracy feem to be preparing punifhments that will require a vaft con-fumption of the above *falutary* vegetable. The *guillotine* is not yet introduced into England.

Heraldry,—a fubftitute for virtue, honor, and integrity.

Hereditary,—worfe and worfe. The claim of folly; the boaft of infamy; and the pride of vice.

Herefy,—an abjuration of nonfenfe and fuper-ftition.

Herefy,—the rights of man, and the promulga-tion of truth.

Hero (Young),—a young prince, without fenfe, without knowledge, and without virtue, who com-mands armies, under the direction of fome officer of fkill and experience.

Hero.—This word, in its literal fenfe, fignifies a perfon eminent for *bravery* and virtue. Accord-ing to the modern reading in England, it fignifies a young prince, from the ftews of debauchery and exceffive diffipation, invefted in an inftant with

the

the command of numerous armies, which he di-
rects at pleasure, without ever expofing his own
precious person within four miles distance of the
least danger. The city of Valenciennes surrendered to the *valour* of the *renowned Dunkirk hero,*
while it is a notorious fact, that this same PRUDENT
commander was never within five miles of the place
during the whole time of the siege. The *heroism*
of this *illustrious Chief* may be more severely tried
before he arrives at Paris; an expedition which
he appears to have so *dearly* at heart. His magnanimous uncle, the Duke of Brunfwick, threatened
in like manner; but neither was that veteran HERO
up to the atchievement. Paris still holds their HE-
ROISM in mockery and defiance, notwithstanding
the brilliant and UNBOUGHT advantage obtained
by the surrender of Landrecies.

Hanover.—From the year 1740 to 1756 it was
a place not to be found in the map, *a poor, pitiful*
electorate; but being the patrimonial territory and
the electoral dominions of our Most SERENE SO-
VEREIGN, must be preferved as a mill-stone about
the neck of England, the ruin of our treasury, and
the grave of Britons. Thus happy are we in our
German connections.

Hero,—the great Duke of York; Philip Aftley,
Esq. of Hercules-hall, Lambeth, Marshal Frey-

I   tag,

tag, Prince of Saxe-Cobourg, the Prince of O.
range, and General Paoli.

Hefitation. " Intermiffion of fpeech." John.
fon. *Squire* Rolle and *Squire* Drake, whenever
they rife to fpeak in the Houfe of Commons, afford
a tolerable idea of *hefitation.*

Hiccius Doccius,—a cant word for a juggler in
any ftation. Juftice Mainwaring is an *hiccius doccius.*

 " An old dull fool, who told the clock
 " For many years at Bridewell-dock,
 " At *Weftminfter* and Hicks's Hall,
 " And *hiccius doccius* played in all;
 " Where, in all governments and times,
 " He'd been both friend and foe to crimes."
Hudibras.

Hideous,—the countenance of William Pitt.

Hierarchy,—an ecclefiaftical eftablifhment, whofe
principles are *pomp, fplendour,* and *revenue.* Jefus
Chrift, the Founder of our religion, on the contrary, preached *poverty, humility, equality. Chriftian* Bifhops delight and revel in wealth and pa-
laces, yet, departing fo wide from its maxims, they
are infolent enough to uphold the excellence and
orthodoxy of the *Chriftian* fyftem. An invention
of *prieftcraft,* which, united with *ftatecraft,* helps
to dazzle and enflave the unhappy, deluded people.
Hint,

Hint,—infinuation; gentle fuggeftion. *Hints* are often as fignificant and expreffive as downright plain fpeaking, and produce the fame effect. Some-times indeed they fail. The combined powers have received *pretty broad* hints, how mad and defperate it is to attempt the conqueft of France. "But in blood they are plunged fo deep, that, "without confulting juftice or humanity, they hold "it now as fafe for themfelves to advance, as to "retire. They will take no *hint.* They have fet "their all upon a caft, and are refolved to ftand "the hazard of the die."

Hireling,—venal, corrupt, defigning men, all thofe who act for intereft—John Reeves, Esquire, &c. &c. &c.

To hire,—to give places, peerages and penfions.

Hiftory,—formerly a true and juft record of paft tranfactions; which if executed now in the fame manner, would be termed a libel, and call down the vengeance of the Attorney-General.

Hiftory,—the relation of paft events.

Hiftoriographer,—hiftorian, paid to conceal THE TRUTH. It feems the ancient defpots had neglected this precaution, to fave their memory from the judgment of pofterity. It is not requi-fite to unite the qualities of TACITUS to be a mo-dern hiftoriographer, but thofe of Dr. Johnfon, Arthur Young, &c. &c.

Holy,

Holy,—the prefent war, the flave trade, the pope, the Archbifhop of Canterbury, and Bifhop Horfe-ley.

Honour,—a quality that will carry a patriot to Botany Bay, a vulgar prejudice: in high life it means the debauching your neighbour's wife or daughter, killing your man, and being a member of the Jockey Club, and Brookes's gaming-houfe.

Houfe,—(though your own), yet in England a place of no fecurity, as ruffians may enter it and pillage it as they pleafe, and drag the owner away to prifon, whenever the Minifter thinks proper.

Humanity,—every fpecies of violence, injuftice and oppreffion.

Humility,—the Marquis of Buckingham.

Hypocrify,—the moft thriving of all qualities.

Hypocrify.—Hypocrify of humanity, is the moft odious of all hypocrifies. Can we behold with-out HORROR, a man who condemns a war, as ini-quitous and unjuft, take upon him the command of an expedition, diabolically criminal, the objeCt of which was to arm citizen againft citizen, and the child againft his parent. When the EXECUTI-ONER lifts his murderous arm againft his fellow creature, he is the inftrument of the law. But what name can be applied to the merit of the unprincipled military favage, who has taken up arms in a caufe which he admits and acknowledges to be unjuft ! *

Hypothefis,

* Earl Moira's expedition to the coaft of France.

Hypothefis,—the Britifh army marching victo-
rioufly to Paris.

I.

To jabber,—to talk idly, to prate without
thinking, to chatter; like young Jenkinfon, Mr.
Canning, Tom Steel and others.

Jacobin,—every man who dares to object to any
part of the conduct of adminiftration; every man
who difapproves of the prefent war with France;
and every man who wifhes for a parliamentary reform and an equal reprefentation of the people.

Ice,—a cold fubftance of which the hearts of
moft GREAT men are compofed.

Idol,—an object of weak and ignorant adoration.
Thus it is often afferted, that a HEAVEN-BORN
minifter is the idol of the people.

Idiot,—poor John Bull, in his prefent ftate of
degradation.

Jewel,—fomething irrefiftably captivating to the
eyes of a pious and chafte Queen.

Jefter,—one who jefts—a Jekyl.

Ignominy,—true patriotifm, philanthropy, and
incorruptibility.

Ignorance,—a committee of fecrecy.

Ill-nature,—ariftocracy, epifcopacy, royalty.

To illuminate,—to darken the human underftanding by every poffible artifice. Thus the minif-

terial

terial newfpapers of the prefent time may be faid to illuminate the public.

Immediately,—in minifterial language, fignifies fome years hence, or perhaps never.

Imminent,—the dangers which threaten ariftocracy.

Immoderate,—the national debt, taxes, tythes, and ariftocratic infolence.

Immutable,—Mr. Pitt and his party; the fyftem of fpies and informers; the loyalty of peers, placemen and penfioners.

Implacable,—all the enemies of liberty.

Impiety,—a faft appointed to be obferved, for the purpofe of inducing the Supreme Being to favor our exertions towards the exterminating of twenty-five millions of the French.

Impertinent,—to pafs a lord without bowing, or to look at minifters with a fmile.

Impoffibility,—for an Englifhman to get promotion on the mere fcore of merit, without intereft.

Importance,—a few yards of ribband ftrung acrofs the fhoulders.

Imprefs,—to take a man by force from his own home and the bofom of his family, and compel him to fight for his King and Country.

Imprifonment,—minifterial argument, or an anfwer to all complaints.

Improbable,

Improbable,—the Duke of York's march to Paris with his army.

Incomprehenſible,—miniſterial operations, Biſhop Horſeley's holineſs, and Lord Loughborough's diſintereſtedneſs.

Independence,—the Duke of Portland, Mr. Wyndham, Edmund Burke, and other FRIENDS of their country.

Independent,—(freeholder) one who, on every election for members of parliament, ſacrifices his conſcience to his convenience, ſets up his dear country, and his darling freedom to the beſt bidder, yet impudently finds fault with his repreſentative, for following ſo laudable an example, nor ſuffers any body to be a ſcoundrel, without reproach, but himſelf.

Infatuation,—is the ſtate of a nation when all the abuſes of its government ſeem to conſtitute its pride, when it glories in its ſhame, and exalts to the ſkies the very men who have undermined its conſtitution, and reduced the people to the moſt abject ſlavery.

Innovation,—a term applied to every ſpecies of improvement, and particularly dreaded by corrupt rulers, as well as by all placemen and penſioners.

Inquiry,—ſedition, a crime of the firſt magnitude, and which is to be puniſhed by *fine,* impriſonment, and pillory.

Inſatiable,

Infatiable,—aristocratic avarice of power, wealth, and titles.

Infenfibility,—those unfortunate military machines, who suffer themselves to be flogged, half starved, and shot at, for the sake of glory, and sixpence *per diem.*

To infnare,—to enlift men for his Majesty's service, by decoying them into houses of ill-fame, then by beating them, and by every species of cruelty forcing them to accept a shilling.

Infolence,—the treafury bench, St. Stephen's.

Ireland,—(the people of) a noble and spirited nation, inviolably attached to us, by every tie of friendship and efteem, and who, on every occasion, hazard both their lives and fortunes in our defence; yet to whom we conftantly make such juft and grateful returns, as to omit no opportunity (however illegal and arbitrary) of beggaring them, though the ruin of their intereft lays a manifeft foundation for the deftruction of our own.

Irony,—a mode of speech, in which the meaning is contrary to the word; as Pitt is a great and worthy character; Wyndham a true lover of his country; the Duke of Portland a wife and independent patriot; Edmund Burke a man of the moft virtuous confiftency.

Juftice and impartiality,—a captain's commiffion to a child not ten years old, while many a
wounded

wounded veteran who have ventured their lives in the fervice of their country are *perifhing through want.*

Juftice,—obfolete.

K.

To kidnap,—to recruit foldiers for his majefty's fervice by delufion, and by inveigling them into houfes of ill-fame, where, fhould the poor wretches fo trepanned make refiftance, or refufe to receive the proffered fhilling of the *nominal* captain who attends there, they are fure to be plundered and beaten, if not killed.

King,—from the Saxon word Kuening, or Kuyning, is but the abbreviation of cunning or crafty, the ufual diftinction and epithet for knaves. According to Swift, a *king* ought to be nothing but a scare-crow placed in the midft of the fields to defend the corn; inftead of which they have almoft ever been the wild beasts which devour it.

King,—the chief magiftrate of a ftate, generally hereditary. Kings were held in utter deteftation by the ancient Romans during the time of the Republic; and they are in like manner execrated by the modern French. A million a year fterling is a mere trifle to fupport a king, who is perhaps feldom feen, and leaves all the trouble of

K   *govern-*

governing to his minifters, who frequently, under
the fanction of his authority, plunder the People
without mercy, and involve them in fanguinary
and unneceffary wars. Kingcraft feems every
where to be now upon the decline, or, in other
words, " *Kings are ripe !*" The chief excellence
however in an Englifhman's character at this time
is loyalty, i. e. royalty, or a love for kings ! ! !

King (infallibility of the).—By the exprefs declaration of our laws, an Englifh prince is a piece
of royal infallibility, incapable of doing wrong.
The pofition that a king can do no wrong, muft
either tax the Englifh nation with great injuftice,
or great inconfiftency. If a king can do no
wrong, why was king James the Second banifhed?
and if a king can do wrong, why the plague are we
conftantly affirming that he cannot ? Either way we
ftand felf-condemned ; and if we are not fet down
as a nation of fcoundrels, we muft think ourfelves
pretty eafy under the appellation of fools.

SWIFT.

King (difaffection to the),—whatever points out
the grievances of the People, and endeavors to
remove a weak and wicked minifter.

To kifs (the breech of perfons in power),—a fure
and fpeedy way to get preferment.

Knight,

Knight,—a ſtrange ſort of an animal into which the king ſometimes transforms a man; thus Sir Watkin Lewes, Sir James Saunderſon, Sir Jeffrey Dunſtan, and Sir Sidney Smith, are knights.

Knowing,—is applied to being acquainted with every ſpecies of ariſtocratic foppery and vice.

L

Labour,—the occupation of the Swiniſh Multitude, who are kept to it twelve hours a day, though it can hardly procure ſubſiſtence for a wife and family, as, conſidering the preſent enormous taxes, ſix or ſeven ſhillings a week is ſcarce ſufficient to provide bread for one. This ſame labour alſo is held in the utmoſt contempt by the uſeleſs great, though at the ſame time they derive all their luxury and excluſive advantages from the exertions of the induſtrious poor. A hard-working man and a poor devil are ſynonimous terms in the language of Ariſtocracy.

Lady,—the wife of any *titled* man; it is ſuppoſed to mean ſomething more than woman. To call a *lady,* WOMAN, would be the higheſt inſult ! ! !

To lament,—the portion of the inferior orders of ſociety; who, however, are told, in compaſſion to their preſent ſufferings, that their reward and happineſs is to come hereafter.

Laſh,

Lafh,—in the plural, is applied to foldiers who commit faults; feven hundred or a thoufand lafhes with a cat-o'-ninetails being frequently beftowed upon them by way of difcipline, and to ftrengthen their loyalty.

To lavifh,—to fpend money like a prince, at the national expence.

Lavifhnefs,—folly in an individual, but robbery and peculation in a prince. Bleffed be God, *our* princes have not THIS SIN to anfwer for among their many ! ! !

Laureat,—a man paid by a king to write odes in his praife.

Law,—a very expenfive commodity, rather more advantageous to the rich and profperous, than to the poor and wretched.

Lawn,—when cut into an immenfe pair of pudding-fleeves, denotes *fanctity* and wealth; it is an outward and vifible fign of an inward and fpiritual grace; it is the glory of the church.

Laws (agreeable to the Conftitution),—acts which are paffed by minifterial influence, and have an immediate tendency to incroach upon the freedom and property of the fubject.

Laws (tranfgreffion of the),—an exertion of that natural right which every man has to a hare or a partridge belonging to his own grounds, and

which

which deftroy both his corn and grafs, by the authority of Parliament.

Lazinefs,—nobility, gentility, epifcopacy.

Leveller,—the man who wifhes to behold the
GLORY OF THE LAWS march horizontally on the
heads of all mankind.

ABBE RAYNAL.

*Liable (to be fent to Botany Bay, or be hanged,
drawn, and quartered),*—all perfons who find fault
with the prefent government, or exert themfelves
to procure a Parliamentary Reform.

Libation,—a minifterial offering to the profperity of Old England.

Liberty and Property,—an indifpenfible neceffity of keeping game for other people to kill, with
pains and penalties of the moft arbitrary kind,
fhould we think of appropriating the minuteft article to the ufe of our own families.

Lie,—a gracious fpeech! a falfehood.

Thou lieft, abhorred Tyrant, with my fword
I'll prove the *lie* thou fpeakeft.

SHAKESPEARE'S MACBETH.

Life,—is a ftate of exiftence which is to be
facrificed by the *lower* orders of fociety whenever
kings and minifters think proper—witnefs the reek-
ing plains of Flanders.

Light,

Light,—in Great Britain a taxable commodity.

Loaves and Fishes,—the great objects of aristocratic contention, the difposal of which conftitutes the chief merit of a heaven-born minifter.

Lord,—a creature made by a king, and which cannot be defined.

Lordling,—a little lord; a lord Montfort; a lord Valletort.

> To lordlings proud I tune my lay,
>   Who feaft in bow'r or hall,
> Tho' dukes they be, to dukes I fay,
>   That pride will have a fall.
>   SWIFT.

Lords (of the ocean),—the fenfible and fpirited people of Great Britain, who have a naval force confiderably fuperior to all the other ftates of Europe put together, yet fervilely do homage to a neft of African pirates, and pay a yearly tribute to a fet of robbers, whom they ought to root out and extirpate from the face of the earth; a much more noble act than the extirpation of the French people.

Loyalift,—a placeman; a penfioner; a lord; a bifhop; a rich man; an Edmund Burke; an Arthur Young; and a Mr. Reeves.

Loyalty,—to hallow in a public theatre for the song of God fave the King! to praife the prefent *glorious*, *juft*, and *neceffary war* ! and to oppofe every fpecies of reform.

Loyalty (true),—extends to one's country as well as to the prince ; and to oppofe tyranny is no breach of *loyalty*, but an effential branch of it. LOYALTY (as the very word imports) is fuch an attachment to both king and people, as is founded on the laws ; and a hair's-breadth beyond law, *true loyalty* does not go.

AUG. TOPLADY.

Luxury,— profufion, debauchery ; Carlton-Houfe.

M

Madnefs,—in political life, an over-heated brain with difappointed ambition. It has lately appeared in diftempered ravings againft the French, in vehement gefticulation, in throwing down a dagger in the midft of an intemperate fpeech, and in writing books full of obfcurity and myfticifm, filled with extravagant fictions and falfe rhetoric. The cafe of one Edmund Burke, who has been lately afflicted with this difeafe, will illuftrate the ordinary phænomena of this mania. See the lift of pa-
tients,

tients, moſt of them incurables, in the hiſtory of
St. Stephen's Hoſpital.

> 'Tis the time's plague when madmen lead the blind.
>
> SHAKESPEARE.

Magna Charta,—an idle word, IDLY made uſe
of by the populace, ſignifying a natural right of
being governed by juſt laws, equally diſtributed,
which they conſtantly ſuffer to be trampled on, and
an inherent claim to the poſſeſſion of thoſe privileges which they have neither ſenſe or ſpirit enough
to poſſeſs.

Majeſty.—This word once ſignified greatneſs of
mind ; but ſince it has been uſed as a title for
kings, it has of courſe acquired a contrary interpretation.   It is indiſcriminately applied to a Trajan and a Louis ; a Harry the Fourth of France
and a George the Third of England.

Majority,—the cattle belonging to the miniſtry ;
or, in other words, a ſet of men whoſe buſineſs it
is to plunder the nation, under pretext of repreſenting it.   The greater part of them, during a
debate, are lounging about the lobbies, or dining
at Beverley's.   When the harangues are over,
they are ſummoned by their keeper, and ranged
in the order in which he wiſhes them to be placed.
Some of them are in a profound ſleep at their own
houſes when they are obliged to attend a diviſion
upon

upon war and peace, or fome other folemn and important queftion; and, having performed their legiflative functions, with unbuttoned breeches and ungartered hofe, they return as expeditioufly as poffible to their beds. But there are always fome who fit in the Houfe to utter "hear him," as loud as they can bawl, when the minifter or Lord Mornington is making a drowfy fpeech. This tribe has been augmented fince the rife of the new fect of Alarmifts. See *Alarmifts.*

Malcontent,—a hog that is fhut out of its ftye on a frofty night, and who grunts to be let in.

Malcontents,—the greater part of this nation; confifting of the laborious poor, from whom the earnings of impoverifhed induftry are fqueezed and torn, for the fupport of our happy Conftitution, the pride of the world! the envy of furrounding nations! &c. &c.

Malefactors,—either in Parliament, or on the highway. The former are fuppofed to belong to a more dignified clafs than the latter. The difference in their fortunes is very great; the one clafs is elevated to places at court, and rewarded with penfions; the other is elevated to the gibbet, and rewarded with a rope.

Malevolence,—a new figure of rhetoric, introduced by Mr. Pitt into his fpeeches.

L

Man,

Man,—a degenerate, degraded animal; the victim of kings, priefts, and courtiers. Born to be
free, yet content to be a flave. *Homo eft duplex
animal,* fay the old fchool-men. When he is independent and free, he is the nobleft work of the
creation, the image of his Maker; but when he is
a fubject to monarchs, and duped by their minifters, he is the vileft wretch that crawls upon the
earth. When he ftarts from oppreffion, and
breaks his chain, he prefents an awful and fublime
fpectacle, on which the gods might look with pleafure; but finking into ignorance and flavery, he is
the fcorn, the difgrace, and the derifion of every
clafs of animated beings.

Manage,—to hood-wink and deceive. " Let
" us alone, and we will manage JOHN BULL, I'll
" warrant you."

SWIFT's Mifcellanies. Hift. of John Bull.

Mangy,—applied to dogs infected with the
mange; and metaphorically to the Houfe of Commons,

Manifefto,—a kind of compofition in which
bullying generals and lying minifters excel. The
Duke of Brunfwick threatened to put all the Pari-
fians to fire and the fword; and he gave the French
notice of it by means of his celebrated manifefto.
But, owing probably to the badnefs of the roads, as
well

well as other unavoidable accidents, his Serene
Highnefs, after having proceeded part of the way,
was under the neceffity of poftponing his journey.

Manifefto,—an affemblage of lies and deceit,
ufed by crowned villains and their military flaves
to juftify their ufurpations, injuftice, and treachery.
That which was publifhed by the duke of Brunfwick, in the names of the Emperor and the King
of Pruffia, exceeds by far every thing of the kind.
If the ancient chiefs of the HUNS and VANDALS
had known how to write, they would have preceded
their invafions by manifeftos lefs barbarous and inhuman, and lefs abfurd.

Manufacturers,—according to the definition of
the minifter, a difcontented fet of men, who, being infected with fedition and Jacobinifm, clamor
againft a juft and neceffary war, becaufe it deprives
them of their trade, and ftarves their families!

March,—a military movement; at fome times
quicker than others. When the Duke of York
marched from Dunkirk, the pace of his army was
what the coachmen would call " the long trot."

Market,—of two kinds; 1. fuch as that in Covent-Garden; 2. fuch as that in the Houfe of
Commons. In the one are fold fruit, vegetables,
&c. in the other, men, confciences, integrity, and
other articles of fmall value.

Mar-

Martyr (a blessed),—a perjured prince, who broke his coronation oath in the most material of all points; governed without a Parliament; imprisoned his subjects for refusing to lend him money; commenced a false, villainous prosecution for high treason against a most deserving nobleman (the Earl of Bristol); reduced his people to the dreadful necessity of taking up arms in their own defence; and, by his shameful dissimulation when he was about to be restored, left it utterly impossible to confide in his honor, his humanity, or his oath, but drove the principal officers of the adverse party, in their own defence, to sit in trial upon, and sentence him to death. Truly, a very blessed martyr! Had this prince been a private man, who would have dared to say a word in his defence?

Mask (of religion),—worn by Sir Richard Hill, Thornton, and Wilberforce.

Mercy (of the law),—see the sentences of Muir, Palmer, &c. Concealing the murderers of young Allen, in St. George's Fields; the pardon of Balf and Macquirk for the murder of Mr. Clark at Brentford, because he polled against the ministerial leech; pardoning the two Kennedys, because their sister was a prostitute to a pampered titled slave.

Merit,—out of fashion at court; an obsolete word; and when met seldom rewarded, and almost universally shunned.

Metaphysics,—a confusion of the brain; Mr. Wyndham is a metaphysician.

Military profession,—the first of all professions in a free country, but the most despicable one in all that are otherwise.

Million,—a small numerical sign in political calculation. Thus, to give the king of Sardinia twenty-five millions sterling is to give merely a trifle, to the support of the *just* and *necessary war*! To talk of extirpating twenty-five millions of Frenchmen is to talk of a very easy and practicable experiment.

Minion,—a courtier; a buffoon; a dependant; H——y D————s; J————n, &c.

The drowsy Tyrant, by his minions led,
Devotes to kingly rage the patriot head.
SWIFT.

Minister,—a word that comprehends all that imagination can conceive of the corrupt, the treacherous, the cruel, the vindictive, and the oppressive; all that is calculated to make human nature hang down its head with sorrow and with shame. Ministers, as Bolingbroke calls them, " are

" the

"the corrupt engroffers of delegated authority."
They muft be fervile, and compliant with every
humor and caprice of the fovereign, and they muft
learn to defpife the rights, and undermine the privileges, of the People. If they can do this, as
Pitt has done, after having cajoled them with de-
lufive promifes and expeclations, they ftand a furer
chance of obtaining the royal patronage and favor; and to add cruelty to perfidy, arrogance to
oppreffion, and infolence to folly, is the polifhed
perfeclion of the minifterial characler. Walpole
was once thought to be too corrupt for a minifter;
but were fuch a man as Walpole to fucceed Pitt,
the utmoft corruption of which Walpole was capable would be innocence and purity itfelf, compared to the black and deteftable policy, the tricks,
the bafenefs, and the low cunning, of his prede-
ceffor.

Minifter.—I do not know how it is, but I never
liked a minifter in all my days. Our friends Oxford and Bolingbroke I had a fincere value for in
their private ftations, but in their public capacities
I looked upon them both as little better than a
couple of rafcals. In facl, I believe it impoffible
for any minifter to be an honeft man: there are
fifty thoufand trap-doors, from the very nature of

his

his office, in which it is next to impoffible but his integrity muft tumble. All *miniſters*, as well as all prieſts, are the ſame.

SWIFT to POPE.

Mitre,—an emblem of fervility, fuperſtition, and bigotry. See *Biſhops*.

Mob (*Church and King*),—a ſpecies of regular militia, kept in pay by the miniſtry, for the protection of property againſt Levellers and Republicans. Some writers fuppofe that they are a conſtituted tribunal, to take a fort of fummary cognizance on Jacobines, Diſſenters, and Preſbyterians; and that they form an important part of our happy Conſtitution. They were very ferviceable at Birmingham, Mancheſter, and other places; and they are, without doubt, the moſt loyal portion of his Majeſty's ſubjects.

Monarch,—a word which in a few years is likely to be obfolete. It fignifies a man, who is begotten by another man, to rule over millions of his fellow-creatures; to trample upon their necks, and to build his own aggrandifement on the mifery and degradation of his ſubjects. They are always the moſt unhappy and miferable men of the community; and at the fame time the weakeſt, and the moſt wicked. The office is growing into difrepute,

pute, and mankind are daily feeing the inconve-
nience and folly of keeping up an humbug, which
is at once ridiculous and pernicious, oppreffive
and contemptible. We have allowed them for a
confiderable time " to monarchife, be feared, and
" kill with looks ;" but their hour is expired, and
the delufion is over. In a fhort period of time,
the nurfe, or the parent, will ufe the term as a bug-
bear for their children: " Hufh, you naughty
" child, the monarch is coming!" *Sic tranfit*
gloria mundi ! ! ! See *Wars, Corruption,* &c.

Monarchy.—Though *monarchies* may differ a
good deal, kings differ very little. Thofe who are
abfolute defire to continue fo ; and thofe who are
not endeavor to become fo : hence the fame maxims in all courts.

CHESTERFIELD.

Multitude,—all fwine, according to the natural
hiftory of kings and nobles.

Multitude (Swinifh),—vid. *People.*

Murder,—fee *War,* &c. &c.

My (pronoun),—poffeffive, if expreffing the
property; as when we fay, MY PEOPLE! *my horfe;*
MY KINGDOM! *my lands.*

Nab.

N

Nab.—To nab a cull is a modern vulgar, though technical term, in the new-invented fyftem of crimping, fignifying, to kidnap for the military fervice any young man who is imprudent enough after dark to frequent the infernal ftews and brothel-houfes, with which the *well-policed* metropolis abounds.

Nadir (*of adverfity*),—in the political world, means that miferable ftate we have been in ever fince the year 1760, anterior to which period we were comparatively in the *zenith of profperity.*

Nænia,—the goddefs of funerals. The laft funeral fhe attended was at the death of Liberty. She died unlamented; and Mr. Burke was the undertaker employed.

Naiffant,—in political heraldry, is applied to a Tyrant's head, which is feen iffuing out of the midft of Britannia's coat of arms. Under it is G. R.

Nakednefs of the Land,—to be feen to great advantage any where in Great Britain, efpecially in work-houfes, houfes of induftry, and in all manufacturing towns fince the war. " To fee the " nakednefs of the land art thou come."

HOLY BIBLE.

Name,—when applied to *great* men, means fame, renown. Thus George III. and Dionyfius, Burke and Thomas Paine, Pitt and Robefpierre, Bifhop Horfley and Bifhop Bonner, have all got names.

Namelefs,—the good deeds of George, Pitt, Dundas, and their myrmidons the clergy.

Nap,—a political flumber, which John Bull is continually afflicted with.

Narcotic,—producing torpor and inaction. Oppreffive proclamations, gold duft, and leaden bullets, are very ftrong narcotics, according to the new political pharmacopœia.

Narrow-minded,—fee *Houfe of Hanover.*

Nation,—a collective term, arbitrarily ufed for a fmall number of people, who, againft the confent of a large number, agree to fubmit themfelves and their pofterity for ever, to the unlimited and uncontrouled tyranny of one man.

National Debt,—three hundred and thirty-one millions of pounds fterling, which is increafing every day, and with it, as we are told, our happinefs and profperity. To give fome idea of this fum, if it was laid down in guineas clofe together in a line, it would extend upwards of fix thoufand miles in length. If it was laid down in fhillings it would extend upwards of five times round the world, and would require feventy thoufand horfes to draw it, at the rate of fifteen hundred weight each horſe.

Natural Enemies (to England),—a nation that governs itſelf without a king, upon the principles of honor, virtue, and eternal juſtice.

Nave of a wheel,—the moſt eſſential parts of the political wheel. 'Thus the King, Lords, and Commons, are all *naves.*

Navy,—a floating hell, conſiſting of an aſſembly of huge, unwieldy, wooden caſtles, well ſtored with artillery, gun-powder, chain ſhot, cannon balls, grape-ſhot, bombs, hand-grenades, ſlugs, leaden bullets, ſharp-angled pieces of iron, flints, glaſs, old ruſty nails, ſalt-petre, brimſtone, com-buſtible canniſters, and every engine of deſtruc-tion that will do execution. Moſt of the ſailors who conduct and manage theſe uſeful machines, are torn by force from their wives and families, to aſſiſt monarchs in executing this only and univerſal object of their whole lives, viz. the extermination of the human ſpecies.

Nebuchadnezzar.—He was an hirſute king, and, like other brute beaſts, ate graſs and potatoes, whence the name of potentate (vide Lemon). It is thought by phyſiologiſts, that it would greatly conduce to the welfare of his people, if the king of *Georgia* was turned out to graſs before the meet-ing of every ſeſſion of Parliament.

Ne-

Neceſſary War,—a war carried on by kings againſt the liberty and happineſs of mankind.

Neck,—that ſlender part that is ſituated between the head and trunk of the body, on which the gentle axe, and gentler guillotine, glided acroſs, and produced a *ſolution of continuity,* in the perſons of the Tyrants Charles the Firſt and Louis the Laſt.

> " Hear it not, *Duncan,* for it is a knell
> " That ſummons *thee* to heaven or to hell."

MACBETH.

Necromancer,—Mr. Pitt, who, by means of charms and ſpells, and his opiate wand, conjures up the Houſe of Commons and the Privy Council to his opinions. For many years, by the force of his incantations, he kept Liberty bound up in a little bottle, containing a ſolution of gold in the *ſudorous acid,* extraƐted from the brows of the laboring poor. This bottle was kept in the Treaſury; and Mr. Windham, going there one day, very thirſty, haſtily opened the bottle for a draught of this precious *aqua-vitæ.* The goddeſs immediately eſcaped and fled to France, on the 14th of July, 1789, where ſhe has taken up a perennial abode, and never means to reviſit theſe inhoſpitable ſhores.

Needy,

Needy,—the virtuous, the honeſt, the induſtrious, and the uncorrupt part of the community.

Ne exeat regno.—In deſpotic countries this is a writ to reſtrain thoſe who are oppreſſed from leaving the kingdom. This is one of thoſe arbitrary meaſures that none but a Tyrant would make uſe of, and none but a baſe-born abject people would ſubmit to.

Nefaſti dies,—thoſe days wherein it is not allowed to adminiſter juſtice. This has been the caſe ever ſince Kenyon preſided in the court of King's Bench.

Negociation,—a treaty or truce between two royal butchers who are at war with each other, to ſuſpend hoſtilities, until the moſt expeditious of them have recruited his ſtrength with men, ſhips, arms, and ammunition enough to renew the maſſacre with freſh vigor of brutality.

Negro,—a black beaſt of the Mammalia claſs, with flat noſe, thick lips, woolly head, and ivory teeth, and with a face ſomewhat reſembling the human. He is a biped, but clearly not a human being, as he is neither a Chriſtian, nor can he talk Engliſh. This animal is very uſeful in our ſettlements in the Weſt Indies, and admirably ſupplies the place of horſes, aſſes, mules, and oxen, in cultivating the produce of thoſe inclement iſlands. The fleſh of their young is very white and tender when

when fricafeed, which the planters in general prefer, for delicacy of flavor, to that of the adults,
which is rather tough and fibrous, from excefs of
labor and coarfe diet.

Neighborly,—to fubfidize Pruffia, Holland, Auftria, and the king of Sardinia. To give flavery
to the Poles, and to exterminate the French.

Nem. Con.—is applied when a motion or bill
paffes unanimoufly, and there cannot be found one
honeft man to ftem the torrent of oppreffion,
which flows from a royal fource, through the
muddy, polluted channel of an arrogant minifter.

Nero,—a king. During the American War,
there was publifhed a caricatur print of a reigning Tyrant, in the habit of a Sultan. Behold the
man! The name of Nero has been proverbially
applied to him, in common with other Tyrants.

Neft-egg,—a fnug finecure place under Government, capable of improvement by extortion and
fraud; fuch as Admiral of the Cinque Ports,
4000*l.* a year, Keeper of the King's Hawks, 1374*l.*
a year, &c. &c. &c. too tedious and too difgrace-
ful to mention.

Nethermoft Hell,—the country feat of Loughborough, Dundas, Pitt, and the whole crew of rafcals round the throne.

Neutral Powers,—thofe ftates which do not perfonally enter the theatre of war, but which promote this infernal trade by fecret plots, machinations and confpiracies. See the hiftory of the
reign of George the Laft; " What! ftab a man in
" the dark! Oh! villain, villain!"

New-fangled doctrines,—thofe which have a tendency to promote virtue, happinefs, and juftice, to
an opprefled and miferable people.

Newgate,—the Englifh Baftille. A large hand-
fome ftone building, elegantly fitted up for the
reception of lords and pick-pockets, phyficians
and ftrumpets, honeft citizens and foot-pads, Ja-
cobites and Jacobines, who form the bulk of the
nation, under the name of Diffenters and Anti-
Minifterialifts.

" Claufi in tenebris cum mærore & luctu, morte
" graviorum, vitam exigunt."

   " Yet think us not of foul fo tame,
   " Which no *repeated* wrongs inflame."

Newfpapers,—journals, for the moft part, under
the immediate patronage and direction of the minifter. It has been computed that about 1000*l.*
a year will buy up a paper; the editor of which, for
this confideration, is bound in a contract to calumniate indifcriminately the whole nation, viz. the
Friends of Liberty, by the name of Levellers;
                     and

and the King, Lords, and Commons, and all the friends of the minister, by the name of Patriots and honest men.

Nick (Old),—a cloven-footed, three-tailed, ' pert, prim, pleader of the Northern race,' who presides in the Tartarus of England—the Chancery.

Nick-name,—to call the king, sapiens; the judges, probi; and the bishops, literati.

Niggard,—a king who has defrauded his needy and starving subjects of nine millions of pounds sterling. " Mercy on us, Mr. Guelph, where do " you expect to go to when you die?"

Nim the Cits,—a technical term among crimps. Vide *Nab the Cull.*

Ninny,—one of the names of John Bull.

No, no!—echoed from the Treasury Bench in the House, and sometimes hear, hear! to confuse or drown the voice of any speaker who is guilty of uttering some unwelcome truths in the hearing of the people in the gallery.

Nobility,—a titled order of men, so called for their hereditary profligacy of manners, abandoned principles, and infernal depravity. Collect, if you can, in one human form, the associations of insolence, ignorance, pride, ignoble ambition, meanness of the basest kind, sordid viciousness, and every thing which is dishonorable, loathsome, and

depraved,

depraved, and you may form some faint idea of a modern nobleman.

Nobility.—Acquired *nobility* is a disease which is made to pass in the blood. " The *nobility*, which " is and always will be the nursery and hot-bed of " the satellites of Despotism, has found in its crimes " its own punishment."

MIRABEAU.

Nobility (privileges of the).—There was a time when the German lords reckoned amongst their privileges, that of robbery on the highways of their own territory. In Scotland they had a right to enjoy the first fruits of all maidens. Every where the lords sold the bondmen, or villains, as they did animals, with the field where they lived, and which they cultivated. The feudal servitude still exists in Russia, Poland, Germany, and Hungary. And there were considerable reliques of the feudal system in France; and there still remains some particles in almost every state in Europe. Nothing has degraded and debased the human species so much as *Feudal Tyranny;* and what remains of this most dreadful plague, is what *Mr. Burke* calls THE CORINTHIAN CAPITAL OF POLISHED SOCIETY.

Nobleman,—one that wishes you should seek in the roots for the fruit which should be found on the branches.

N

Nod,

Nod,—a quick declination of the head, by which the minifter *perfuades* the Houfe of Commons to a concurrence with him in opinion.

Noli me tangere, Touch me not,—the motto to Pitt's coat of arms.

Nominative cafe,—the firft cafe of declinable nouns. HARRIS.

George and Pitt are nominatives, becaufe they are both in the *firft* cafe, and both *declinable;* but, they are nominatives *abfolute.*

Non-conformifts,—all thofe factious and evil-difpofed perfons who refift " the Oppreffor's " wrong," and will not conform to a fyftem of intolerance and injuftice. " Coftoro hanno un " animo in Piazza, & uno in Palazzo."

Nonjurors,—thofe who foolifhly fcruple to fwear damnation to themfelves. See *Papifts.*

Nonplus,—the ftate of Pitt's mind when fober, and on the opening of the budget.

Noofe,—a running knot, which is capable of fitting necks of all fizes, Very convenient for the People to have by them when fummary juftice is adminiftered to wicked kings and corrupt minifters.

Nootka Sound,—famous for the produce of a few cat-fkins, which we quarrelled about with the Spaniards. But happily for this country, our able
minifter

minifter prevented a war by an armament which coft only four millions! " Incidit in Scyllam cu- " piens vitare Charybdim."

Nofe,—a cartilaginous protuberance in the human face, to which (in Parliament men) is fixed a fmall wire, for the accommodation of the minifter, to guide them at his pleafure.

Notes (Bank),—fmall flips of thin, filky paper, on which are engraved ftrong and forcible arguments in favor of arbitrary power. They have been much ufed of late, and poffefs wonderful powers of conviction. It is death, however, for the Swinifh Multitude to *take off* thefe arguments.

Novitiate,—the time in which the rudiments of corruption are learned; exemplified in young Jenkinfon and young Canning.

Nuifance,—vide *the Clergy*.

Numfkulls,—Judge Afhhurft, Judge Rook, Garrow, and the Dunkirk Hero.

Nuncio,—a meffenger from the army to inform us how far our troops have retreated, and how many victims are left unfacrificed, but ready for killing.

Nurfery,—the court, for rogues and thieves, pimps and parafites.

Obe—

O

Obedience,—that obfequioufnefs and blind fubmiffion which in countries on the decline of freedom men in power demand from the People. When Paul le Mefurier demanded (according to the ancient cuftom of his nation) houfekeepers to imprifon their lodgers, he demanded *political obedience.*

Obedience (paffive).—To put your perfons in prifon, your necks in the halter, and fuffer yourfelves to be fent from your country, to fight and be butchered *againft your wills, but according to the will of your Tyrant,* and pay heavy taxes for all this ABUSE, without murmuring, is PASSIVE OBEDIENCE in reality.

Œconomy,—a pitiful manner of furnifhing the royal kitchen, and a profufe method of expending the money of the nation.

One.—Among men you fee the ninety and nine toiling to gather a heap of fuperfluities, for ONE, getting nothing for themfelves all the while but a little of the coarfeft of the provifions which their own labor produces; and this ONE too, oftentimes the feebleft and worft of the whole fet, a *child,* a *woman,* a *madman,* or a *fool;* looking quietly on, while they fee the fruit of all their labor fpent or fpoiled; and if one of them take or touch a particle

ticle of it, the others join againſt and hang him for the theft.   Vide *King*.

ARCH. PALEY.

Oppoſition.—It is ſaid that in England there is *oppoſition* to every thing except Shakeſpeare ; but ſhortly we may likewiſe except the *Government*.

Oppoſition,—a ſet of men leagued to thwart the meaſures of the reigning miniſter ; contriving falſe ſtandards of popular freedom to the nation, and then deceiving them ; pretending to ſacrifice their intereſt to the People's good, but in faɛt *ſa-crificing* nothing but *principles* and *veracity.* The nation ought, in golden letters, to place before their eyes the fable of the lark and her young ones.

Orator,—in the preſent age, the member with ſtrong lungs, aſſiſted by an extenſive memory, re-tailing *ſentences* of Cicero *by inch of candle* in St. Stephen's Chapel. " *Happy the man who hath his* " *quiver full of them.*"

Orgies,—the Bacchanalian repaſt of Billy the Tory, and Scotch Harry, during receſs of buſi-neſs ; and of infinite uſe to ſecure them from French Atheiſm.

Orthodoxy,—the adherence to thoſe tenets and dogmas by which the animal is enabled, by pa-tronage, corruption, and influence, to extend his

views

views from the country church to the summit of the cathedral.

Ostentation,—the art of securing attention by blue ribbands, embroidered garters, journeys to St. Paul's, and Weymouth excursions.

Oversight,—the retreat of able generals from before the walls and battlements of Dunkirk; of experienced commanders from Tournay; and *brave patriots* from Toulon!

Overtures of Peace.—History has delivered to us the quarrels of potentates, and the vices of monarchs; it hath informed us of the mean arts used by princes, when war has no longer become practicable, either from the emptiness of the treasury, or from the remonstrance of their subjects. At this period, kings complimented each other, restored the conquered territory, and ended where they began. In the present time, different overtures must be adopted; new language had recourse to. We are contending, not indeed with the vicious Louis, or the haughty Charles; we are warring with a great and free people, who will alike disdain the artifice of courts, and the hypocrisy of statesmen. Our overtures, when we relinquish the system of conquest, must be open, manly, and generous.

Outcast.—Such is the fate of the man, whose reputation bore his name to the closet of every politician

tician in Europe; fuch defervedly the lot of that
general, who, entrufted with the fafety of the
French nation, relinquifhed his honor for mercenary reward. He trufted to the principles of Cobourg, of Clairfayt, of ariftocracy!—trufted to
ariftocracy! how weak his mind, how futile his
experience, who accufed nobles of virtue, integrity, or veracity. May the paths of Dumourier be
the paths of apoftacy.

P

Pacification,—by Dr. Johnfon, termed the art
of making peace. In modern cabinets, this word
has no accurate definition; in faft, by them it is
an art frequently talked of, but feldom practifed.

Pageant,—a fpeftacle, by the lure of which a
minifter may draw money for himfelf and his
friends; by amufing the public mind; fuch, for
inftance, was the Spanifh armament in 1790; fuch
the Ruffian armament in 1791; and whilft the
People of England tamely fuffer their privileges
to be reftrained, their rights pillaged, and immuni-
ties plundered, the fame pageants will be erefted,
and the fame fpeftacles difplayed.

Painite,—every individual who will not fign his
teft in Mr. Reeves's Affociation; will not conde-
fcend to kifs the minifterial rod, held out to punifh

him,

him, or agree to arm for the fake of a conftitution fervilely adulized, and pompoufly extolled.

Palace,—the ufual refidence of monarchs, reigning (to quote an elegant author) in contempt of the People. Could we unite in one idea, the luxury and voluptuoufnefs of aldermen, the mean-nefs and avarice of parifh officers, and the igno-rance and fervility of courtiers, we fhould form a juft conception of the lodging and inhabitants of a royal palace!—*in Spain ! ! !*

Pannic.—Political inftances may be fhown in the examples of the Duke of Richmond's fortifica-tions, Edmund Burke's prophecies, Mr. Pitt's crufade, and Judge Afhhurft's *mild fentences* for fedition.

Pantheon,—formerly ufed for the purpofes of fuperftition, in a collection of fabulous deities and ennobled gods; lately ufed on the continent for the reception of falfe virgins, myfterious Jefufes, and pretended faints; at prefent exalted to the nobler defign of conveying to pofterity the names of great men, who have embellifhed fcience, de-cried fuperftition, or have promoted the beft inte-refts of man.

Papacy,—almoft forgotten, until the foldiers of England protected the offices and dignities of the church of Rome;—until convents were permitted in this Proteftant and religious country; and until

the

the Bifhop of Rome, the defcendant of St. Peter, gave his holy benediction upon the united ftandards of Auftria, Pruffia, Holland, and Spain, to curb anarchy, and re-eftablifh defpotifm.

Pardon,—in politics, denotes the forgivenefs of an individual who, belying all his prior profeffions of patriotifm and juftice, forfakes the People's caufe for a ministerial bribe, and is feated on the right hand of Billy Pitt, *whofe mercy endureth for ever.*

Parliament,—a word founding far, and fignifying little; formerly it was freely confidered as a check upon executive power, or as the bank which prevented the inundation of arbitrary caprice; at prefent it ferves the purpofe of miniftry, by fanctioning thofe meafures which their ignorance or vice has performed. It gave our ally Pruffia money for which he is not accountable; it repaid the expenfive armaments voted ufelefs by the nation; and it gave fanction to a war difaftrous in its effects, and ruinous in its confequences. Such are your Parliaments; fuch your Reprefentatives.

Parfon,—formerly a refpectable character, practifing the mild precepts of the Chriftian religion, of which clafs a few remain. At prefent it denotes an animal vifiting the univerfity, fubfcribing to articles he has not yet digefted, refigning the right of reafoning, confidering *the Defender of our*

O *faith*

faith at leaft as infallible as the Romifh Bifhop, and finally beholding with enraptured eye the lawn fleeves and crofier of his Holinefs the Archbifhop of Canterbury.

Partition,—well exemplified in Poland by the Royal Gaoler of Europe, and the Northern Bear; at prefent a word rather in difrepute, fince the failure of this practice in a neighboring Republic.

Partition.—The partition of Poland, by the three combined crowned thieves, is the moft famous partition of modern times. That of France, which was thought fo eafy, notwithftanding all the Duke of Brunfwick's fkill in tactics, ftill remains a problem.

Partnerfhip.—This word, by L'Eftrange, is called, " the union of two or more in the fame " trade." *Quere.* Will the firm of the houfe of Meffrs. Auftria, Pruffia, and Co. fatisfy the demands of their creditors; or, where muft they apply for a ftatute of bankruptcy?

Party.—There never was any party in which the moft ignorant were not the moft violent; for a bee is not a bufier animal than a blockhead. However, fuch inftruments are neceffary to politicians; and perhaps it may be with ftates as with clocks, which muft have fome dead weight hanging

at

at them, to help and regulate the motion of the finer and more ufeful parts.

SWIFT.

Party Jury,—means, in law, a jury of half fo-reigners, half natives;—in political practice, it means a Winterbotham jury, * * * * *, * * * * *, *cetera defunt.*

Paftime,—the fport or amufement by which fome kings are diverted; as by armaments, battles, fieges, and maffacres.

Patience,—is a virtue faid to belong peculiarly to *cuckolds* and to *affes*, in company with whom we with juftice may place the People of Eng-land.

Patriot,—not the individual feeking perfonal emolument by temporary profeffions, nor the op-pofitionift who votes the fupplies for the war he condemns. It is the man, " juftum & propofiti " tenax," *who dares be honeft in the worft of times;* whom no threats can difcourage; whom no temp-tations can fubdue; who can behold the tide of popular opinion ebb and flow without a dereliction of principle; who can, if called upon, facrifice even life itfelf for the good of his country.

Patriotifm.—In the times of the Romans, it confifted in facrificing upon the altars of the coun-try all who were not Romans, under the name of

O 2

Bar-

Barbarians. Among the English, it consists in treating as enemies all who are not English, under the name of *Foreigners.*

Patron,—one who countenances the apostate, protects the informer, and supports the dependant; whose patronage extends not to the friend of virtue, the opposer of tyranny, or the lover of justice; but, on the contrary, seeks to enrich the man who sells his country for a bribe, or courts the wretch who disowns his principles for the pavilion of ambition.

Peace,—to a nation, is as contentment to an individual; it is a gentle stream running with smooth and easy current, fertilizing the land through which it flows, and enriching the country whose labors have made it navigable; it is the trunk of the vast oak, furnishing shade to the flocks, and food for the cattle; it is so necessary an ingredient in the mixture of national happiness, that without it no people can be flourishing or virtuous, any more than the rich individual can procure ease without contentment, or happiness without virtue.

Peacock,—a fowl eminent for the beauty of his tail, and deformity of his voice; in other words, a great parliamentary orator, whose volubility amuses, but whose arguments displease, and whose arrogance disgusts.

Pecu-

Peculator,—a robber of the public money. Is not, however, the robber of public freedom equally deformed; and the filcher of national reputation equally culpable?

> Who steals my purse steals trash;
> 'Tis nought; 'twas mine, 'twas his,
> And has been slave to thousands.
> But he that filches from me my good name,
> Steals that which nought enriches him,
> But makes me poor indeed.
>
> SHAKESPEARE.

Peerage,—that hereditary body of men to whom the public virtue and national freedom are entrusted. These *guardians* of public liberty, these political priests, have indeed been the *nomina rerum,* the butterflies of the hour. Thus,

> ********, of Commons' House a stupid wretch,
> Whose mind to A, B, C, can scarcely stretch,
> Has, by a monarch's all-creating word,
> Become a very decent lord.

Peerage,—in former days, an honor conferred upon such as had rendered themselves conspicuous for their merit, and eminent for their virtues; but in the more modern ages it has been, in general,

the

the ufages of venality and corruption, and a diftinction not to be purchafed at a fmaller price than
everlafting infamy and difgrace.

Peers.—The generality of Peers, far from fupporting themfelves in a ftate of independent great-
nefs, are but too apt to fall into an oblivion of
their proper dignity, and to run headlong into an
abject fervitude.

BURKE.

Penfion.—In England it is generally underftood
to mean pay given to a ftate-hireling for treafon to
his country.

JOHNSON.

Penfion.—This word has been well defined by
Addifon, to be "an allowance made to any one
"without an equivalent." Had not penfions, as
it were, obtained a fanction by long and continued
ufage, we fhould have decried the meafure as an
abfurdity; and the man who fhould have propofed
it, more fitted for the cells of Bedlam than the
departments of the ftate. It is, however, with
civil abfurdities as with religious ceremonies,
whofe fetters are firft made eafy by chaplets of
rofes, and afterwards retained by prefcriptive
rights. The time, indeed, may arrive, when the
ceremonies of the latter, and the abfurdities of the

former,

former, may moulder into duſt, and be known only from the recording page of hiſtory.

Penſioner,—a ſlave of ſtate, hired by a ſtipend to obey his maſter.

JOHNSON.

In Britain's Senate he a ſeat obtains,
And one more *Penſioner* St. Stephen's gains.

POPE.

People.—It is the *People* which compoſe the human ſpecies. All which is not the People, is of ſo little conſequence that it is not worth the trouble of counting.

ROUSSEAU.

People,—the commonality; the vulgar; the *Swiniſh Multitude;* or whatever the *ennobled race* may, in their *infinite goodneſs and mercy,* be pleaſed to term them.

Permit,—a ſmall piece of paper, for which, at Harwich, you pay 13*s.* 4*d.* to be divided between the twenty-four electors of that paltry borough, for the liberty of paſſing and re-paſſing from thence to Helvœtſluys.

Perſecution.—We reſerve this definition until we can collect the experienced authorities of Eaton, Winterbotham, Muir, and Palmer. We promiſe

mife its appearance in the next edition of this Dictionary.

Perfpicuity.—We refer our readers to a work juft publifhed by Sir James Murray, compofed in Flanders; fpecimens of which may be feen in fome Extraordinary Gazettes.

Petition,—a form of prayer, unprofitable, inconvenient, and ufelefs, when directed from the People to the minifter; but fure, certain, and infallible, when in the form of a parliamentary act it requefts money from the nation.

Pillory,—a very forcible argument, ufed by men in power to divert the attention, and refcue the imagination from the abfurd and dreadful notion of a Parliamentary Reform.

Placeman,—Mr. Pitt, and his heaven-born family, Mr. Rofe, Henry Dundas, and others.—A heavenly, difinterefted, and honorable Adminiftration! *Quere.* Is it the king that has made them rogues, or they who have made the king a ———?

Pluralift,—the man who, under the facred name of religion, contrives to gain from the farmer his produce; to pillage mankind of their reafon; and to plunder from the ftate its religious liberty.

Poet Laureat,—one who takes the place of *buffoon,* or *fool,* in moft courts in Europe.

Police,

Police,—the art of erecting *military baſtilles,* i.e. *barracks,* in every county in the kingdom.

Poor,—both in ſpirit and in purſe, the People of England.

Poor,—ſelf-evident; ſearch your own purſe, and look round and ſee.

Popularity,—the means by which Pitt got into power; *i. e.* the reforming of Parliament, and deſtroying abuſes; but, his turn ſerved, the apoſtate is diſcovered, and who hitherto attempts to delude and deceive by aſſerting that this is not a proper time, nor that a proper time; in ſhort, no time is proper whilſt he is in adminiſtration.

Popularity,—the heaven-born miniſter, and a hanging thief.

Power (arbitrary).—Where any one perſon or body of men, who do not repreſent the whole, ſeize into their hands the power in the laſt reſort, there is properly no longer a government, but what Ariſtotle and his followers call the abuſe and corruption of one. I look upon *Arbitrary Power* as a greater evil than *Anarchy* itſelf; as much as a ſavage is a happier ſtate of life than a ſlave at the oar. Whoever argues in defence of abſolute power in a ſingle perſon, ought in all free ſtates to be treated as the common enemy of mankind.

SWIFT.

P

Precedent,—a kind of argument, which we muſt not confound with *example.* PRECEDENT is only brought in proof to favor the claims and in-tereſt of kings, miniſters, and the privileged claſſes. It is abſolutely inſignificant, and of no force, when the maintaining or recovering the Rights of the People is in queſtion. This is what diſtinguiſhes *precedent* from *example,* which applies equally to all.

Prejudice (national),—is the moſt common, and the moſt allowable of all deviations from juſtice; it is a near, though an illegitimate, relation of patriotiſm.

Prerogative (a regard for the royal),—a worn-out pretence to infringe upon the laws, and a glar-ing deſign upon the privileges of the People.

Preſs (the),—formerly the palladium of Engliſh Liberty; what it is at preſent let facts declare. Mr. Holt, of Newark, in the year 1793, was tried, convicted, and impriſoned, for re-printing the Duke of Richmond's Letter to Col. Sharman, and Mr. Pitt's Reſolutions in the year 1782. *O tem-pora, O mores!*

Preſs (licentiouſneſs of the),—the candid me-thod of repreſenting the ſufferings of the king-dom, and the ſpeedieſt means of having them re-dreſſed.

Prince,

Prince,—a being nurfed by Luxury, reared by Affluence, educated by Flattery, and degraded by Servility.

Princes,—in their infancy, childhood, and youth, are faid to difcover prodigious parts and wit. Strange, fo many hopeful princes, fo many fhameful kings! If they happen to die young, they are prodigies of wifdom and virtue; if they live, they are often prodigies indeed, but of another fort.

SWIFT.

Prifoner,—among others, the man who, originally indebted a few fhillings, fhall, by the villainy of attorneys, and chicanery of law, fpend in the gloomy cell thofe years which might have been confoling to his family, and ufeful to his country.

Proclamation,—a fuppofed letter from the king to his People, in which they are informed when they are happy, and by which they learn an increafe of taxes to be an accumulation of comfort.

Prudence and Œconomy,—an increafe of taxes at the conclufion of an expenfive war; and lavifhing that treafure upon profligate favorites which fhould be applied to difcharge the public debts of the nation.

P 2

Qua-

Q

Qualification,—implies frequently, the quantum of money neceffary for a reprefentative in Parliament to poffefs, before he fhall be fuppofed to have fufficient knowledge to give his aye or no upon the weighty affairs of the nation.

Quarrel,—in political affairs, means nothing more than the defire of two potentates to try each other's force;—a fyftem perfectly rational, and freely confiftent with that which gave it birth!

Queen,—the poor wife of a king, who miferably hoards up riches, and counts her gold, guinea for guinea, with the avaricious, covetous mifer her hufband; who is greatly belied if fhe ever did a generous or meritorious act in her whole life; and, for the bleffing of the nation, has contributed all in her power to make a bad *thing* good for nothing.

Quorum,—a bench of Juftices; who affemble at fome hall, or fome inn, to do juftice; and there pafs orders to convey a man, his wife, and twelve children, two hundred miles off, becaufe he was not born, or ferved apprenticefhip, in this town, although he is efteemed the beft workman, and bears the beft of characters, under the apprehen-

fion

fion that he or his family may become chargeable to the parifh!

O MAN! ARE THESE LAWS JUST?

Or to fentence a man to tranfportation, or fine, or, from inability of payment, to imprifonment, for having knocked down a hare which was devouring his cabbages in his garden; or fining a man ten pounds, for not being worth a hundred a year, and for carrying a gun without a licence!

R

Rabble,—an affembly of low-bred, vulgar, and riotous people; otherwife the *Swinifh Multitude,* fo called by St. Edmund, becaufe they dare to grunt their grievances even at the foot of the throne. The Englifh rabble, when once roufed, are very faucy and unmanageable, but they have the remarkable quality of the moft paffive forbear-ance, as it is not a little will difturb their flumbers.

> Sincere, plain-hearted, hofpitable, kind,
> Yet like the muftering thunder when provok'd;
> The dread of Tyrants, and the fole refource
> Of thofe that under grim oppreffion groan.

Rack,—an engine of torture, commodioufly fitted up with cords, pincers, flefh-hooks, &c. &c.

ufed

ufed chiefly for extorting confeffion from innocent men. In England the rack has been out of ufe ever fince the mild reign of Tyrant Elizabeth, but, it is reported, has been propofed in the Cabinet Council to be renewed for the accommodation of the Jacobines of the prefent day. It was introduced here by a duke of Exeter, in the reign of Tyrant Henry VI. and has, from that circumftance, been called, " The Duke of Exeter's " Daughter ;" fo that it fhould be exercifed only on the nobility, as it would be highly degrading for a duke's daughter to have a *criminal* connection with any but of noble or royal blood.

Rain.—The prefent long and fatal *rain* in England has entirely ruined the country paft redemption, unlefs it fhall pleafe Heaven to put a fpeedy end to it. All vegetation is checked, the poor are ftarving for want of bread, and the bountiful lap of nature no more fupplies us with her accuftomed bleffings, for nature herfelf feems to riot in the general devaftation; and all owing to this curfed *rain.*

Rank.—Kings are perfons of the firft rank on earth, and very *rank* indeed they are; fo much fo, that I know not one who could not confciencioufly exclaim with the royal murderer in Hamlet :

' Oh! my offence is *rank;* it fmells to heaven !'

Ran-

Ranſom,——priçe paid for redemption from captivity or puniſhment. If unfortunately the Duke of York ſhould be taken priſoner in this *glorious* and *neceſſary* war, the French would gladly ranſom him for a ſans-culottes drummer.

Rapier,——a military ſpit, long enough to transfix at once a tyrant king, his infernal miniſter, and one or two judges or biſhops.

Rara-avis,——a *thing* next to impoſſible to exiſt; as a pious prieſt, a good king, a wiſe lord, or a virtuous Parliament man.

Raſcal,——ſee *Wedderburne*.

Raſhneſs,——to attempt to ſubjugate a free people, by oppreſſion, intolerance, and bloody proſecutions for imaginary crimes.——" The ſame pretended " power which robs an Engliſh ſubject of his birth- " right, may rob an Engliſh king of his crown." —Tyrants, beware!

Razor,——an inſtrument very proper for crazy kings to make uſe of, when their *will is* encompaſſed with *evil*.

Realm,——all of a country that is governed by one Tyrant.

Reaſon,——a faculty of the ſoul, which the People of England never make uſe of till too late. They ſhut the ſtable door when the horſe is ſtolen.

Re-

Rebellion,—an unfuccefsful attempt of the People in a generous ftruggle for liberty and equality
of the rights of nature.

Recefs of Parliament,—an interval between the
feffions, when the prime minifter may hood-wink
and tyrannize over the People, lavifh their treafures, and commit any enormity, not only with
impunity, and without controul, but likewife with
popularity.—So much for the Englifh !

Reckoning,—that awful account which all wicked kings and their minions may expect to be called
upon to make by an injured People, whom they
lord it over with an iron fway.

Recruit,—to inveigle young men by martial
mufic, to make them drunk, and then flip into
their pockets a fhilling of the Ty——, of the King's
money, I mean ; or if all thefe allurements be not
fufficient, they then kidnap them.—See the words
Crimp and *Nab.*

Rector,—a grave and fanctified human being,
clad in fable, who lives by extortion and fraud,
attacking the prejudices of men, keeping them
from the truth, and inculcating, with a pious countenance, falfehood and impofture.—One of the
engines of Defpotifm.

Redrefs of Grievances,—what an opprefled People can never expect from a venal Parliament, or
from

from any other fource but their own will, and a vi-gorous execution of that will.

Reeves,—every thing that is corrupt, flagitious, depraved, and abandoned, affociated into one human form. In competition for villainy with Lough-borough and Juftice Clerk.

Reform in Parliament,—an object moft devoutly to be wifhed, but which a fpirited People would no more *petition* for.

Refugees,—Englifh Patriots, as Dr. Prieftley and family, Mr. Cooper, of Manchefter, &c. &c. who, in the years 1793 and 1794, were obliged to quit a country pregnant with bigotry and perfecu-tion, to fpend the reft of their days beyond the reach of Arbitrary Power, in a more genial foil, and in a kinder atmofphere, in the calm regions of tranquil liberty and uninterrupted harmony.

Regent,—one Tyrant who governs a kingdom in the abfence, or during the minority of another Tyrant.

Regicide,—any brave fellow who dares con-fign an anointed defpot to his native regions be-low.

Regifugium,—a feaft held in ancient Rome, in memory of the expulfion of their kings by Lucius Junius Brutus. There is generally one at the lat-ter end of every century in England. The regi-fuge we at prefent celebrate is on the 4th of No-

Q   vember,

vember, as on that day, in the year 1688, Tyrant
James II. may be faid to have been expelled from
the throne. Mr. Pitt is paving the way for a new
feaft to celebrate.

Regiment,—a body of hired affaffins, who enter
into partnerfhip together in the trade of war. Thus
for fix-pence a day one human being lets himfelf
out to murder as many others as he can. The Bifhop of London fays truly,

" One murder makes a villain, thoufands a hero."

Religion,— a fuperftition, invented by the archbifhop of hell, and propagated by his faithful dio-
cefans the clergy, to keep the people in ignorance
and darknefs, that they may not fee the work of
iniquity that is going on. Under the mafk and
pretext of duty to God, they preach up the divine
right of kings to tyrannize, and enjoin us to paffive
obedience and non-refiftance to oppreffion.

Wherever God erects a houfe of prayer,
The devil always builds a chapel there ;
And 'twill be found, upon examination,
The latter has the largeft congregation.

Remonftrance to the King,—the fecond mode of
the People, when they appeal for the remedy of
fome political evil. " Their firft appeal is to the
" *integrity*

" *integrity* of their Reprefentatives; the fecond to .
" the King's *juftice*; the third and laft argument
" of the People, whenever they have recourfe to
" it, will carry more weight perhaps than perfua-
" fion to Parliament, or fupplication to the
" throne."

Reprefentative,—one who neither cares for your
interefts nor your welfare, provided he can get a
fhare of the general plunder. If he can *not* get
a fhare, he becomes all at once a flaming patriot,
harangues againft corruption and venality, till,
like the noify maftiff, he receives an opiate morfel
from the thieves whom he was placed there to guard
againft. This puts me in mind of boys running
after a coach, who, when they are driven away by
thofe who have already got a place, bawl out, Hil-
loa, Coachman! whip behind!

Reprefentatives of the People.—The king is the
reprefentative of the People; fo are the lords; fo
are the judges; they are all truftees for the people, as well as the commons; becaufe no power is
given for the fole fake of the holder; and although
government certainly is an inftitution of divine
authority, yet *its forms*, and *perfons who adminifter
it, all originate from the People.*

BURKE.

Reprobate,—an abandoned wretch, loft to all
fenfe of virtue; e. g. It has been faid of Pitt,

that

that while he was begging his mother's blessing
on his knees, at her death-bed, he stole her
purse out of her pocket, underneath her pil-
low.

Republic,—a popular government, founded on
the eternal and immutable principles of liberty
and equality, truth and justice. A monarchy
is quite *toute autre chose,* and directly opposite to
this.

Republic,—a government which is conducted
with a tenth or twentieth part the expence, throughout every department, that it costs a monarchical
one. There is scarce such a thing known as corruption of rulers; and the rulers being stationary,
have no occasion of attempting such ruinous
schemes to rob their fellow-citizens of their rights,
as in such case they would destroy their own. In
truth, a Representative Republic must be the best
government, as it appears the most rational.

Requiem.—When Pitt dies a requiem will be
sung or said by the Aristocrats in all the churches
in this kingdom, and in our town of Berwick upon
Tweed, to intercede with his Grace the Archbishop of Hell to take his dear departed soul out
of purgatory, and to request some loyal ghost or
other to dip his finger in water to cool his tongue,
as he must be tormented in that flame.

Re-

Refignation (minifterial),—a fallacious method of efcaping from the hatred of the Public, and an artful contrivance in a favorite to make others refponfible for meafures which are guided by himfelf.

Reftoration,—the 29th of May, 1660; the faddeft day England ever faw; on which the reftoration of regal and epifcopal government took place under Tyrant Charles II.

Retrogade,—the marches of the Dunce of York in Flanders againft the fons of Liberty.

Revolution,—the fudden overturning of an arbitrary government by the People. Tyrants change a free government into a defpotic one, by flow gradations; but it is a comfortable reflection to the patriot, that a united nation can overthrow in a moment the work of whole ages of Tyrants. The Revolution of 1688, no good and wife man can applaud. It was the defpicable patch-work of a few addle-pated, whig noblemen. The People foon found they had only made an exchange of Tyrants; in fact, it was out of the frying-pan into the fire.

Revolution,—change in the ftate of a government or country. It is ufed among us for the change produced by the admiffion of king William and queen Mary, fays Dr. Johnfon; but that was only an amendment, and a very partial one it was.

A Re-

A Revolution is a total alteration of the forms of governments, and a re-affumption by the People of their long loft rights; a reftoration of that equality which ought always to fubfift among men.

Reward of merit,—places and penfions to fuch as had fcandaloufly fold the intereft of their country, and fupported the tyranny of a prefumptuous minifter.

Rights,—thofe claims which belong to us by nature and juftice. They are quite obfolete and unknown here. It has, indeed, been a fubject of difpute among learned political antiquarians, whether fuch things ever exifted in this ifland.

Riot Act,—read by a magiftrate (or, if he cannot read, by the bell-man) in times of tumult, whenever more than three people are feen talking together;—a very convenient inftrument of ftate to prevent any redrefs of grievances.

Rival Nation,—the Ruffian to our's, in cruelty, intolerance, and bloody perfecution.

Robbers,—Eaft and Weft India plunderers, Prime Minifters, Judges, and Bifhops.

Robbery.—Many people confound *robbery* with *conqueft:* they contend, that it confifts equally in poffeffing by force the property of others. But there is a prodigious difference. A robber is frequently folus in his enterprizes, or at leaft has but

few

few affociates: it is commonly an individual poffeffed of neither title nor crown. The *conqueror,*
on the contrary, is almoft always a prince or a
king, and is followed by thoufands of men: and
the pirate who was bold enough to compare himfelf
to ALEXANDER, regarded the difference as nothing. Yet hiftory, both ancient and modern,
proves it fufficient to render ROBBERY infamous
and difhonorable, whilft CONQUEST is held both
lawful and glorious.

Rope,—in revolutions, an article in great demand among the canaille, or Swinifh Multitude,
when great men are put in a *ftate of requifition,*
by a few moments *fufpenfion* from their titles and
honors.

Rofe (red and white),—by way of diftinction
between two factions, who deluged this country
with blood through a feries of above thirty years,
in order to eftablifh a permanence of tyranny on
the throne. The houfe of York had for its badge
a white rofe; that of Lancafter a red one. They
were both emuloufly revengeful, cruel, unjuft, ambitious, and bloody-minded. As each in turn got
the afcendant, the fcaffold was the fource of a conftant and never-failing ftream of blood; and
there were alternately attainders in every noble
family in the kingdom, which were as frequently
reverfed. The remote caufe of all this blood-

fhed

shed was Tyrant Henry IV. surnamed Boling-broke, who depofed, and then murdered, Tyrant Richard II.

Royalift,—among the ignorant part of mankind, fignifies a perfon attached to regal government; among artful courtiers it is a veil for their own ariftocracy.

Royalty,—the curfe of God Almighty in his wrath to man. Where this office exifts, the whole country is pale, fickly, and unfruitful. The poor lucklefs inhabitants miferable, melancholy, and almoft mad with defpair. Emaciated through hunger, fpiritlefs through fubjection, and depraved to the utmoft poffible, by mimicking the aban-doned profligacy of the court.—See *England.*

Ruftic,—the poor laborer, who toils all the live-long day, to procure, by the fweat of his brow, enjoyment for another. He tills the ground, and fows the feed, but another comes to reap the har-veft. He is mocked with the beautiful profufe-nefs of nature; but denied to partake of her bounties. He cultivates her flowers, but cannot fhare her fruits. Great God! if this is ever to be the ftate of man on earth, happy had it been had he never been born!

Sans-

S

Sabbath,—a day appointed by Chriſtians (from the Jews) for public worſhip, which is employed in works of piety, inſtead of works of labour. This hebdomodal fit of devotion among Chriſtians returns regularly every Sunday, when they diſcharge in whining prayers and diſcordant hymns, the accumulation of the week, and empty themſelves in copious evacuation, much in the ſame *neceſſary* manner that a gormandizing alderman does after a feaſt. In different parts of England, various ways are adopted of expreſſing to the Creator, the devotional fervor of the people. In the metropolis the city apprentices, journeymen, and their maſters generally pay their tribute of adoration, in a ſhilling ordinary at Hackney, or ſome other neighbouring village, a row in a boat to Putney, or at the Dog and Duck. The higher orders of ſociety, in a ride in Hyde Park in the morning, and at a gaming-table in the afternoon. In the country, the athletic villagers generally engage in a game of cricket, trap-ball, or long-fives ; and the boys amuſe themſelves at marbles, or at toſs-halfpenny on a tomb-ſtone in the church-yard. In the churches you will find a few old bachelors, old maids, and other poor deluded wretches (who think to atone for the ſins of a whole life, by going to church twice in one day in the week, and cheating

R all

all they can the other fix) liftening with open mouth
to the dogmas of an illiterate prieft, who is bound
apprentice to Implicit Faith, Efq. a wholefale merchant, both in religion and politics ; and afterwards
becomes an *acting* partner in the extenfive commercial houfe of Meffrs. Superftition, Fraud, Hypocrify and Co.

Sacerdotal,—belonging to the priefthood. A
generic term for the moft abominable vices, the
moft confummate depravity, and the moft bloated
corruption that either the mind or body is capable
of. See *Les Crimes des Papés.*

Sack.—To fack a city, is when it is taken by
ftorm, and left to the ravages and indifcriminate
plundering of the foldiery, and when the fair fex
is not treated with that decency and *decorum* which
is ever due to it. At the recapture of Toulon by
the French, an Englifh lady of virtue, very coolly
went up to a French officer, and as compofedly
afked him, " Pray, Sir, can you tell me when the
" ravifhing begins?"

Sack-cloth,—is a kind of *pickling* fhift, which is
impofed on the backs of finful heretics who im-
pioufly attempt to refift the unlimited authority of
the prieft, over all their thoughts, words, and actions. The Jews firft wore them by way of *mortification of the flefh,* and after them, thofe who
follow the religion of the Whore of Babylon at
Rome.

Sacrament,

Sacrament,—the Euchariſt, the holy Communion, the celebration of the Lord's Supper, which generally takes place about eleven or twelve o'clock in the morning, when (according to the doctrine of the Romiſh or Popiſh church) the prieſt (in a manner worthy of Breſlaw, Hymen Palatine, Katterfelto, or of any other moſt accompliſhed conjuror) after muttering a myſtical abrácadabra of Dog-Latin, actually changes a piece of half-baked dough, and a bottle of good old port, into the real body and blood of Chriſt!

Sacred.—Excluſively every word which comes out of the mouth of that infallible, though human being, called a prieſt.

Sacrifice,—any thing which is offered up to heaven, by way of ſtaying the rage of the Deity againſt ſinners; " and the ſame lamb which was offered up " to appeaſe an irritated Deity, ſerved to appeaſe " the appetite of the hungry prieſt."

MANDEVILLE.

In modern times, human ſacrifices have been uſed by pious princes, inſtead of thoſe of the brute creation; and ſome faithful generals, obedient to the mandates of their truly Chriſtian maſters, have ſacrificed twenty and thirty thouſand of human beings in a day; which plainly ſhows that they have always the fear of God before their eyes.

R 2

Sacrilege.

Sacrilege.—To deprive God's vicegerents here on earth, the clergy, of a tittle of their poffeffions would be facrilege; " they toil not, neither do they " fpin," but they do much more, they provide for us eternal falvation, in a fnug birth in the *other* world, merely by a word or two, fpoke in a canting *drant*, and with thofe additional and irrefiftible pleaders in favour of their petition, " the lifted " whites of both their eyes;" and for fuch a kind office as this, they ought to have a tenth of the produce of all human induftry, and a tenth of the bountiful gifts of nature.

Sailor,—a feaman who is taken *voluntarily by force* from his native home, to fight for a country which he is indebted to for nothing, except it be mifery and wretchednefs.

Saint,—a devotee who, before men, reprobates fwearing, lying, cheating, thieving, and whoring, but practifes them all at his leifure, undetected and even unfufpected.—*Vide Clergy.*

Salute,—a gentle declination of the head, hat off, when you meet a perfon. Some time ago, Mr. Beaufoy, M. P. for Yarmouth, was actually brought to tears, becaufe Mr. Pitt did not return his falute. It was a hard cafe.

Sanctuary,—a facred afylum, not for kings and prime minifters alone, but for rogues of *all* defcrip-
tions.

tions. The Houſe of Commons is the ſanctuary of Pitt, George and Co.

Sans,—without.

> " Talents, in Alfred's lofty mind,
> " Were with integrity combin'd;
> " In the laſt Henry, talents ſhone
> " *Without* integrity, alone :
> " But lucklefs George, alas! we ſee,
> " *Sans* talent, *ſans* integrity !"

Sans-Culottes.—Breeches are deemed a neceſ-ſary appendage to decorum; but among our more northern brethren are conſidered as a degrading ſhackle upon natural liberty. At the ſame time we forbad the Scotch to carry arms, we compelled them to wear *breeches.*

Satellites.—In aſtronomy this appellation is given to ſubordinate bodies, called Moons, revolv-ing about a ſuperior orb. In the political world, it is applied to Dundas, Jenkinſon, Windham and to about $\frac{118}{355}$ of the Houſe of Commons, who (al-though they cannot bear the thoughts of a *revolu-tion)* revolve round Mr. Pitt once in every ſeſſion. The word moon, which is uſed in aſtronomy, is evidently a corruption from the word man—moons, mons, mans, man.

Saviour.

Saviour.—George III. is the Saviour of this country, and it was a particular difpenfation of Providence, in his kindnefs towards us, to blefs us with fo wife, fo pious, and fo good a king. For in this happy reign not more than two hundred and fifty millions of money and of lives, a number exceeding the prefent population of the country, have been expended in *juft and neceffary* wars.

Scabbard.—One of the maxims of Chriftian kings is, " Draw the fword, and throw away the " *fcabbard.*" This is in obedience to the commands of our bleffed Redeemer, " I came not to " fend peace on earth, but a fword." And as he mentions nothing about a fcabbard, it is evident he had no intention fuch things fhould be ufed by true Chriftians.

Scaffold,—an elevated ftage covered with black cloth, and elegantly fitted up with a gallows and rope, a block and ax, a coffin and fhroud, and a bafket of faw-duft for the head to roll into. This mode of execution is only ufed for great malefactors, fuch as kings, bifhops, and prime-minifters. England and France feem (from hiftory) to take it by turns to execute their kings. France produced the laft inftance.

Sceptre,—one of the enfigns of royalty, which Pitt appears to have a longing after, if we may judge from the following foliloquy, in which he was

over-

over-heard one night, in a perturbed fleep, when his mind had got the political night-mare :

" Is this a *fceptre* which I fee before me,
" The handle toward my hand?——Come, let me
      " clutch thee ;
" I have thee not, and yet I fee thee ftill."

This happened, as I am informed, during the king's m——, illnefs I mean.

Scots,—the name of North Britons, who are celebrated for fair promifes and non-performances, fair faces and black hearts. They are whited fepulchres ; and God Almighty has placed them in a country as barren of the fruits of nature, as their fouls are barren of virtue and honefty.

Scoundrels,—a clafs of men exceedingly ufeful in polifhed focieties, and happily they are very numerous. There are many things which could not be done without fcoundrels ; there would be neither fpies nor informers, nor Leaches of the London Coffee-Houfe, nor minifters ; in fhort, without them the reformers of government would be deftroyed, and the focial fyftem totally overthrown.

Scramble.—At the Treafury there is a fpacious apartment, where Mr. Pitt amufes his *friends,* fometimes with a fcramble, and fometimes with a *hug and a bite.*

Scrawl.—How many thousands have loft their lives by a *scrawl* of two letters? witnefs, amongft others, the *scrawl* of G. R. at the bottom of a death-warrant! Oh! God! is it for this that human beings are born?

Scripture (Holy),—the Bible, which is the *vade-mecum* of priefts, who put common fenfe to the rack (and men too, where they can) by torturing the meaning of obfcure paffages, by their *à pofte-riori* conclufions, and will juftify any thing that is expedient, whether it is robbery or murder.

Seamen.—Judge Fofter juftifies the impreffing of feamen, by the following argument: that " all " orders of men ought to contribute to the fupport " of the ftate; that thefe men have been ufed to a " fea-faring life, that confequently they can be of " more fervice than raw, inexperienced land-lub- " bers, THEREFORE that they ought to be *made* to " go, if they will not go voluntarily."—No matter how they are fituated in their domeftic concerns! How long will this iniquity laft?

Seafon for Reform.—*Not* when we are at war, for then all is hurry and confufion, and our minds too heated and agitated to fet about fo ferious an affair. *Not* when we are at peace, for then it would be madnefs to difturb the tranquillity of the nation.

Seat in Parliament,—from the unbiaſſed ſuf-
frages of independent electors for 4000l.—" A
" little leaven leaveneth the whole lump."

HOLY BIBLE.

Second-Sight,—the power of ſeeing things to
come, ſaid to be peculiar to Scotſmen; *e. g.*
when Loughborough ſeized the ſeals, almoſt an
univerſal bankruptcy took place, and he, in a
very ſhort ſpace of time, iſſued out upwards of
400 commiſſions of bankruptcy, at the moderate
rate and profit of 10l. each commiſſion. " How
" are we ruined ?" 10 times 400 is 4,000l.—" How
" are we ruined ?"

Secretary of State,—a great officer, in whom
crimes are no crimes; and who, by a political ſpecies of infallibility, can exerciſe acts of oppreſſion,
without ever dreading the rod of correction, or
regarding the poignancy of general reproof.

Sedition,—any thought, word, or action of
your life, if brought into a court of—juſtice, and
determined ſo by a corrupt judge, and *ſettled* ſo
by a packed jury.—Dreams may be ſeditious !

Sedition (a ſower of),—one who tells honeſt
truths, and is above the reach of miniſterial influence and corruption.

See,—the reward of *blind* and bigoted prieſts.

Senate.—In ſome countries, is an aſſembly of
the ſcum of the earth, who will ſtick at nothing

S

that

that is depraved and difhonourable, to increafe
their treafures by plundering the people, depriving
them firft of their wealth, and then of all the
fweets of liberty, and all the comforts of domeftic
life.—In England the fenators are all honeft men,
" all honourable men!"

Senfe of the kingdom,—the dictates of an arbitrary minifter, and the defpicable arguments of
his mercenary advocates.

Sepulchre.—See the infide of Pitt's heart.

Sermon,—a little thin book, with a black cover,
" wherein one may read ftrange things," fuch as
arguments in favour of damnation, eternity of
hell-torments, and other matters equally amufing.
They are made fo as to laft exactly fifteen minutes
by the clock. The deliverer of thefe entertaining
and inftructive lectures, is, for the moft part, a
black-legs; though fome are good kind of men; but
I have feen " fuch *things* that mount the pulpit
" with a fkip, and then fkip down again."

Shuttle,—an inftrument *formerly* in much ufe
among the weavers; but ever fince the war began,
the Englifh manufacturers have had no occafion
for them; fo all the weavers from Manchefter,
Norwich, &c. are gone for foldiers " to weave the
" crimfon web of war," rather than ftarve at home.

Sickle—a reaping hook, to cut the corn at
harveft.—This is another inftrument, the ufe of
which

which is daily declining; as *gentlemen* of landed property are got into a way of parcelling out their land into sheep-walks, lawns, and parks for deer to run about in. Besides this, the rustic, instead of cultivating the earth (the produce of which he may scarcely be said to share) amuses himself by entering into some volunteer corps, where he gets a horse and a pewter watch, a suit of clothes, and the *name* of a gentleman!

Simony,—the mode of disposing of church preferment.

Sine-cure—a kind of civil *benefice,* more numerous in England than *ecclesiastical benefices* are in *Italy* and *Spain,* &c. no kind of worth or merit is required of the incumbents, and they are not obligated to any honest duty in return. In short, a black friar is a most useful man in comparison with a fine-cure.

Slave.—In the West-Indies, is a human being, who is marked upon the back with the initials of his Christian master's name. He is torn from his native country, from his friends and connections, from the arms of an aged parent, a beloved wife, or his dear children, never to behold them more.— And yet God suffers this!

Slave,—a human creature, made by law the property of another human creature. Many princes desire, as *Sancho Panca, in the promised island,*

that

that their subjects might be all blacks, because they would sell them.

Slavery,—the state of ninety-nine out of a hundred of the human race. In England we profess to love freedom; and yet we are the chief agents of wickedness in the infernal traffic in human flesh! And so accustomed are we now to the tale of woe, which belongs to the little history of thousands and tens of thousands of Negroes, that we are wearied with the mention of their sufferings, and a noble lord, Carhampton, (who is a disgrace to the human species) in the House of Commons, openly and publicly, and with the clamorous approbation of some other shameless members, laughed at, and ridiculed the Quixotic humanity of Mr. Wilberforce and the rest of the members who had the feelings of human beings interwoven in their natures: and further took what he thought a parallel case, by an infamous and cruelly sportive allusion to the situation of a common prostitute!

Slaughter,—massacre of the human species. Invented by priests, and practised by kings.

Sleep.—Would to heaven that Englishmen could forget all their cares and all their miseries, and rest their perturbed souls in oblivious sleep! But

" Methought I heard a voice cry, sleep no more !
" *King George* doth murder sleep— innocent sleep!"

Society,

Society,—a union of community linked together in one general intereft. But Pitt, that murderer of human happinefs! that butcher of liberty! that deftroyer of all the deareft ties of love, harmony, and friendfhip, has diffolved at once all the bonds of love and affection, and fet up father againft fon, and fon againft father, to perfecute each other with unrelenting fury—and all—for a difference of opinion!

Soldier,—a man inveigled into a banditti of hired affaffins, by means of martial mufic and a few guineas. This miferable portion of fubjects is inclofed within barracks, feparate from the reft of fociety, from which it has a particular and diftinct intereft. Soldiers have no privileges, no rights, no feelings of humanity to guide them to action, no fentiments of regard for their fellow-men! They are a diftinct order, kept apart, that all fenfibility, all fympathy for the fufferings of others, with them may be extinct. Hear it, O man! This is the intereft of all kings and priefts, in order to keep up the delufion of human adoration!

Sovereign—is a man " clothed in purple, and " that fares fumptuoufly every day," bedizened out with ermine, fattin, velvet, filk, and gold fpangles. Thus dreffed up, he excites the adoration of thofe who thus deck him out; and when they approach
him,

him, they fall down on their knees, kifs his hand, and pay him that fame kind of homage which in other places the prieft ordains us to pay to three fuperior Beings. This man has the power of life and death over his fubjects. The frogs petitioned for a king, and they had a ftork fent them. Would to God that human kings were no worfe than ftorks. I rejoice within myfelf wherever I ob-ferve a tyrant king ; for that abject people that endures a defpot, deferves to be enflaved, and to be made wretched.

Sponge.—Oh! iniquitous fon of Chatham, go on in thy deeds of darknefs, finifh thy diabolical projects. There is yet much blood to fpill, and much treafure yet to wafte! Be not in a ftate of in-quietude, for

" A *sponge* will wipe out all, and coft you nothing."

Spy,—an underling of government, fent to watch over the words and actions of innocent men ; to excite them to intemperate expreffions, and then to inform of them, bring them into a prejudiced court before a loyal jury, and, if poffible, fwear away their lives, to fatisfy the bloody vengeance of an infernal minifter. An *avowed* fpy of govern-ment (Watt) is taken up I find on a charge of high treafon, who, they fay, has gone fo far as to

order

order pikes, and to lay before a society a specific plan of revolt and rebellion. I know the present ministry so thoroughly, that I should not wonder if they were to sacrifice this man, though their friend, in order to prove the existence of a conspiracy. And yet it cannot be ; human nature can never be so depraved. But if it was to happen, I am sure such a man would die unpitied and unlamented. His fate would be something like that of the Santon Barsisa.

Squire.—Every squire, almost to a man, is an oppressor of the clergy ; a racker of his tenants ; a jobber of all public works, very proud, and generally illiterate. The squires take the titles of great men, with as little ceremony as Alexander or Cæsar. For instance, the great *Conolly*, the great *Damer*, &c. Swift.

Stage.—If any one wishes to observe the vitiated and corrupt state of the age, let him repair to our theatres, especially Covent-Garden, and he will be surfeited with the servile effervescence of the most brutish loyalty, and with the empty frivolity of sentiment with which the new pieces all abound. A declining stage in taste and morality, is invariably the proof of a declining empire.

Standing Army.—It is directly against the principle of our blessed and glorious constitution to keep up a standing army, and yet we have an immense menfe one, which is renewed every year under the fiction of a mutiny-bill. What an infult upon the people! What a mockery of juftice! What a faithful adherence to the caufe for which our fathers fought and bled! Who can view with a complacent eye, thefe locufts of the earth, " eating up " the people, as it were bread," thefe drones that are armed with the fting of the bee, to plunder with impunity, and fatten on the fpoils of other's induftry, not to defend the well-earned pittance of their own!

Staple-commodity,—of this country, wool was formerly, but fince the war, the ftuff and woollen manufacturers have had no other ufe for this ftaple article, than to make flannel fhrouds for our gallant countrymen in Flanders.

Star-Chamber.—Till the 17 Car. I. this was a criminal court, calling itfelf a court of equity, in which all ftate delinquents were thrown, when any offence was given to the king or his minifters. The penalties chiefly impofed by this infamous tribunal were fine, imprifonment, pillory, and lofs of ears. The cabinet-council of modern days, has fuperfeded the ufe of the ftar-chamber of ancient days; and I fhould fcarcely be furprifed if part of the houfe of commons were to form themfelves into a kind of fecret committee for the fame purpofe.

Star-

Starvation,—what two-thirds of the people are actually reduced to, unless they choose to go into a workhouse, or for soldiers. The poor " may die " like dogs in ditches," and yet our king is as merry as a grig!

Statue,—the solid representation of a living being. The Hon. Mrs. Damer has gained much credit by her masterly *execution* of the king in a marble bust; which idea gave birth to the two following impromptu's.

I.

Lord! what a lumpish, senseless thing!
And yet 'tis very like the king!

II.

Why strive to animate the marble rock,
His sacred majesty's more like the block!

Statutes,—acts of Parliament. The *lex scripta;* or, for the most part, gradual incroachments upon the liberty of the subject.

Stiletto,—a short dagger, which Pitt always carries about with him, in order to cheat the executioner; as he expects to be impeached whenever he goes out of place, and I think there is little doubt when that happens, that he will be hanged. Some time ago St. Edmund, the Jesuit, brought

T

one of thofe convenient inftruments into the Houfe of Commons, but he 'did not ufe it as he *might* have done. He only drew it from under his coat in a furious theatrical attitude, and with much vehemence of action threw it on the floor. " Hic *crazy* eft, hunc tu Romane caveto!"

Subject — can only with propriety be applied to a member of a ftate, whofe government has been inftituted by foreign conqueft, or the prevalence of a domeftic faction. *Citizen* is the ancient appellation given to the members of free ftates.

Subjects,—a body of people who fubmit to the tyranny of one man; and yet they complain !

Suborn Witneffes,—on ftate trials, is to procure falfe witneffes to fwear away the lives and property of innocent individuals who wifh for a reform in Parliament. A real Statefman-like Minifter will always have a ftore of fuch witneffes by him, to ufe them when wanted.

Subftitute.—I knew an inftance of a Roman Catholic being drawn for the Militia. The Magiftrates would not fuffer him to be fworn in and ferve, and yet made him procure a fubftitute, which coft the poor fellow nine guineas !

Succeffor.—All monarchs are infected with the ftrange wifh, that their fucceffors may turn out bad princes. Good Kings defire it, as they imagine that their glory will thus appear the moft

fplendid;

fplendid; and the bad defire it, as they confider
fuch Kings will ferve to countenance their own
mifdemeanours.

Sugar and Coffee,—vegetables which have been
the ruin and mifery of two parts of the world;
America has been unpeopled to get land to plant
them in, and Africa is unpeopled to cultivate
them.

Suicide,—felf murder, very prevalent in England, and which I think is wholly afcribable to
Government. For when men have married,
and find they cannot fupport their wives and families, they are thereby driven to this act of def-
peration. Under a perfect form of government,
a poor man would be an anomaly, a phenomenon.
The character of a nation is certainly influenced
and determined entirely according to the adminiftration of the government. I never was fo much
affected as at the relation of a fact which took
place a few years ago on the coaft of Africa. Some
Englifh fhips appeared on the coaft. This amongft
the tribes, was the fignal for war. After the battle,
upwards of forty victims, who had been taken
prifoners, knowing their fate, burft from their
chains, rufhed into the woods, where they all
committed fuicide together,—Oh! Englifhmen!
have ye hearts to feel, and yet continue this traffic?

Super-

Superstition.—Come forward, ye reverend crew! and answer for your crimes! Ye priests of Satan, it is you that have lighted up the torch of intolerance; it is you that have set fire to the faggot; it is you that have erected the funeral pile of martyrdom! It is you that have ordained religious massacres! you have strewed the fields with human carcases, and deluged them in blood; and yet you have done it all to the glory of God! False religion, false morality, false reverence for idle ceremonies, and false worship, are all the children of the priesthood, and have been, are now, and I fear, ever will be adopted, by foolish and unreflecting men!

Surplice,—a white garb, which priests wear when they are humbugging the people.

Swinish Multitude,—an epithet applied by Mr. Burke, the Jesuit of St. Omer's, to the English people, because they tamely suffer their rights to be wrested from them, and their wrongs to remain unredressed.

Sword,—a weapon of offence and defence, put into the hands of mercenary troops, to deal destruction to all within their infernal reach. The tyrant, William III. ordered the massacre of Glencoe, in which neither age nor sex were spared. A similar event, it has been reported, took place, a few years since, at Lexington, in America. Of

what

what materials are Princes made ? I fhould much like to know whether their anatomy and phyfiology be the fame as in other men !—How can they ever procure men to murder for them at fix-pence a day ?

Sycophants,—a long ftring of rafcals, from Loughborough down to Windham.

Syftem of Courts,—to keep the people in ignorance ; becaufe if they were fuffered to be enlightened, " Othello's occupation's gone !"

" Where there are Kings, there muft be Courts,
" And where there are Courts, there muft be
corruption."

Therefore long live corruption ; may corruption live for ever.

T.

Tale-bearer,—one who gives malicious and calumnious intelligence.—Windham is tale-bearer and lying alarum-bell to the Houfe. In December, 1792, at that extraordinary meeting of Parliament, he bafely afferted what he knew to be falfe. In the violence of his declaration againft his enemies, the friends of liberty, he faid, " it was notorious that there was a criminal correfpondence between the Jacobins of England and the Jacobins of Paris;

that

that there was a regular confpiracy, and that, like the accomplices of Cataline, they were bound to fidelity by the folemnity of a horrid oath (here he was interrupted by fome Members who exclaimed, *prove, prove!*) The orator then proceeded to ftate his authority, which, he faid, was unqueftionable, no lefs than that of an honourable Member, but "*the faCt was not of much confequence.*"

Tally.—The little boy's tonkay bean, that grew up to the moon, would fcarcely be long enough to cut a *tally* upon, of our national debt.—But it is all for the beft, as Dr. Panglofs fays.

Tartarus,—a place in hell, fet apart for Englifh Kings and Minifters, who lord it over their fubjects with an imperious, cruel, and iniquitous domination.

Tattoo.—The roar of cannon is the Devil's Tattoo, by which thofe *generous-hearted* men (called foldiers, who are paid fix-pence a day to fhoot and to be fhot at,) are warned to appear at their *laft* quarters. *Can any one pity them?*

Taxes.—Thefe are impofts laid on the common bounties of nature, and on the bleffings of Providence, in order, as is pretended, to defray the *neceffary* expences of a ftate, but, in fact, to affift defpots in carrying on bloody and internecine wars againft human life, human liberty, and human happinefs. In this country our unrelenting tax-

masters

masters and task-masters, as if studying a refinement of cruelty, inflict upon the mute and patient
people, the worst of all punishments, disease, by
taxing the light of heaven, that grand essential to
health.   This tax alone is the remote cause of the
premature mortality of nearly one hundredth part
of the nation.   To superficial observers this may
appear incredible ; but to the enquiring and scrutinizing philosopher, it is a sad and melancholy
truth.   Oh! People, People ; when will ye open
your eyes ?

Tear,—a crystal drop of water, which at once
involuntarily starts in the eye of the philosopher,
upon the bare mention of the word King, or Priest!
I declare to God I almost wish that I possessed the
gloomy eloquence of Hegesippus, that mankind,
by that sad alternative, might be for ever relieved
from those scourges of the human race !

Te Deum,—a hymn of praise and thanksgiving
offered up by Christians to the God of Peace, in
celebration of those massacres called victories.   I
have studied the English people thoroughly, and I
verily believe they are very rapidly indeed merging towards Popery; nor should I be astonished
to see the English church a real church militant, its
Priests at the head of armies carrying the bloody
banners of war into the churches, to be consecrated

at

at a polluted altar, and an Auto-de-fe to crown the whole.

Temper of the Times.—What a wonderful fource of contemplation! What an endlefs field of fpeculation to the thinking man! In the times of Junius, in that period when the prefent Chamberlain of London was a man, and at the reluctant clofe of the American war, what national energy was difplayed! What fpirited refolutions were entered into! What manly remonftrances! Every man was permitted to exercife the faculties of man! He might *then*, with impunity declaim againft iniquity, oppreffion, and military maffacres! A King was not then divine, a Prime Minifter infallible, or a Prieft the Vicegerent of God! It was not *then* libellous to expofe the conduct of corrupt Judges, nor was it treafon to cenfure the blind and mifguided, yet perfevering, policy of a crowned man.

" Tempora mutantur et nos mutamur in illis !"

Temple,—the refidence of legal monfters, who difguife themfelves when they are bent upon plunder, for the fame reafon that highwaymen do, to prevent detection. The attornies (a body of men, which, taken collectively, are a difgrace to human fociety) are their parafites and their Panders.
Doubtlefs

Doubtlefs there are many, very many valuable members of fociety in both thefe communities, but one cannot help abhorring the general *efprit de corps* which is their charaĉteriftic.. It is a great confolation, however, to me, that the rifing gene- ration of lawyers (I fpeak of thofe intended for the bar) are for the moft part, young men of libe- ral and enlightened minds, and from whom much may be expeĉted.

Temporal.—The Lay-lords might juftly be cal- led both temporal and eternal. Temporal, becaufe not ecclefiaftical ;. and eternal, becaufe their titles and poffeffions defcend by hereditary right in eternal fucceffion.

Temporize.—" Thefe are the times to try men's " fouls," and when, to *temporize* is a heinous rime.

Tent,—a canvas awning extended upon poles, under which, upon the cold and damp earth, a wifp of ftraw is thinly ftrewed, to make a bed for five creatures of a human *appearance,* whofe bodies are ftretched upon this *downy* couch, forming radii of a circle, with their feet wedged together in the middle like the fpokes of a wheel. Here they all join in the glee, " How merrily we live that fol- " diers be." ! !

Tenth.—As an adequate reward for thofe ftrong dofes of intolerance, bigotry, fuperftition, and fa-

U　　　　　　　naticifm

naticifm, which are adminiftered from the pulpit,
and as a reafonable compenfation for the general
error and mifchief which is fuperinduced in the
minds of the ignorant and deluded, the wily prieft
demands one *tenth* of all the bountiful gifts of cultivated nature. And he will tell you with a grave
face and uplifted eyes, that eternal damnation is
the *fine qua non* of a refufal to this *facred* demand ! ! !

Teft-Act.—This is one of the many Acts of Parliament that difgraces our Statute Book. It en-
joins, that no one, except he is of the eftablifhed
Church, fhall enjoy any place, penfion, or emolument in office, under government, unlefs he
has previoufly eaten a piece of *confecrated* bread,
or drank fome *confecrated* wine, which is by the
magic of the prieft, conjured into the *myftical* (not
real as the *true* Chriftians affert) body and blood
of Chrift ! !

Tetrarchy.—The object of this juft, and neceffary war, is to change the wild anarchy of France
into a glorious tetrarchy, under the kind and particular difpenfation of Providence to the crowned
men of Pruffia, Spain, Germany, and England !
Demoberos Bafileus ! !

Theatre.—I. of War, is a large plain where the
flefh-plant grows to perfection, and likewife a new
plant perfectly unknown to Linnæus, hitherto
a *Non-*

a *Non-Defcript*, but which I fhall have the ho-
nourof firft acquainting botanifts with, and there-
fore proceed to give the following defcription
of. I clafs it according to the Linnean fyftem.
Clafs and Order. Monandria. *No* gynia.
Genus and Species. Miles. Sanguinarius.
Generic Charaɛer. Pugnat et trucidat pro
    auro.
Figura. Humana, et emittit vocem humanam.
Calyx. Galeatus, plumis, fanguineo colore, de-
    coratus.
Corolla. Ovata; nafo, et ore, et lingua, et
    mento, et pube in mentum tamquam in ani-
    male humano, et duabus auribus, et duobus
    oculis, ornata.
Cortex. Coccinatus.
Caudex. Cruralis, brachiatus, et *braccatus.*
Stamina. Plerumque ab auris frigidis et hu-
    midis, etiam exhalationibus terræ exitialibus,
    debilitata.
Piftilla. Duo, cum pulvere et ballis chargeata.
Pericarpium. Folliculus, cartridgis expletus.
Fulcra. Arma. Mufketa bayonettata; et gla-
    dius anceps *fine* vagina.
Habitat. In barrackis fætidiffimis, et in agris
    humidis, varies.
Frutex eft perennis, parafiticus; et fæpiffime
    mutilatus invenitur, e. g. fine capite, fine
    cruribus, fine brachiis, &c.

U 2   Florefcit

Florefcit optime in Orbe Chriftiano.

Theatre.—II. Dramatic. The common fewer for the moft beaftly and the moft depraved fentiments of loyalty, that a bafe born, abject people, can make ufe of! A temple of worfhip, where the little, fceptered and tinfelled creature is adored with more veneration and reverence, than the great Creator! It is in thefe places that a moft impious, and blafphemous fong is fung, during which time the obedient People are compelled, by force of arms, to ftand up, uncovered, as if they were in a church !

Theologian,—a *Profeffor* of Divinity, which is fynonymous to a practifer of chicanery, fraud, and hypocrify. For ample examples, apply to the *heads* of Colleges in our Univerfities of Oxford and Cambridge.

Thirteen—United States of America ; which bravely threw off the Englifh yoke, and like all good Republicans, renounced the bug-bear of royalty.

Thoufand.—When fpeaking of Englifh foldiers flain in battle, a mere milk-fcore, not worth a King of England's thinking of! " What! what! " what! Pitt! only a thoufand! only a thoufand! " Heh! Go a hunting? Go a hunting? Heh! " Heh! Son's a fly dog, fly dog, fly dog! Takes " care of his flock. Ha! ha! ha! Good Bifhop !

good

" good Bifhop! Ha! Ha! Ha! Go and tell Char-
" lotte! tell Charlotte! and then tallio, tallio !!
" Ha! Ha! Ha! What, What! What! only a
" thoufand! Dutiful fon, though! Heh! Pitt, Heh!

Thraldom.—The human mind has been in a
conftant ftate of *thraldom*, (for what reafon I know
not) ever fince that fatal year for England, 1760.

Throne,—a fumptuous, richly furnifhed, and
elevated feat, which is placed upon a platform,
with fteps to it, and would ferve as well for a fcaffold, as any thing elfe; but it is made for a King
to fit on. A man, fantaftically dreft out in ermine,
velvet, gold and filver tinfel, gold and filver fpangles, fquirrel and rabbit fkins. Thus tricked out,
like the wooden god of Otaheite, having fcarcely
the refemblance of a human being, it is no wonder that men fhould be fo deluded, as to think him
more than mortal, when it requires fo little of
imagination to metamorphofe him at once into an
object of worfhip. Under this impreffion, when
they approach the throne, they are ftruck with
awe and difmay, and addrefs this bundle of fine
clothes with bended knee and an humble voice, as
if they were attempting to appeafe an irritated
Deity. If the addrefs pleafes the oracle, a great
red hand is protruded from under this now animated
bundle, which the priefts, who are ftanding around
the altar, and affifting at thefe folemn rites, tell the

lowly

lowly fupplicant he is to kifs!! To kifs? Heaven
and earth, muft I remember?—To kifs? And yet
if you afk one of thefe defpicable wretches, after
having gone through this pantomimic fcene, whether he is a lunatic? " No," he will tell you,
" I'm a loyal man." Pitiful, forry wretch! loyal
thou mayeft be, a man thou canft never pretend to
be!

Throttle.—A *curfory ftricture* on the throttle of
that monfter Pitt, and of fome other great men,
would, I think, be well received by all parties,
upon an *authentic* publication to the world.

Thrum.—In Manchefter, Norwich, and in other
manufacturing towns, it formerly meant a loom's
work, curioufly done up, and ready for the weaver,
but the word is now nearly obfolete, and the meaning of it only known by obfcure and imperfect
tradition. And where the bufy weaver, in days of
yore, plied at his cheerful labour, the no lefs bufy
little fpider now weaves its filken veil of oblivion!

Tick,—the way that government pay their
debts!!

Tomb,—a certain, and, I believe, the only
afylum for mortals, from the tyranny and oppreffion of Kings; and the depravity, hypocrify, and
intolerance, of priefts! When I pafs by a burial
place, I think I fee engraved upon every tomb-
ftone, " Come unto me all ye that labour, and I
" will give you reft."

Torture.

Torture.—Invented by monks, and practifed on by priefts on unbelieving heretics at an Auto-de-Fe, in order to bring thofe finful renegades within the *pale* of the Chriftian Church. Whence the term *impaling* ! ! But as their fouls are faved by it, it is all very right ! !

Tower,—the Englifh Baftille for State Prifoners who are in the Oppofition, and for friends of freedom. It is policy to put fuch men in the Tower, as they will prize Liberty the more when they come out.

Trade,—a mean way of getting money, upon that account much and fuccefsfully difcouraged in the prefent reign.

Tragedy.—The hiftory of Kings of all ages and all countries, is one continued deep and difmal *tragedy.*

Train-bands,—a curious collection of brawny, greafy-faced old ladies, dreffed up in men's clothes, and accoutred with large bread and cheefe knives.

Traitor,—any man who ftrives to reform either Church or State.

Tranfubftantiation,—one of the fuppofed tricks of thofe arch-conjurers called priefts, by which dough and wine are changed into flefh and blood !

Treafon,—any undefinable offence which crown lawyers chufe to call fo, provided they can pack

accom-

accommodating juries to bear them out. In the reign of the Stuarts, corrupt Judges were eafily to be procured, and juries were fo compliant to the arbitrium of a Judge, that to accufe, was to convi&. In more modern times, however well the bench may have been ftocked, with Trefilians, Empfons, Dudleys, Jefferies, and Scroggs, yet I have too good an opinion of a modern Englifh Jury, if colle&ed with but tolerable partiality, to fuppofe, that they would fend innocent men out of the world, merely becaufe they oppofe the adminiftration for the time being.

Treafury.—I. *Prints,* are thofe newfpapers under the pay of the Minifter for the time being. For which confideration the editors applaud and attempt to juftify every meafure of government indifcriminately, reprobate all reform of abufes, every amendment of the conftitution, and abufe all reformers as-levellers, and every innovator as a traitor to his country.

II. *Bench,*—is the feat on the right hand of the Speaker in the Houfe, on which are arranged in order, in regular feniority of corruption, thofe members who have the fingular good fortune *always* to coincide with the Minifter in all his meafures whether it be to overawe the people of this land who wifh a reform, by the introdu&ion of foreign

troops,

troops; or whether it be to fuspend the Habeas Corpus Act.

8. *Letters*,—are ftrong, admonitory, and argumentative epiftles, in favor of any *particular* bill the minifter wifhes to pafs the houfe, or againft any bill he wifhes to have negatived. It was the cuftom formerly to inclofe in thefe letters a few fcores of lottery tickets; but the arguments are now-a days penned in Algebraical and arithmetical fymbols, which afford a decided and mathematical proof of the arguments propofed in the *given* fubject. Nothing indeed can exceed the beauty and admirable concifenefs of thefe Algebraic equations, which I am told are fometimes fent with blank *cheques* on the bank of England, to be filled up at the difcretion of the *dominus refpondens !* I fhall fubjoin two Algebraic equations by way of illuftration, with an explanation appended.

Equation I.

$$\sqrt{SHCA} + S = 50 \, LT + P - SD.$$

Equation II.

$$\sqrt{A} + GSAF - AMEG = BC + P - GE + P \times RS.$$

Explanation of the Firft Equation.

Voting for Sufpenfion of Habeas Corpus Act, *plus* a Speech, *is equal to* 50 Lottery Tickets, *plus*

X a Pen-a Penſion, *minus* a Small Drawback when Pitt goes out of place.

Explanation of the Second Equation.

Voting for the Addreſs, *plus* a Good Speech Abuſing the French, *minus* Abuſing the Miniſters of the Engliſh Government, *is equal to* a Blank Cheque on the Bank of England, *plus* a Peerage, *minus* a Good Eſtate to it, but *plus* the Promiſe of one, *multiplied* by Royal Smiles.

IV. The *Treaſury* is a large ſpacious apartment, filled with guineas, which the *miniſter* for the time being, and his *friends* and the friends to *Church* and *king* have conſtant acceſs to, whether it be to purchaſe perjury againſt an innocent friend to liberty, or whether it be to gain over an untractable, doubtful, or *unſtaunch* jury.

" *Nemo omnium* gratuito *malus eſt.*"

Treaty,—of king and king, is a negotiatory compact between two ſtates, in order to be firſt broken by him whoſe intereſt it is ſo to do.

Tree of Liberty—*Habitat* where kings are not, and where prieſts are not.

Trial,—a pantomimic farce, where there is a *ſhow* of juſtice, who is repreſented full of eyes, like Argus,

gus, to exprefs her *impartiality*, and a *fpy-glafs* to each eye to fhow that fhe has an eye upon all. In the centre, upon a kind of *bench*, fit three old ladies, with cardinals on, by way of a *cloak*. Round a green table are fitting ten or a dozen priefts in fable, with bands on, who expound the myfteries of the place to the old ladies, and to twelve lean, hungry, grunting pigs. In the centre of this groupe, and oppofite to the old ladies, fits Innocence in a reclining pofture, pale and emaciated, fad and melancholy through long confinement, and bound hand and foot. At the clofe of the pantomime the pigs grunt out fomething of an articulate found, for the moft part, as they are *taught* to do by the three old fchool-miftreffes.

Trinity,—the incomprehenfible union of three perfons into one Godhead. Whofoever will not believe this will be damned. *Therefore*, whofoever does not believe what is incomprehenfible will be damned. Q. E. D.

Triumph.—In Chriftendom human maffacres are folemnly celebrated in churches by way of *triumph* ! !

Truce,—a mutual accommodation between two royal butchers: from the verb *trucido*.

Trumpet,—a long tube which is founded in battle here on earth, to chide Clothe and Lachefis for

X 2

their

their idleness, and to tell Atropos to get her scissars ready.

Truth.—What kind of a government must that be where it is *judged* libellous to tell the truth of the *creature*, but praise worthy to calumniate the *Creator*? What kind of government, or rather what kind of tyranny must that be, where the noble and investigating mind of man dares not promulgate known truths, where the scrutinizing eye of the philosopher has penetrated, but where that eye dares only see in secret? What can we think of a state where our religion is the patch-work of priests, and our system of policy the Dagon of a few wily and idolatrous knaves called statesmen? Where, upon the only subjects worthy of disputation or minute enquiry, all the noblest faculties of the soul are hushed into silence, and fettered down to the received opinions of an age of superstition and prejudice, on pain of the most cruel and vindictive punishments? Truth in such a country is a stranger; she wanders up and down like a houseless pilgrim, not having where to lay her head; and if she chance to stray into some lowly cottage, she is driven out with unrelenting fury, by some loyal brute or other, in the person of an ignorant, hot-headed magistrate, or a bigotted intolerant priest! Thus persecuted, and thus driven from all society, she droops her head in piteous languishment, yet still struggles ftruggles againft the oppofing tide, each ftruggle fainter than the former, and her fate ftill tumbling in the balance, till at laft fhe is overwhelmed at once by the ftrong arm of power, and plunged into the pitchy fhades of everlafting night!

Tyrant.—For examples look into hiftory, no matter of what country !

U.

Ubiquity.—It is curious to hear priefts talk of the *ubiquity* of the Deity, and yet at the fame time furioufly deny his *material* exiftence. What is this in fact but denying his exiftence at all ? For, if the Deity is fpirit, the Deity is nothing, or a non-entity ; for a fpirit is nothing which can either be defcribed or pencilled. Therefore there is no God (according to their dogmas) unlefs it can be fup-pofed that there is an immaterial *fomething* floating about, which however occupies no fpace, has no parts, no folidity, extenfion, nor any other proper-ties of matter, and yet this nothing is fomething, and poffeffes volition to real action. Priefts only make this problem ; they alone can folve it. However they may reafon away any difficulties of this kind ; they can never, with any face, deny that there is in England an *ubiquity* of priefts who cringe, fawn, and tyrannize ; that there is an *ubiquity* of fpies and informers, who live by calumny and perjury ; an

ubiquity

ubiquity of loyal magiſtrates who ſupport them ; and laſtly, an *ubiquity* of treaſury gold which ſupports them 'all.

Unconquerable,—the human mind. In ſpite of the tyranny and intolerance of kings and prieſts, in ſpite of the infernal machinations and combinations of crowned conſpirators, if a great and mighty nation wills only to be free, ſhe muſt be free in ſpite of all earthly interference. France ſaid, Let there be freedom, and there was freedom ! And I hope to God that liberty there is *unconquerable.*

Uncrown.—What a pity it is that kings never conſider that reaſon and juſtice can as well co-operate to *uncrown* them, as well as ignorance, weakneſs, and credulity did to crown them.

Unction Extreme.—In the Popiſh or Romiſh or *Baby*-loniſh Church, this is the ceremony of daubing, with linſeed or lamp-oil (I don't know which) the body of a dying Roman Catholic. It however is of uſe, as it ſerves very well as *baſting* before they are *roaſted,* which is what Divines call, " king-" dom come."

Uncultivated,—one third part of England. Huzza ! Long live poverty and miſery ! Huzza !—— Church and king for ever !

Unenvied,—the virtues of the king, the morality of the Lords and the independence of the Commons ; the humanity of the Biſhops, the impartia-

lity

lity of the Judges, and the learning of the Clergy ; the generofity of the Queen, the economy of the Prince of Wales, and the courage of the Duke of York! Honi foit qui mal y penfe.

Unhanged,—Pitt, Loughborough, Windham, and a long, long et cætera ; and yet they are all, and every of them, what the French call, "vrai gi-" bier du potence."

Univerfity,—a place where ignorance is *taught.* This is abfolutely the cafe at Oxford and Cambridge, where you may fee monks, fenfual, beaftly, hoggifh monks, wrapped up in all the ignorance, as well as the fuperftitious garb, of the 9th centu-ry ! Heu ! meminiffe dolor !

Unking,—an European cuftom, much practifed towards the clofe of the 18th century.

Unlighted,—as *yet* the torch of intolerance and the funeral pile of perfecution, but the priefts are high bufy in getting the faggots ready. Bigotted priefts ! take care what you are after, for the fame devouring flame that is kindled for a heretic, will confume a bifhop !

Unprincely,—any action that is performed from motives of benevolence and humanity.

Unfatiable,—the thirft of *fome* princes after gold and human blood.

Unfold,—the freedom of the people, and the members of the two houfes ! ! !

Unfuccefsful

Unsuccessful War.—Nothing demonstrates to me
so much the incivism, and the sordid weakness of
men, as applying the epithetic term of *unsuccessful*
to the war, by way of argument against the principle
of it. What, have governments nothing to do with
morality or justice? *Unsuccessful!* Is that all that
can be said against a war which had for its *first* object, the extermination of a great and noble minded
people? A war which was begun in iniquity and
blood-thirst, carried on with true, savage, and Chri-
stian-like ardor, and will be ended with true Christian charity, *viz.* when all our resources are dried
up by this raging, parching fever, and the soldiers are
sick of blood. Woe be to him in whose dark and
sanguinary mind this cruel war was first projected!
But the age of delusion is not *yet* gone! Man is *yet*
contented to forge his own fetters, by way of getting
a livelihood!

Unthrone,—an obsolete word which is getting
into use again.

Uproar.—This is a Dutch word, and if Dumourier had not been a traitor, the Dutch by this time
would have given us an application for this term.
But perhaps " *tempus erit quando, &c.*"

Usurping Powers,—Russia, Prussia, &c. &c.—
who, under the subterfugal pretence of preserving
peace, good order, and good government in the
kingdom of Poland, have from time to time, with
unhal-

lowed hands and unblushing hearts, seized upon
the beft and moſt valuable part of the King's do-
mains, and are even now, like an equinoctial tide,
rapidly encroaching on and overwhelming the
whole furface of the country.

V.

Vacation.—I. In the Univerfities, is that interval of leifure, when thofe Voluptuaries the Heads
and Tutors of Colleges indulge themfelves in the
excefs of every fenfual and beaſtly enjoyment.

II. Among lawyers, is that period when, if you
take a walk in the Temple, you may fee clouds
of needy Barrifters pacing up and down with a *co-
loured* coat and waiſtcoat, and black rufty breeches
and ſtockings. This is both their *Lent*, and bor-
rowing time.

III. In the fenate, although there is and muſt
be fo much important bufinefs to tranfact, yet the
vacation with them is eight or nine months in the
year. I wonder much that King Pitt does not
vote the Parliaments ufelefs at once. And yet
thefe doughty Patriots, thefe Wife Men of Gotham, have the impudence and effrontery to call
themfelves Friends to the People, and men—men
who confult the welfare and happinefs of the poor
and the nation at large !

Vaffals

Y

Vaſſal.—In Poland the peaſants are all vaſſals, at this preſent day, and in England the eſſence and ſpirit of vaſſalage is kept up, although the name of it be aboliſhed. But if the nation wills it, I ſay, long live the Feudal ſyſtem ! !

Vendible,—a ſeat in the Houſe of Commons, which is as marketable a commodity as a pig or a gooſe, through the medium of venal and corrupt boroughs. The preſent price is about 4,000 guineas, which is much more than given under former adminiſtrations; but Pitt, as Mr. Drake ſays, is an immaculate and heaven-born Miniſter.

Vicar,—a prieſt who gets a good fat benefice by deluding the People, and teaching them to look upon the King and the Clergy as objects of infallibility, awe and adoration.

Vice Chancellor.—In our monkiſh Univerſities this is a man, *ſecond* only in iniquity, who takes care that the ſtudents ſhall be ſo involved in mathematics and divinity that they can find no time to inveſtigate ſubjects of greater import. And if any of the gownſmen ſhould be found out in reading politics or polemics, to difcountenance, or get a *grace* to expel him, becauſe ſuch irreverent arrogances, as Kenyon would ſay, is *contra bonos mores* !

Vice-gerent.—In days of yore, the Monks, alias Prieſts, would tell you, under pain of the faggot

if

if you denied it, that they were God's *Vice-gerents.*
In modern days, nay even now, they would enforce the fame, but——they dare not.

Vice-Roy.—In Ireland this is an Englifh nobleman fent over there by our monarch to play the
king. A country at the fame time remarkable for
the fervile venality of the nobles and the noble
fpirit of the People !

Village,—is a collection of two or three miferable huts, whofe wretched inhabitants can but juft
keep their clay in an animated flate, by the fcanty
pittance of the coarfeft and moft unnutritive diet.
However fmall the village is, *one* locuft of fociety
at leaft you are fure of meeting, and *one* temple of
Ignorance at leaft you are certain, erects its grifsly
and monkifh head above the woods and plantations
of the Squire, in which temple the name of the
God of Peace is invoked again and again to go
forth with " our Fleets and Armies," and to
" give us the power over our enemies" by their
deftruction. Oh God! Oh God! Is this humanity ? But hold my impious tongue—it is Chriftian
charity.

Violet.—" The king is but a man, the *violet*
" fmells to me as it does to him." Shakefpeare had
no proof in *his* time that kings were men, and in
obedience to the doctrine that they govern *jure divino,* I fhould really think that no legal king is
human,

human, but juft the contrary, *inhuman* by their very office.

Volunteer,—a loyal fubject and king's-man, who enters into a fociety of armed men to oppofe by force and arms any Reform, or attempt to a Reform of the Reprefentation of the People in Parliament, and further, to be ready at any riot, to pull down the houfes of all Jacobins and Diffenters, who either oppofe our holy Religion, or our holy political Inftitution, which they *call a* Government!

Vulgar,—the ariftocratic epithet given to the moft ufeful, the moft induftrious, and the moft valuable part of the community.

W.

Wafer,—myftical pafte, which, among the Romanifts, is changed by that arch-conjuror of all conjurors, the prieft, into the *real* body of Chrift, and given to that deluded mafs of mankind, under that idea and with that impreffion in one of their communions called the Eucharift. Oh! man, man! " have you eyes?"

War.—Of all things in this world, it feems to me moft ftrange, that men, large parties of men, perfectly indifferent to, and ignorant of the merits of the difpute, fhould voluntarily enter into the fervice of a fanguinary tyrant, and, as far as in them

lay,

lay, to maſſacre and deſtroy their fellow-creatures who are oppoſed to them, and who are as innocent and as ignorant as they, of the whole ſubject and occaſion of quarrel. Is it that the ſound of fife and drum, the trumpet and bugle-horn, or any other martial muſic, poſſeſſeth ſuch a ſavage charm? I am a man, but it has no ſuch an effect on me. Is it that the gariſh ſplendor of a camp, the emblematic veſtment of the ſoldier, the glittering of arms, the roar of cannon, the diſplay of gaudy colours, or any other military trappings, poſſeſs ſuch a ſavage charm? I am a man, but they have no ſuch effect on me. Is it that the leiſurable, eaſeful life of the military, the mildneſs of their diſcipline, or the profligate diſſoluteneſs of their manners, poſſeſſeth ſuch a ſavage charm? I am a man, but I confeſs theſe things have no ſuch effect on me. Or, is it that theſe men are ſectariſts, and have doctrines, creeds, and opinions peculiar to themſelves; that love war, bloodſhed and rapine, and internecion in the abſtract? I am a man, ſubject to frailty in common with other men, but I could never yet convince myſelf, that the deſtruction of the human ſpecies was a lovely and deſirable occupation, ſo that a man could liſtleſsly enter into it, as into a trade, by way of getting a livelihood. Whence then this fond deſire, this madneſs after ſlaughter? Is it any conſolation or

solace

solace when wounded, to see your enemy by your side extended breathless on the plain? Oh soldiers, soldiers! lay not the flattering unction to your souls, that you are heroes! You are nothing but murderers; butchers. When you began to be soldiers, you ceased to be men! Do you delight in blood, and in the sweet tuneful groans of dying animals? set up the trade of butchers at once; there must be such men in civilized society. But do not murder man for gold. If ye are soldiers, ye cannot be virtuous men. *You* are more abandoned and depraved even than the priests. Let them then gain the summit of their wishes and their ambition, viz. the ascendant in human depravity, the acmè of human wickedness, the climax of mortal guilt. Bow to them with humility, leave to them the crimson palm, they are your superiors in *invention*, and would be in *action* if they dared! Still I am bewildered how to account for this universal and brutal rage for massacre, which seems to have stagnated and palsied every human sentiment, and stopped at once all the noble workings of nature which *once* glowed in your bosoms! I have only one way more to account for your unjustifiable dereliction from all principle of virtue, only one cause more that could possibly induce you to such a dreadful effect, and that cause is, want. If this be the cause of your joining a lawless band of hir-

ed

ed affaffins, then you are exonerated from a load of guilt; ftill however burthened with a load of remaining guilt, for you cannot be virtuous if you are foldiers. It is then to you, O iniquitous Governments! that mankind is indebted for this awful calamity! You ftarve your people, and then the loud calls of Nature force them into a compliance and concurrence with you in plunder and murder! You take away their earnings, and deftroy their commerce, and then inlift them under your bloody banners! You depopulate the world, and then hie to your corrupted churches, to pay your filthy adoration to an all-benevolent God, to thank him for what *he* has done, as if he was a cruel and vindictive being like yourfelves! Why don't you ordain your priefts to drink hot blood at the altar, and devour human carcafes, by way of celebrating the Lord's fupper? You will want but little of imagination then to believe in tranfubftantiation! They'll do't if you order them. It will infpire your troops with the true bloodhound vigor; and you may then, with fome effect,

" Cry havoc, and let flip the dogs of War."

Weal.—The common *weal*, the public *weal*, the general *weal*, fo much regarded in Saxon antiquity, is now out of date, and fneered at by our

legif-

legiflators; infomuch, that if a man talks of the public weal, he is a vifionary; and if he, by actions, ftrives to promote the general weal, he is a rebel, and a leveller; fo changed are the times, fo perverted is the reafon of man, and fo abject his fubmiffion to priefts, and the " Powers that " be !"

Wealth.—Although it is as perceptible as the meridian fun, that in England the riches of the country are merging in the hands of one order of men, yet, in fpite of the alarming increafe of the poor, and the fynchronous decline of manufactures and manufacturers, that loyal fool John Bull is made to believe that the country was never fo rich, and commerce never fo thriving! If a People will fuffer Oppreffion to trefpafs on their common rights, which even brutes enjoy unmolefted, they deferve it.

Weaver.—Let the moft unfeeling, the moft hardened, the moft cruel and inflexible of our ftatefmen, (I don't know which to choofe, Windham, or his mafter Pitt, for they are both fuperlatives) pay a vifit to any of our manufacturing towns, where this ufeful clafs of citizens, *once* were feen with bufy faces, carrying their looms-work home to their employers; it matters not where, whether at Manchefter, Norwich, Leeds, Halifax, or any other manufacturing town, ftill it is the fame; nothing

thing but misery and wretchedness; he will do well to avoid stumbling over shuttles, weavers' beams, looms, and every other, the implements of a lost occupation! Let this man Windham, if he be really a man, lift up the latchet of the door of one of the thousands of miserable huts which abound in every one of these *flourishing* towns. After satiating his gladdened eyes with the misery before him—after glutting his ravished sight, in the voluptuous luxury of beholding wretchedness in its maximum—let him thus address the starving groupe in the true and sincere language of his heart—" You are a set of factious and discon-" tented fellows, who are always complaining—" never satisfied. You are as well off as you de-" serve to be ;—there always must be poor people " in all countries, and *Providence* has selected you " to be of the number ; therefore it is impious as " well as disloyal to murmur. If it be true, that " you can get no work, and are starving, go to " the workhouse."

Wedlock.—This is that happy and enviable state, which but few can enjoy in wicked and unprinci-pled governments. I know not how or why it is, but upon turning to the page of history for a few years back, I find a great many evils that date their chronology from the year 1760, and this evil, among the myriad, that two-thirds of our

Z

youth

youth are in a ftate of celibacy at the age of twenty-nine. I need not here ftate to the philo-fopher, that government muft of neceffity be the root of this evil. Under a more perfect inftitu-tion of government, the human male and female would enter upon the happy ftate of *wedlock* at fixteen and fourteen. A good king would encou-rage early marriage; a wicked king will difcou-rage it, by wars, which impoverifh a People, and by the natural prohibition of it, by means of heavy burthens, luxuries, and by curbing the natural noble fpirit of the People, by unequal impofts, partial laws, interdictions, and reftraints. What is the confequence? It drives the women to proftitution, and the men to the moft abandoned and avowed concubinage. This indifcriminate commerce entails on them difeafe, fordidnefs, and mifery. They are hurried to an early grave, with a total lofs of conftitution many years previous to their diffolution, with a total lofs likewife of virtue and morality.

Whig,—a perfon who prefers the influence of the Houfe of Hanover to the prerogative of the Stuarts. I am an enemy to both; but if we muft languifh under one or the other, I would, without hefitation, prefer the prerogative of the Stuarts, and for this reafon—where prerogative is, the de-fence and juftification of an arbitrary act, all the

odium

odium which fuch an act would incur, is attached to the king himfelf; whereas, when this fame arbitrary act is induced, through the medium of influence, the odium refts on no one in particular. If our Parliament, for inftance, was to vote the fufpenfion of the Habeas Corpus Act (not that I think the People would fuffer it), this would be effected by influence, but the odium could not be perfonally applied, as no one could tell who voted from influence, and who from erroneous conviction. And further, here the People have the fhow, the fiction, of a reprefentation, it would therefore be, oftenfibly, or *feem* to be, the People's own act.

Widow-maker.—A crowned man whom I could name, is *Grand Widow-maker* to Europe!

Woolfack,—in the Houfe of Lords, the feat of the Judges. After a long refearch I have at length afcertained the meaning of this cuftom. It is to remind them of their duty to their fovereign, viz. that they fhould do all in their power to keep the ftaple commodity of the country *under.*

Workhoufe,—the abode of wretchednefs and defpair, filthily fitted up for the reception of decrepid old men and women, orphans, and widows, of thofe who have been killed in battle, fighting for defpotifm and tyranny. The poor are firft deprived of all means of fubfiftence in the commercial

way,

way, by the deſtruction of trade, and then thrown
into this filthy ſtew, to be eaten up by vermin, the
offspring of naſtineſs and a putrid atmoſphere.

World,—a collective term uſed to ſignify all the
nations of this vaſt globe. Here is an immenſe
field of inveſtigation for the philoſopher. It is
ſtrange, but no leſs true, that all nations, without
any exception, are ſubject to and the ſlaves of, ſome
error or ſuperſtition which is the fundamental of
unhappineſs to the people. Experience, knowledge, hiſtory, in vain afford them leſſons, what
paths to follow, what to ſhun. Blinded by the
warring paſſions, and ſtupified by their love of
ſenſuality, they ruſh on headlong into the abyſs
of vice and folly, and think to extricate themſelves
from theſe pitfalls by heaping crime upon crime,
till they find themſelves even with the reſt of the
world. The grand and ſtedfaſt enemies to the
happineſs of mankind, are religion and government. The firſt is the offspring of fear; the latter,
the child of depravity; and if it were not for the
intervention of prieſts and tyrants, mankind would
ſtill have had to bleſs the halcyon days of a natural government and a natural religion. It is
worthy of remark, that a ſtandard of truth is erected
by every little tyrant, in every little ſtate, and
though truth is immutable, ſhe is a very Proteus,
diverſifying and variegating her ſnowy garb in
every

every foil, in every climate, among every tribe, and in every age. What is a virtue in one country, is a crime in another; what is truth in one, is falfehood in the next; what is juftice here, is injuftice there; what utility here, injury there; what laudable here, culpable there. Thus the axe and the halter, the rack and the wheel; the faggot and the crucifix are the infallible umpires, the unerring oracles, the unchangeable ftandards of truth, the grand determiners of right and wrong! Treafon and integrity, religion and fuperftition, reafon and error go hand in hand in the world, and the tyrant and the prieft of every pitiful territory arbitrarily decide *by law*, which is truth, and which is error. " Oh! world, thy flippery " turns!"

Wrongs, Public.—If all the wrongs that exift in this world under different governments were to be written down, the whole earth, to ufe the language of fcripture, " would not be able to contain the " books that might be written." As a fpecimen of fuch a vaft voluminous work, it would take to record the public wrongs of England, more than ten hundred thoufand millions of folio volumes, fmall print, and no margin!

Yoke,—of flavery, is what men of all nations bend their necks to with cheerful fubmiffivenefs, and to fuch *things,* that lap-dogs would not fubmit

to,

to, but contemptuously wag their tails at. State minifters and church minifters are yoke-mafters to the whole of the civilized world, and man is now fo accuftomed, fo wedded to it, that he would think himfelf robbed of his rights, if deprived of it. Year after year, day after day, he renews his toil for others to enjoy the fweets of that labour, and goes as mechanically to it as the ox to the plough, and fucceeding generations claim the yoke as an hereditary privilege.

Youth.—It is much to be lamented that more attention is not paid to the education of youth. Thofe who in the wane of life are counting on the joys of hereafter, fhould confider it one of the firft of duties to warn the rifing generation againft their thoughtlefs prodigality of time, that greateft of earthly treafures. If half that wide lapfe of time, which at once confumes itfelf and the health of the body in exceffes were fpent in the improvement of the mind, what a wonderful change, what a revolution would be produced! kings would not then tyrannize over their fubjects, and be idolized for it; nor would priefts plunge the bulk of mankind in darknefs and ignorance, and be revered for it! Our univerfities are nothing but monkeries, where real knowledge is trodden under the hoofs of an affemblage of ignorant, fuperftitious, bigoted, intolerant friars, and
where

where the partial knowledge of words is preferred
to the knowledge of things, and of men and manners! 'Tis ignorance that is the tyrant! 'Tis ignorance that is the prieſt! 'Tis ignorance that lights
the torch of intolerance, that fans the flame of the
faggot! becauſe it is ſwiniſh, ſottiſh, ignorance
that ſuffers it!

F I N I S.

Annotations

p. 1

Absurdity. *Mr. Pitt's surplus fund*: After taking office in 1784, Pitt introduced a number of new taxes by which he created an annual surplus of income over expenditure. In May 1786, he introduced the so-called Sinking Fund, which was used to alleviate the national debt accumulating since the American War. New capital was raised as the Government paid in £1 million each year for the Fund's commissioners to buy up Government stock. With the outbreak of war in 1793, however, the scheme had become an 'absurdity', as the Government was now forced to borrow money at high rates of interest to give to the Fund's commissioners so that they could redeem the debt at a much lower rate.

his Majesty's civil-list: The Civil List Act of 1698 gave the king an allowance to cover the costs of the areas that were counted to be under his command. At the end of the eighteenth century, this not only included the uphold of his property and household, but also civil government departments, legal offices, pensions and sinecures, as well as home and foreign secret service (for an exhaustive list; see Sainty, 'Introduction').

to restore ... in France: When Britain joined the Coalition against France with other European kingdoms in 1793, the Government was keen to emphasize that it was to protect British interests of safety, trade and the BALANCE OF POWER – not to revenge or restore the Bourbon royal family to the French throne. The signals were, however, mixed. When Toulon was captured from the French (see ADVANTAGE), the British Government issued a statement of 29 October 1793 in which it was proclaimed that the port was held in trust for the return of a French 'hereditary Monarchy' (*PH 30*, col. 1060) – but with no specification of what kind this should be.

Abuse. *privileged orders*: The various aristocracy, nobility and gentry taken in contempt by the radicals. See, for example, Joel Barlow, *Advice to the Privileged Orders, in the Several States of Europe, Resulting from the Necessity and Propriety of a general Revolution in the Principle of Government* (1793–95). Part II was printed and sold by Pigott's publisher, Daniel Isaac Eaton.

Adam. Supporters of King and Government used examples from British history as well as the Bible to prove that the model of constitutional monarchy was justified by tradition and divinely sanctioned, whereas opponents used other chapters in the same sources to claim that kings were a corruption of historical liberties. In *Rights of Man*, Paine charged Burke with having 'set up a sort of political Adam, in whom all posterity are bound for ever' (p. 94). Pigott's idea that Adam in Genesis was the only 'man of his time' is related to Paine's attempt to trump the many 'historical' arguments by tracing the history of man to his most original state: 'Why … not trace the rights of man to the creation of man?' If the antiquarians who ransacked constitutional history would go back all this way, they would arrive at a point when there were no aristocratic titles, but 'Man was his high and only title, and a higher cannot be given him' (p. 117). In *Politics for the People*, Eaton included a 'humorous account of the ORIGIN OF JACOBINISM', which aligned the breaking of God's law with resistance to monarchical tyranny. Adam and Eve were 'Sans Culottes, consequently Jacobins, for which they were kicked out of Paradise', and the Devil was described as the 'first Jacobin, for which he was hurled neck and heels out of heaven' (12 [1793], p. 173).

Address. To check the surge of radical activity, Pitt secured the Royal Proclamation for the preventing of tumultuous Meetings and seditious Writings on 21 May 1792 (printed in *PR* 33, p. 130–32; *PH* 31, cols 470–71). This was welcomed by addresses of thanks to George III, which flooded in from loyalist associations all around the country. The *Annual Register* reported that by 1 September, the King had received 341 loyal addresses in support of the Crown and the constitution (*AR*, 1972, Chronicle, 37). In *Jockey Club* III, Pigott observed that no king since the tyrannical Charles II 'has received so many Royal addresses as King George' (pp. 31–2). It was in reaction to these loyalist addresses that Paine wrote his inflammatory *Address to the Addressers, on the Late Proclamation* (1792).

Admiralty. The office of First Lord of the Admiralty (the Minister for the Navy) was given to Pitt's elder brother John Pitt (1756–1835), Earl of Chatham, in 1788. Criticism of his management was fierce, and in December 1794 he was removed for inefficiency.

Advantage. *the evacuation of Toulon*: In 1793, royalists at the French town of Toulon called for help against the revolutionary government in Paris. On 28 August, Coalition forces under the British navy commander Lord Hood occupied the important naval arsenal there. However, the attempt to lift the French siege of the town failed, as a young Napoleon Bonaparte led an assault on Point L'Eguilette, which overlooked the inner harbour. On 18 December, Lord Hood agreed to evacuate. Hence, French naval skills brought defeat to the Coalition fleet and showed the British that their so-called 'blue-water' strategy did not give them a decisive advantage.

   retreat from Dunkirk: In 1793, before the attempt to take Toulon, the Allied forces had suffered another defeat. The Duke of York had been appointed to command a force of just over 6500 men into the Netherlands against the French. After capturing Famars Camp and contributing to the seizure of Valenciennes on 28 July, the Duke of York was commanded from London to proceed to Dunkirk, with the objective of capturing the naval port so a free passage through the Straits of Dover could be secured. On 24 August, the English army established itself before Dunkirk, but the Duke lacked the heavy artillery required to seize the port. It arrived eight days after an attack would have been advantageous. When the allied Austrian army was defeated at Hondschoote on 8 September, the Duke had to embark on a speedy retreat to Furnes. The failed mission showed the inefficiency of the British war administration and was humiliating for the Government domestically as well as internationally.

Earl Moira's expedition: On 12 October 1793, Earl Moira was appointed commander of a joint expedition of British and French émigré soldiers, which sailed on 30 November to aid the insurrection of royalists in Brittany. Although the expedition reached the coast of France to the east of Cape la Hogue, no landing took place. At the time, the Government had made the decision to allocate forces and artillery to capture the West Indies. This meant that Moira had to wait well into December for stores to arrive, only then to learn that the opportunity had been lost. After waiting a month at Guernsey, the expedition returned to Portsmouth in the beginning of January 1794.

p. 2

Alarm. It was the official Government line that Britain was not concerned with the internal state of France and the restitution of aristocratic estates. Officially, war was declared to curb the rising power of the French in Europe, a fear of an invasion and a protection of trade. Anxiety that revolutionary ideas would be exported to Britain led the Government to introduce restrictive legislation, which included the outlawing of radical publications, correspondence and meetings by Royal Proclamations of 21 May 1792 (see ADDRESS) and 1 December 1792 (printed in *PR* 34, pp. 31–2), the latter in response to rumours of a plot to provoke a rising in London, for which the militia was called out to protect vital interests.

unconstitutional augmentation of the army: In March 1794, Home Secretary Henry Dundas had distributed a circular letter with an address to all Lord Lieutenants of the counties asking them to initiate a programme for voluntary subscription to the militia. The militia could only operate on the mainland, and was called upon in two situations: if there was a threat of foreign invasion or 'in cases of Riot'. Facing an escalating number of riots up and down the country, the militia had become an important arm of Government control. Dundas's letter outraged the Foxite Whigs, who saw his initiative as unconstitutional and attacked it in Parliament. Also, reformist meetings around the country protested. The Opposition believed it not only put pressure on those in Government service, but that it was also 'absolutely illegal, and supereminently dangerous to the constitution' (Plowden, *History ... 1793*, p. 69). To overcome the criticism, Pitt passed a Volunteer Bill for the statutory raising of a Volunteer corps in the summer of 1794. The immediate background for the subscription programme was the fear of invasion that had already sparked the formation of many new regiments especially around the coasts.

introduction of foreign troops: Another measure attacked as 'unconstitutional' was the introduction of non-British troops in Portsmouth, the Isle of Wight and other regional centres to bolster the defence against a possible French invasion. The quartering of Hessian troops on the Hampshire coast in January 1794 led to a lengthy debate. In February, a Bill of Indemnity to Ministers was, however, thrown out of Parliament (*PR 37*, pp. 550–83). In a speech, Stanhope proclaimed that he 'trusted the people would resist' the Government initiative 'by opposing force to force' (*The Speech of Earl Stanhope in the House of Peers on February 19th. 1794* [printed and distributed for free by the London Corresponding Society], p. 4).

barracks: The erection of barracks was a measure taken to increase the mobility of troops and help avoid the old problem of quartering them on the populace. It is important to note that the barrack-building programme began before the war and was as much a response to the domestic political situation as it was to the demands of a war against an external enemy. Out of the seven barracks built in 1793, six were in industrial towns where there had been outbursts of active radicalism, the seventh was in Hounslow, from which troops could easily be brought into the capital (Emsley, 'Military and Popular Disorder', pp. 17–18).

Alarmists. In the first issue of the conservative magazine *The Alarmist* (J. Owen, 1796), the editor explained his choice of title: 'The Modern Whigs [i.e. followers of Fox] have coined the term Alarmist to describe one whose understanding is for ever disturbed by visions of imaginary public danger' (p. 6). He corrects, however, that an 'alarmist' should rather be seen to be one who 'inculcates that provident care of the public safety, which represses Sedition before it has ripened into Treason, and Treason before it has broken out into Rebellion' (p. 8). Of the about one hundred Opposition Whigs, nearly two-thirds of that number followed their nominal leader, the Duke of Portland, in voting with the Government on alarmist measures. In February 1793, Portland and Windham had declared their separation from Fox. Although the Portland Whigs stayed on the Opposition benches until June 1794, their support for the Government was evident. Both Windham and Powys sat on Pitt's Committee of Secrecy, which was constituted in May 1794 to monitor and prosecute the radical organizations. When a formal coalition was agreed upon in June 1794, Portland became Home Secretary and Powys made Junior War Minister.

Two other Whig defectors also took office. One was George John, Earl Spencer (1758–1834), who became Lord Privy Seal. He had former strong Whig connections, but joined Burke in criticizing the Revolution and voted with Pitt in support of the war and alarmist restrictions on personal freedom. The other was William Wentworth, Earl Fitzwilliam (1748–1833), who was made Lord President of the Council. He was a former friend of Fox (who had intended him to head his proposed new India Board in 1783), but Fitzwilliam had shifted his allegiances to Pitt in the years leading up to the war.

Alderman. In the legislative body of the City of London, the Court of Aldermen had 26 members, normally elected for life. William Curtis (1752–1829) held one of these seats and also, from 1790, represented the City in the Commons, where he was a supporter of Pitt. The corruption that secured his return to Parliament made him a victim of many satirical jibes. John William Anderson (1736–1813) was Alderman for Aldersgate Ward. He was the Justice who examined Pigott when he was brought to Guildhall on accusations of uttering seditious words in the London Coffee House (*Persecution*, pp. 12, 34n). Paul Le Messurier was the alarmist Lord Mayor of London (1793–94), who actively tried to contain radical activity in the metropolis. Sir James Sanderson (1741–98) was an MP for London and, like many City Aldermen, a wealthy merchant. With his brother and partner, Timothy, he was in the biscuit baking business. Their factory at Wapping had secured a contract with the British navy for provisions, and Sanderson's suspected motives for wanting a British war were attacked in contemporary caricatures (see, for example, *BMC*, 7676). In 1792–93, he had been Lord Mayor. For these people and other City posts, see *Kent's Directory for the Year 1794* (R. and H. Causton, 1794). Aldermen were traditional targets of satire due to their legendary extravagant lifestyles and misuse of public funds. This included indulging in lavish feasts. One that was reported in the Government papers was William Curtis's annual June celebrations of the anniversary for his election to Parliament. In 1792, this took place in the London Tavern (*Public Advertiser*, 27 June 1792). Several City taverns like this kept live turtles ready to be picked for their patrons' indulgence (Murray, *High Society*, p. 172).

Ally (new). Since the establishment of Protestant hereditary to the English throne, the King and Rome had been enemies. However, in their attitude to republican France, both Pope Pius VI (Giovanni Angelo Braschi, 1717–99) and George III shared the same hope that the old order of King and Church would be restored in France. Pius VI was against the Civil Constitution of the Clergy (1791), by which French officials of the Church were subjected to civil authority. He was also powerless to prevent the loss of the Papal State of Avignon in 1791. Mutual antagonism was exacerbated in February 1793 when a French envoy was assassinated in Rome.

Furthermore, the Pope helped to orchestrate opposition to the French during the Italian campaigns of 1794–97.

America. *state of prosperity*: The success of the American economy was often invoked as invective against Britain and her Allies' war with France, which had a negative effect on trade. On 21 January 1794, Sheridan reminded the Commons that 'America remains neutral, prosperous, and at peace … thrives at this moment in a state of envied tranquillity, and is hourly clearing the paths to unbounded opulence; America has monopolized the commerce, and the advantages which we have abandoned' (*PR* 37, pp. 121–2).

p. 3.

Ambassador. Ambassadors received their salaries from the King's Civil List and were counted as members of the Royal Court. They were His Majesty's Ministers abroad, and bore the King's credentials to foreign royal courts at a time when these were the centres of power. Diplomacy was often complemented with bribery and spying (see Black, *British Diplomats*). They were often extremely active in the countries to which they were envoys. Examples were the Dutch crisis of 1787 and the Turkish crisis of 1791 (Duffy, *Younger Pitt*, pp. 166–78).

Ankerstrom. On 16 March 1792, Johann Jakob Anckarström attempted to assassinate Gustavus III of Sweden. The King died from his wounds on 29 March. *Brutus* (6th century BC) was the main conspirator to the assassination of Caesar and was often hailed as the founder the Roman republic. In *Politics for the People*, Eaton published an anti-Government satire entitled 'Budget of the People', which concluded with the wake-up call to all Britons: 'Brutus thou sleep'st' (9 [1793], pp. 130–32).

Apostate. General Dumoriez was the French military commander who defected to the Austrian side in April 1793 and made plans for a coup d'état to overturn the Girondists in Paris. Pitt had in the early 1780s moved bills for parliamentary reform according to Whig principles. Years later, as a seasoned Prime Minister, he blocked reform. In *Jockey Club* III, Pigott calls Pitt the 'GRAND APOSTATE' (p. 55). Edmund Burke was the most notorious example of a reformist Whig who turned to favour the existing order in response to the French Revolution. Charges of apostasy were part and parcel of radical discourse. James Mackintosh, the author of *Vindiciae Gallica* (1791), wrote in 1792 a *Letter to … Pitt on his Apostacy from the Abuse of Parliamentary Reform*, which was sold by the publisher of the *Jockey Club* series, H. D. Symonds. The turn away from former principles of reform was also what had compelled Pigott to write *Strictures on the New Political Tenets of the Rt. Hon. Edmund Burke illustrated by*

Analogy between his different Sentiments on the American and French Revolutions in 1791. Earl Moira's appointment as naval commander in the war with France came as somewhat of a surprise, as he had abandoned his support for the Government back in 1787 and had since associated with the Whig-friendly Prince of Wales, especially during the Regency crisis, when the Whigs had tried to topple Pitt's Government.

Argument. Since the Royal Proclamation against seditious correspondence of May 1792, the Government had attempted to silence enemies of the establishment. *Botany Bay* was a penal colony established in New South Wales, Australia, in 1787. The lawyer Thomas Muir, founding member of the Scottish Association of Friends of the People, was sentenced to 14 years' deportation there on 31 August 1793 by the Justice Clerk Lord Braxfield at the Court of Justiciary in Edinburgh. The dissenting minister Thomas Fyshe Palmer was tried before the circuit Court of Justiciary at Dundee and sentenced by Lord Braxfield on 13 September 1793 to seven years' deportation. Both had been active in organizing a national convention for British reformist societies. Radical Whigs in the Commons made pleas to the Government to intervene in Lord Braxfield's decision. Muir and Palmer were now referred to as martyrs, and the parliamentary speeches were popular enough to be published separately (see *Speech of William Adam in the House of Commons March 10th 1794* [J. Depress, 1794]). On 24 February 1793, Sheridan presented a petition to Parliament which described the transportation as 'unconstitutional'. The petition failed. When the Pitt Ministry, against the many protests, finally decided to uphold the sentences on 25 January 1794, it was protecting 'banishment' as punishment for sedition as a special feature of Scottish Law. The men were transported on 2 May 1794. At the time, Muir and Palmer arrived in Botany Bay, nearly 2000 convicts were held there, most of them convicted of minor theft. *Newgate* prison became residence for many English radicals. Often prison sentences for radical activity were accompanied by fines, which sometimes kept prisoners in gaol beyond their allotted time. William Hodgson, with whom Pigott had been arrested in the London Coffee House, remained in gaol beyond his two-year sentence for his inability to pay the fine. See PILLORY.

Army (standing). The British army was kept to a minimum in peacetime. It was believed that a standing army would increase the power of the Crown. On the eve of the declaration of war, when it began to seem sensible to prepare for expected hostilities, the issue was raised in Parliament. On 22 January 1793, M. A. Taylor, MP for Poole, proclaimed that 'in no free country could a large standing army be kept up, without danger to liberty ... history affords innumerable instances ... in this country, the same army which raised Cromwell to the Protectorate, restored Charles the Second' (*PR* 34, p. 560). This sentiment was supported by the source Pigott quotes here: Sir John Dalrymple, *Memoirs of Great Britain and Ireland*, 2 vols, 2nd edn

(W. Strahan et al., 1771–86). The passage cited is Dalrymple, quoting from William III's speech of 1698, in which the King denounces 'the attempt of Charles I and Cromwell to destroy the constitution by means of an army' (2, p. 125). In a pamphlet published by Eaton, it was stated that a standing army was 'dangerous to the Liberties of the Country' (*Letters on the Impolicy of a Standing Army in Time of Peace and the Unconstitutional and illegal Measure of Barracks* [1794?])

Ass. George Louis Leclerc Buffon (1707–1788) was a French naturalist historian who wrote a number of important studies of the earth, anthropology and mammals. The English translation of his *Natural History* was advertised in the opposition paper the *Morning Chronicle* in January 1794. In *Jockey Club* III, Pigott had described Charles I as a tyrant grabbing the people 'by the ears (asses ears)' to 'drive them as he pleased'. To this he added that George III's 'character is now the same'. Pigott cautions the ruling orders, however, that 'John Bull is a less mercurial and patient animal, the harder he is driven, the more tame and docile he becomes, nor is it till the last gasp, when almost pressed to death, that he resists the reins, and exerts his natural strength' (pp. 9–10). *John Bull* was a stock-in-trade personification of the English people, often depicted as a simple country bumpkin, who is easily deceived.

p. 4

Assertion. *king's speech*: George III's speech to Parliament on 21 January 1794 was reported in the Opposition paper the *Morning Chronicle*: 'His majesty reflects with satisfaction on the progress made by the arms of the Allied Powers, more especially since the British troops were sent in aid of the Common Cause.' This was against the French republicans, who are 'arbitrarily seizing on and disposing of the lives and properties of a numerous people'. For this reason 'His majesty regrets that a continuance of the war is necessary; but he should think himself wanting in attention to the welfare of his subjects were he to think of making any peace.'

combined powers: The First Coalition of nations against republican France, which from 1793 comprised Britain, Russia, Prussia, Spain, Holland, Austria and Sardinia. It was officially dissolved in 1797, but ineffective since 1795.

British Constitution … unprecedented prosperity: After the booming years of 1789 to 1792, when English exports rose by nearly 50 per cent, Pitt would on 17 February 1792 give a famous optimistic budget speech, in which he had praised the constitution as something 'we cherish and value, because we know that it practically secures the tranquillity and welfare both of individuals and of the public' (*PH* 29, cols 816–40). Cf. Pigott, who made the following observation on 'the boasted prosperity of England': 'There are this very day (12 February, 1794) 27000 prisoners confined for debt in his Majesty's different gaols throughout this island; and in the year 1793, four million eight hundred thousand pound sterling was found an inadequate provision for our national poor, notwithstanding the prodigious number of starved objects to be seen in every part of this metropolis and its environs. If however, the country be really so prosperous, as we are forever told it is; does it not reflect everlasting infamy on the higher orders of the nation, that the sum of poverty existing therein should exceed the utmost stretch of human credibility?' (*Female Jockey Club*, 134n).

madness of reform: The alarmist reaction in Britain meant that many motions for reform, which had seemed likely to pass into law in the preceding years as a matter of course, became tarred with the brush of revolution and were conferred. Many believed that any admission to reform would open the floodgates to the anarchy perceived to exist in France. One casualty was the repeal of the Test and Corporations Acts (see TEST-ACT). When it was motioned on 8 May 1789 in the Commons, it was lost by a narrow majority of 122 to 102 (*PR 26*, p. 128). When it was motioned again on 2 March 1790, it was lost by 294 to 105 (*PR 37*, pp. 139–96) – the increased number of voting members reflecting the seriousness with which reformist causes were now perceived.

Association. See 'Introduction'.

four years: This was the maximum sentence passed for sedition in England during this period. William Winterbotham was convicted to Newgate for this term; see *Trial of Wm. Winterbotham … before the Hon. Baron Perryn, and a Special Jury, at Exeter on the 25 of July, 1793, for Seditious Words*, 2nd edn (D. I. Eaton, 1794). Such sentences were the outcome of some of the Government's prosecutions against organized reformism in the early 1790s. The corresponding societies, such as the London Corresponding Society of which Pigott was a member, were checked by Pitt's introduction of the Royal Proclamations against seditious correspondence (21 May and 1 December 1792), which gave the Home Office powers to monitor reformist societies through the use of spies, infiltration, the opening of letters and so on.

Friends of the People: In April 1792, a group of liberal Whigs fronted by Charles Grey formed the Society of the Friends of the People, which included 28 MPs and three peers. They argued for the kind of moderate reform which Pitt and Richmond had once endorsed, hence the comparison here. By November of the same year, there were 87 branches of the Society in Britain.

Pigott's complaint that Pitt supports 'associations', such as that formed by the ultra-loyalist John Reeves: In November 1792, Reeves, a lawyer who had held a number of minor Government positions, established the Association for the Preservation of Liberty and Property against Republicans and Levellers. This was not, as Pigott claims here, formed under Pitt's 'immediate sanction'. In fact, evidence suggests that the Government was not aware of its establishment, but quickly saw the usefulness in subsidizing the Association for its own ends (Duffy, 'William Pitt and the Origins of the Loyalist Association Movement of 1792', p. 945). Reeves's organization would, by the end of 1793, consist of as many as 2000 local societies. Adverts were placed in newspapers to encourage informers to report anyone who published, circulated or expressed seditious views to the Association's headquarters at the Crown and Anchor Tavern in the Strand. Hundreds of letters, often anonymous, were sent to Reeves, hence making him 'the Prince of Spies'. Pigott's antagonism against loyalist associations was heightened by the fact that they were looking into prosecuting *The Jockey Club*, as it was reported in Parliament on 4 May 1793 (*PR* 35, p. 6). Eaton, who became Pigott's publisher, was brought to court on the behest of Reeves's Association in 1793 (*The Trial of Daniel Isaac Eaton, July the tenth 1793* [Eaton, 1793]). For George Savile, see 'Cast of Characters'.

  preservation of game: In Britain, Game Associations first saw the light of day in the 1740s, but hundreds of them sprang up during the late 1780s and early 1790s (Munsche, *Gentlemen and Poachers*, pp. 90–92). These were formed to safeguard the privileges of the landed classes. They were subscription societies which used the contributions for prosecutions and for rewards for information leading to the conviction of offenders who hunted for game on the land that belonged to them. The right to kill 'game' depended on obtaining a Game Licence, which was granted on the basis of income. For this reason, the Game Laws were considered some of the most glaringly class-biased legislation on the English statute books. Pigott suggests here that a poor freeholder who killed animals might not always be poaching for revenue at the market, but simply trying to protect his crops on the land he rented from the landowner. A legal distinction between gaming and the killing of vermin existed, and was sometimes tried in court. The absurdity of the laws made it questionable whether a small freeholder, who did not meet the financial requirements for obtaining a Game Licence, could get rid of partridges, pheasants or hares on his land at all. The freeholder could not kill them, because if he did, and if anyone else killed these animals without the lord of the manor's permission, he committed a trespass. The Game Laws were not repealed before 1831. Cf. LAWS (TRANSGRESSION OF THE).

p. 5

Attornies. In *Jockey Club* II, Pigott dealt at length with the evils of the judicial system, focusing on the judges. The hedge '(for the most part)' may favour the celebrated barrister and politician Thomas Erskine, who successfully represented several radicals throughout the 1790s. On Erskine; see *Jockey Club* II, pp. 124–35.

Author. The Duke of Leeds had tried his poetic talents in a pro-war composition for the stage: *New Song, sung by Mr. Bannister ... performed for the benefit of sailors* [sic] *widows*. This song was later printed and sold in London at the beginning of 1794. Hervey Redmond Morres, Viscount Montmorres (1746?–97) was a peer in the Irish House of Lords, who anonymously wrote *The Prodigy: A Comedy* (1794). Francis North (1761–1817), son of the former Government leader Lord North, was a lieutenant in the army and a patron of the stage. His *The Kentish Barons: A Play in Three Acts interspersed with songs by the Honourable Francis North* was first performed at the Theatre-Royal, Hay-Market on 25 June 1791 (later printed in Dublin by Byrne et al., 1791). Colonel George Hanger (1751–1824) had served in the war in America with the Hessian Jäger corps. He was an infamous dandy and a crony of the Prince of Wales. Pigott probably refers to a satirical piece entitled 'Ode to Bacchus' printed in *The Times* on 27 July 1787, supposedly written by Hanger and performed at the Marine Pavilion in Brighton in front of the Prince of Wales and several prominent politicians of the opposition. John Williams, who had served in the entourage of the Earl of Barrymore, later included it as a 'dream' he had in ('Anthony Pasquin') *The New Brighton Guide*, 6th edn (H. D. Symonds, 1796), pp. 132–40.

Balance of Power. One of the main reasons the Government gave for Britain entering into Coalition against France was the maintenance of the *balance of power*. Eighteenth-century political theory proscribed that European States existed in equilibrium comparable to the balance that operated in the natural world, and that no State or alliance of States should be allowed to gain a military advantage that would threaten this equilibrium. Pitt had used the theory in the crisis of 1791, when he proposed an increase in British naval forces to support Turkey against the superior power of Russia. Pitt's 'balance of power' policy was, however, attacked in Parliament, and he had to see his argument defeated (see PAGEANT). Pigott suggests here that the Coalition forces went to war less to restore a 'balance' than for self-aggrandizement. Cf. the radical writer William Fox's definition: 'Balance of Power means perpetual war, on a series of the most extravagant and incongruous pretexts: it meant King William's ambitious project of conquering France, it meant carrying on a bloody expensive war for the emolument of the Duke of Marlborough, and it meant annexing Bremen and Verden to Hanover' (*On Jacobinism* [M. Gurney, 1794]).

Bankruptcy. In March 1793, the alarm over the French Revolution, combined with the stoppage of exports to France, caused apprehension among speculators and led to what Pigott described as 'bankruptcies of a most alarming nature, unbounded in their extent [which] multiply through the nation' (*Treachery no Crime*, p. 151). The *Annual Register* commented that a 'general distress' spread throughout the country (1793, British and Foreign History, p. 73). One historian has counted 1956 commissions of bankruptcy in 1793 against only 934 the year before (Levi, *History*, p. 69n). Figures elsewhere differ, but there is consensus that the number was at least doubled in the first year of the war.

Dundas's speeches: In a debate on 30 April 1793, Home Secretary Henry Dundas argued that 'the present embarrassment of public credit' was not the effect of war, but that the 'very circumstances of the present stagnation [of credit] was a proof of the power and energy of the country'; its cause should be ascribed to the optimism of merchants who had gone beyond their capital and thereby 'occasioned distress' for others (*PR* 35, p. 335).

p. 6

Bargain. The word was often used to head newspaper advertisements.

ministerial loans: The Government's war efforts were primarily funded by loans rather than taxes. The first loan of the war was taken out in March 1793 and was for £4 500 000 (Newmarch, *Loans*, pp. 7–8).

Brook Watson's contract: See CONTRACTORS.

200,000 l … Sardinia: It was Britain's war strategy to subsidize its allies for them to provide troops for the war on the European Continent while many of her own soldiers were employed in colonial conquest in the West Indies. On 25 April 1793, the British Government struck a deal with its ally Sardinia to provide 'an army of fifty thousand men' for the protection of their own dominions. This was secured by an annual British subsidy of £200 000 (treaty printed in *Jordan*, 4, pp. 20–22). As George III was also Elector of the hereditary German electorate of Hanover, 14 000 Hanoverian troops were taken on the payroll in 1793 at the cost of £492 000, raised to 560 000 in 1794. The subsidy to Hessian troops was 190 000 in 1793, and 437 000 in 1794 (Newmarch, *Loans*, p. 51).

Jesuit of St. Omer: In 1765, enemies had accused Burke of being a crypto-Catholic educated by Jesuits. Though this was untrue, he offered Rockingham, the then Prime Minister, his resignation, but was refused. In Eaton's *Politics for the People*, the satirical song 'Mr. B—ke to the Swinish Multitude' contains the lines: 'My education has been such / That few can boast of one so good: / St. Omer's taught me very much / To hate the Swinish Multitude' (2 [1794], pp. 15–16). St Omer was a college in France, which had served as a safe haven for English Catholics seeking education. As the political climate improved, it moved to England in 1793. *Jesuit* had the general meaning of cunning intellectualism, an accusation often levelled at Burke. There is no evidence to suggest that Burke received a pension before it was announced in August 1794 (£1200 a year for him and his wife), but the figure of £1500 was quoted by Paine in *Letter Addressed to the Addressers* (1792). This related to the rumour that Burke had received a secret pension for speaking the Government's cause, which Paine had helped popularize in *Rights of Man* (see pp. 88, 102, 226).

Gilbert Elliot (1751–1814) was one of the younger Portland Whigs, who defected to the side of the Government. In 1793, he first accepted Pitt's offer of Commissioner at Dunkirk, then the Commissionership of a captive Toulon. As both Dunkirk and Toulon had to be abandoned by the British, Elliot's services were symbolic. Yet for the latter he was given a salary of £7500 a year, and 40 shillings a year for life (Plowden, *History ... 1793*, p. 341). On 4 January 1794, the *Morning Chronicle* commented that 'the expensive establishments formed for Toulon are not concluded by the evacuation of the place. As they were made for the purpose of rewarding Gentlemen for changing their opinion, they are made fixed and permanent.' The article went on to criticize Elliot's pension as well as other Government officials involved in the failed capture for having 'bargained for pensions beyond the date of their own existence'. On 28 January 1794, Elliot's reward for his abortive Commissionership was discussed in Parliament when Sheridan addressed the Government with a request for information on the matter (*PR 27*, p. 195).

Baronet. Sir Francis Molyneux (1774–1840) was Gentleman Usher of the Black Rod – an officer of the Order of the Garter with a seat in the House of Lords. He took the title of seventh Baronet of his family line in 1781, at the age of eight. His fondness for the turf made him one of Pigott's original targets in *Jockey Club* I, pp. 36–8. The simple mention of his title here is to be seen on the background of Pigott's attack in the *Jockey Club* pamphlets on the nobility for lacking all the noble qualities one should expect from titled men.

Barrister. In *Jockey Club* II, Pigott writes of the Attorney-General William Garrow (1760–1840) that the 'insolence and presumption of [barristers] is fully exemplified in the pert loquacity of this conceited, ignorant upstart'. It is these rather dubious qualities that make him a 'Paragon of the Law' (pp. 77–9). Garrow was the judge presiding in the trial against Eaton for selling Paine's *Rights of Man* on 3 June 1793 (see *Trial of Daniel Isaac Eaton* [Eaton, 1793]). On this occasion, Eaton was acquitted.

Bastille. The fourteenth-century fortress in Paris, taken by the French insurgents on 14 July 1789, epitomized the abuse of power in popular imagination. With acts of 1784 (24 George III c. 54) and 1791 (31 George III c. 46), Pitt had provided for the rebuilding of gaols. *Newgate* was London's main criminal gaol, where prisoners awaiting trial or execution were held. It was notorious for its overcrowding and the squalor which poorer prisoners suffered. A rebuilding of Newgate had begun in 1767, but after being ruined by fire in the Gordon Riots of 1780, its completion was delayed until 1785. In the pamphlet *Extermination, or an Appeal to the People of England on the Present War with France* (printed by Eaton), the Bastille is described as a place 'where every man who was obnoxious to the Monarch ... was shut up without any public accusation whatever'. To this the anonymous author adds: 'This Country also may now boast of a Bastille, as the new Prison in the Spa Fields has the same terrific appearance' (p. 5). *Coldbath Field's Prison* was a correction house, which was undergoing extensive rebuilding in 1794.

Beggars. *Spitalfields* had become a byword for poverty, as the London silk weavers who were concentrated there suffered recurrent difficulties. Many weavers had to beg for a living, and Spitalfields had some of the most overcrowded workhouses in England. Silk was a volatile market, and their plight was partly an effect of a change in fashion away from silk dresses. Yet the *Morning Chronicle* (14 December 1793) blamed the weaver's distress specifically on the war (Emsley, *British Society*, pp. 30–31). So did Eaton's *Politics for the People*: it was the Government's 'present war', which had closed foreign markets and 'robbed' weavers 'of all means of support' (7 [1794], pp. 110–14).

Blindness. *'none ... won't see'*: The line appears in Jonathan Swift's *A Treatise on Polite Conversation* (1738), Dialogue Three.

Bombast. Accusing one's political opponent of using high-flown rhetoric to cover up for empty arguments was a common strategy in political debate. The political writer Anthony Pasquin wrote on Pitt as an orator that he 'is not so remarkable for vigor of dictions, as aptitude of expression', but that 'he is most adroit, when circumlocutory' (*Legislative Biography; or, an Attempt to Ascertain the Merits and Principle of the most Admired Orators of the British Senate* [H. D. Symonds, 1795], p. 11). Pitt's cousin, the academically gifted Lord Grenville, had a keen interest in and extensive knowledge of classical literature and was judged an apt parliamentary speaker.

Boxing. In the eighteenth century, boxing was a gentleman's sport. Many lords took lessons in Gentleman Jackson's room in Bond Street, and in 1788 the three eldest sons of George III took up the sport. The royal princes and noblemen were behind organizing the fights, at which large bets were taken (Ford, *Prizefighting*, pp. 65–75). Pigott places prizefighting with the lust for gambling which Pigott criticizes throughout. In 1795, Eaton published a pamphlet entitled *The Political Progress of Britain; or, an Impartial History of Abuses in the Government*, in which it is asserted that 'Thirty, forty, or fifty thousands pounds are sometimes betted among the spectators, on the prowess of a favourite champion' (p. 123).

p. 7

Braggadocio. 'A vain-glorious fellow, a boaster' (Grose). The connection between Pigott's targets here is their claim to military accomplishment. Sir Banastre Tarleton (1754–1833) had been a General in the American War, where he served under Lord

Howe (see BRAVERY). For many years, he was Mary Robinson's lover (see DULLNESS). Together they edited his *History of the Campaigns of 1780 and 1781* (1787). Tarleton was attacked in *Jockey Club* I, pp. 105–7. Sir Watkin Lewes (1736–1821) was a Colonel in the Artillery Company and a commander in the Blue Regiment and the London militia. He had served as Sheriff of London. Roger Curtis (1746–1816) served under Lord Howe in America and was re-employed in the military campaign against the French as Howe's First Captain. Sir Sidney Smith (1764–1840) served under Lord Hood in the siege of Toulon. Having organized the burning of the captured French fleet, he was pronounced a hero of the new war upon his return to London in January 1794 (Pocock, *Thirst for Glory*, p. 33).

Brass. Slang expression for money. Home Secretary Henry Dundas was Treasurer for the Navy from 1783 and a member of the Board of Control for the colonial business in India from 1784. Notoriously, he was also a virtual despot in his native Scotland, where he controlled Government patronage (see, generally, Fry, *Dundas Despotism*).

Bravery. *Royal Dunkirk Hero*: See HASTE. Earl Henry Phipps Mulgrave (1755–1831) was a soldier by trade and, in Parliament, a supporter and personal friend of Pitt and Dundas. In the failed British occupation of Toulon, he was land commander. When the overall command of this operation was taken over by another officer, Mulgrave refused to serve in a subordinate position and went home. He had to defend this conduct in the House of Commons on 19 April 1794 (*PH* 31, cols 250–55). Earl Richard Howe (1726–99) had led a number of uncoordinated campaigns during the American War. In February 1793, he was appointed Admiral of Channel Fleet. For five months after the outbreak of war, the fleet under Howe's command was still at Spithead (which was partly due to the valid problems of manning the ships). When he finally set sail, he was beaten back twice by gales during the first few weeks he was at sea. The press saw this as an evasion of the French, and this impression was reflected in the drawings of Gillray and Cruikshank (*BMC*, 8352, 8353).

Briton (True). The *True Briton* was a conservative morning paper started in January 1793 on the initiative of George Rose and the Treasury, which subsidized it. Like the evening paper *The Sun*, whose proprietors were Pitt and friends, it was used as a means to regulate public opinion. It was edited by John Heriot.

Brunswick (Duke of). Charles William Ferdinand, Duke of Brunswick was ruler of the Duchy of Brunswick and a senior commander in the Prussian army. On 25 July 1792, a declaration was issued under his name, known as the 'Brunswick Manifesto'. In this, he threatened the French towns that 'their houses shall be demolished or burned' if they raised a resistance to his invasion army. Republican Frenchmen were also admonished that he would 'inflict on them the most terrible punishments' should they harm the Bourbon royal family (*Declaration ... to the Inhabitants of France*, printed in *Jordan*, 1, pp. 256–60). As a propaganda exercise, it was miscalculated, provoking a popular sense of defiance in revolutionary France. In turn, it triggered the French Declaration promising brotherhood and aid to all peoples wishing to 'recover their liberty' (19 November) and the determination (3 December) to commence the trial against Louis XVI. Pigott reasons here that after the execution of Louis XVI on 21 January 1793, Brunswick's threats must apply to all 'twenty-five million' Frenchmen. After some initial military successes, Brunswick's troops suffered defeat at the Battle of Valmy on 20 September 1792. It was seen as somewhat of a sensation that the untrained volunteers of republicans could defeat the Allied forces so decisively.

Brutality. *thief-takers*: Before an efficient police force was in place, semi-professional gangs operated in the metropolis, apprehending wanted felons and collecting the rewards. As the felons had often taken to crime out of poverty and their punishments were severe, thief-taking was not always considered an honourable career. The two Bow-Street Runners who arrested Thomas Hardy, the Secretary of the London Corresponding Society, were also thief-takers (Hardy, *Memoir ... written by himself* [James Ridgway, 1932], p. 31).

keepers and turnkeys of gaols: Prison officers were known for their brutality, often keeping prisoners in chains and under squalid and dirty conditions. As a result, many died of gaol fever (typhus). Prisons were run privately for profit, and gaolers turned their own rackets. Wealthy prisoners could thus buy themselves privileges, whereas poorer inmates were exposed to iniquitous treatment (see GARNISH). The brutality of imprisonment was used by the prison reformer John Howard (1726–1790) to pass the Gaol Distemper Act of 1774, which regulated the conduct of the gaolers and improved the conditions for the inmates. This was largely ignored, however.

FIVE SHILLINGS: Larceny from a house to the value of five shillings was a capital offence according to 39 Elizabeth c. 15, ss1 and 2 (Blackstone, *Commentaries*, 4, pp. 241–2). No child under seven could receive capital punishment, but in several instances children under fourteen were executed. Henry Fiennes Clinton, Duke of Newcastle (1720–94) was a Knight of the Garter with several sinecures. The Game Laws made it possible that a person sentenced for repeated offences became liable to transportation for seven years and, under special circumstances, fourteen years. A lord of the manor could bring a case of poaching before a local Justice of the Peace to have the offender fined and sentenced. But, after 1772, he could also choose a civil prosecution in a court of record (usually King's Bench or the Exchequer).

Lord Advocate Robert Dundas's speech on upholding the harsh transportation sentences of the Scottish martyrs Muir and Palmer (see ARGUMENT) was delivered to the Commons on 10 March 1794 (*PR 27*, pp. 520–26). Although it was considered somewhat distasteful, noblemen were known to frequent the *cockfighting* pits in Hewin Street, Hockcliffe, the Royal Cockpit in St James's Park and elsewhere around the capital.

Hunting was a popular royal pastime. At Richmond or Windsor, George III delighted usually once or twice a week in hunting until 1788. The royal chase included both the stag and the hare, but not foxes, which did not become generally accepted in the south of England before the nineteenth century (Ayling, *George III*, p. 183).

drayman: Usually a driver of a brewer's dray.

Earl of Darlington, William Henry Vane (1766–1842). In *Treachery, No Crime*, Pigott wrote in connection with a discussion on *inequality*: 'Earl of D—l—ng—t—n, born to millions, without talents or virtues whatever' (37n). Darlington had a seat in Parliament in the 1790s, but was better known as a sportsman who spared his animals no expenses when he went hunting. He also spent much time at the turf (*DNB*). Pigott appeals to a sentiment against heartless cruelty to animals, which was given increased attention in the eighteenth century. Writers often connected cruelty to animals with larger philanthropic issues of moral character, and, as part and parcel of educational literature, kindness to animals was used to teach social benevolence (Pickering, *John Locke*, pp. 3–39).

p. 8

Budget. On 9 January 1794, the Opposition paper the *Morning Chronicle* featured 'A short Account of the Rise and Press of the National Debt, with some remarks on the ruin that must inevitably succeed'. It commented that 'Mr Pitt took every advantage that all those favourable opportunities gave him, and loaded the people with such heavy, partial and grievous taxes that no Ministers ever before attempted even in times of war. His shoptax, fustian tax, his tax on the poor servant maids, the extention [*sic*] of excise laws, his commutation tax, and others equally obnoxious'. In *Jockey Club* II, Pigott wrote: 'Every addition to the revenue naturally produces an increase of influence of the C[row]n' (p. 23). The assumption here is that additional revenue gained from taxing the people is used to patronize with sinecures and pensions those young heirs of wealthy families who showed loyalty to the King.

Bully. Lord John Hervey (1757–97) was Envoy Extraordinary in Florence from 1787 to 1794. In *Female Jockey Club*, Pigott writes that he 'executed the mild equitable orders of his English masters, in bullying the grand Duke of T[us]c[a]ny and the G[o]v[ern]m[en]t of Fl[o]r[enc]e' (p. 25). The duchy of Tuscany, which remained neutral, was by Britain considered of importance in Mediterranean affairs, as its port was a natural outlet for supplies and transport of troops by sea if required. Lord

Hervey pressed Florence's Grand Duke Terriflori hard for an alliance, but the duchy contained a strong Francophile faction, and the presence of the French army in Savoy (taken on 27 November 1792) was strongly felt; the Duke therefore declined. Lord Hervey was told by Foreign Secretary Grenville in July to relax his diplomatic pressure (Ehrman, *Pitt*, 2, pp. 281). The correspondence between Hervey and Terriflori was printed in *Jordan*, 3:415–18. Also high on the list of British war priorities was an alliance with the neutral Switzerland. Not only did it occupy a place of great strategic importance, it was the home of some of the best-trained soldiers in Europe. In the last weeks leading up to the war, some of the cantons were approached to gauge their willingness to commit their troops against the French; but the country as a whole was too much under French influence to enter into an alliance. When Sardinian forces gained some ground in Savoy, some of the risk of a French invasion was removed, and Robert Fitzgerald, His Majesty's Minister in Berne, would in the summer of 1793 work hard to secure a deal. In September he was still optimistic, but later in the autumn, he was forced to admit that a deal was not imminent (Ehrman, *Pitt*, 2, p. 282). Fitzgerald's correspondence was published in *Jordan*, 5, p. 379, and 6, p. 96.

Burden. *Civil list:* See ABSURDITY.
   Standing army: See ARMY (STANDING).

Butchery. A reference to the Bristol Bridge Riot of 1793. When the townspeople were told the bridge tolls would not cease, as they had been promised the year before, a mob riot broke out during a few days in late September. The Herefordshire militia opened fire on the crowd, killing ten and wounding over fifty. The casualties were the largest since the anti-Catholic riots in London in 1780.

Candour. For Earl Moira, see APOSTATE. Pitt managed the British patronage system with great skill. During his time in office, he made several promotions and created a significant number of peers, 135 in total (Duffy, *Younger Pitt*, p. 109), which was criticized as a way of extending the influence of the Crown, as the recipients were expected to vote loyally with the King's Government. This bolstered the system he had himself attempted to reform in the early 1780s (see ASSOCIATION).

p. 9

Chancery. The court of highest judicature presided over by the Lord Chancellor. It was used when the Common Law courts failed to deal fairly and equitably with disputes between parties. Lord Loughborough had broken with the Whigs in 1792 and now voted with the Government. When Loughborough accepted the Chancery bench on 28 January 1793, he was the first of the Whig defectors to accept a ministerial office under Pitt.

Chaos. In his writing, Pigott refers several times to Montesquieu, in whose influential *Spirit of the Laws* (1748) the separation of powers was discussed. Reformers often invoked this work to explain how the necessary separation was not observed in Britain. Pigott may also be seen to rebut Burke, who had contrasted the 'order' of the British system of government with the 'strange chaos of levity and ferocity, and of all sorts of crimes jumbled together with all sorts of follies' introduced in France (*Reflections*, p. 92).

Charity. Due to disruptions on the world market in the early war years, there was a rise in poverty levels in Britain. Despite pleas from the Opposition, poor rates were not regulated. At the same time, huge amounts were paid to keep the war machine going: £8137 million in 1793 and £16837 million in 1794 (Mitchell and Deane [eds], *Abstract of British Historical Statistics*, Ch. 14, Table 2). Britain provided military assistance to the royalists who rebelled against the revolutionaries in Paris on several occasions: for example, Toulon, Brittany, Sardinia and so on.

Chastity. Queen Charlotte was conspicuously 'virtuous' in her abstinence from the carousing and revelry enjoyed by the royal princes and the cronies at the Court. The political commentator Anthony Pasquin wrote of her that 'she is benign – as a Christian meek, as a mother, affectionate – as a wife, chaste' (*A Cabinet of Miscellanies* [H. D. Symonds, 1795], pp. 61–6).

Church. The Church of England was a prop of the political order. It was expressed by Paine in *The Age of Reason* (1794–95), in which he charged the 'adulterous connection of church and state' and railed against the fact that 'religion is very improperly made a political machine'; this machine being 'the political church' (*Complete Writings*, 1, p. 451).

Citizen. The French-style republican address, which became common coin among British radicals, especially the members of the London Corresponding Society.

Clemency. In 1792 until the first half of 1794, the Government had successfully convicted radicals at the Court at the King's Bench for sedition, passing sentences of between two and four years. In Scotland, the Court of Justiciary passed harsh sentences of deportation (7–14 years) on charges of sedition.

Coalition. In January 1793, about twenty-five MPs, led on by Portland and Windham, deserted the Opposition to form a 'third party', which voted with the

Government. The former Whig Lord Loughborough accepted the office of Lord Chancellor the same month. In May 1794, Pitt established the Committee of Secrecy to monitor radical activities, which included several Whigs. Later, in July 1794, an expected coalition was negotiated. Defected Whigs took up another five out of thirteen Cabinet posts. The Foxite Whigs remained opposed to Pitt, but, as Pigott indicates here and elsewhere in *A Political Dictionary*, a real radical alternative party no longer existed. The anonymous author of *An Outline of the British Constitution; or, the Poor Man's Political Library* (T. Dolby, 1800) made the comparable observation that 'the Fox party and the Pitt party, are expected to grapple with each other as soon as Parliament meets; but we may be assured that neither of these parties will do any thing that shall effectually relieve the country, – it will be a mere quarrel about sharing the spoils' (p. 29).

p. 10

Cock (game). In the November 1793 issue of *Politics for the People* (pp. 102–7), Eaton printed the political allegory 'King Chaunticlere; or the Fate of Tyranny', by the radical lecturer John Thelwall. It was a fable about a game cock described as a 'haughty, sanguinary tyrant, nursed in blood and slaughter from his infancy, fond of foreign wars and domestic rebellions, into which he would sometimes drive his subjects'. The solution was to cut off his head. In the indictment, which Eaton published separately in 1793, the Prosecution had after each mention of the Cock inserted the sentence '… meaning our said Lord the King' to clarify that the allegory was seditious in referring to George III. At the trial, the celebrated lawyer of the radicals, Thomas Erskine, successfully argued that it was impossible to ascertain whether the allegory really did refer to George III, and Eaton was acquitted (see *Trial of Daniel Isaac Eaton* [Eaton, 1793]).

Company (East India). The East India Company held a virtual monopoly on trade in India and the Far East. Its officials made large profits, most often through accepting bribes and striking deals with local rulers at the expense of local populations. Besides the Company's commercial interests, it also helped to establish Britain's military and political authority on the subcontinent. The East India Company's ill-gotten gains were exposed in the lengthy trial of its General Governor Warren Hastings and in the accusations levelled at returned adventurers such as Francis Sykes (see FAMINE).

Confidence. In *Treachery no Crime*, Pigott complained that 'Nations, like armies, have ever been the wretched dupes of catchwords, thrown out by their leaders.' Of 'the terms at present in vogue', Pigott nominates 'CONFIDENCE' as 'that which rules with most absolute sway'. This word is invoked by ministers of the State with the intention to persuade the people to blindly trust the Government's 'standards of delusion'. With the 'sanction' of this 'magic auxiliary', Pitt 'calls forth his vassal to rally round his standard of delusion' and 'all enquiry is crushed; the spirit of reform is construed into treason' (pp. 41–2, 48). The immediate backdrop for Pigott's comments was the financial crisis that followed in the wake of the declaration of war. During the spring of 1793, trade disruptions led to 'stagnation in every species of commerce' (p. 151). The whole financial system threatened to collapse, but Pitt's economic rescue plan was successful in restoring investors' confidence, and the depression was avoided (see NOTES (BANK)). At a time when economic solidity meant social stability, the Government's confidence trick showed how much society relied on a question of mere belief.

Consequence. Pitt was First Lord of the Treasury and, while in power, his spending of public funds was used to uphold the present system of government.

full-dressed: An expression used to describe a formal parliamentary debate in which important speeches are delivered on each side of the House.

Consistency. Pigott had earlier been sympathetic to Fox, but had adopted a more radical Painite stance from the time he wrote *Jockey Club* III. In this, Fox was now seen to have shortcomings in terms of introducing needed reforms, and was dismissed as a 'lukewarm friend ... more hurtful to a cause than an open enemy' (p. 30n). In Ireland, Henry Grattan (1746–1820) was leader of the Irish 'Patriots', who in 1780 had given the Irish Parliament self-determinacy. Although Grattan had long been a staunch opponent of Pitt's Government, he did not oppose the war against France when a peace treaty was put to the vote in 1794. In 1793, he agreed to a proposed augmentation of the militia in Ireland. Grattan was also criticized for having received 'the immense sum of fifty thousand pounds from the very Government which he had so industriously maligned' (Pasquin, *Legislative Biography*, p. 34n)

Constitution. As Britain has no singular constitutional document defining the rights of citizens, it was largely left to the judges to develop legal practice in the country through the creation of precedents. Lord Lloyd Kenyon (1732–1801) (criticized in *Jockey Club* II, pp. 46–53) was Chief Justice of Court at the King's Bench and a supporter of Pitt in the House of Lords. Kenyon presided as judge in the trial of Paine on 18 December 1792 (see *The Trial at Large of Thomas Paine for a Libel in the Second Part of The Rights of Man* [J. Ridgway, 1792]), after which Paine was outlawed *in absentia*. William Henry Ashhurst (1734–99) was also judge at the King's Bench, and had presided in the Old Bailey on 24 February 1794 in the case against Eaton for publishing John Thelwall's political allegory 'King Chaunticlere' (see COCK (GAME)).

The ultra-loyalist Association for the Preservation of Liberty and Property against Republicans and Levellers (see ASSOCIATION) published Asshurst's *Charge to the Grand Jury for the County of Middlesex assembled in the Court of King's Bench, on Monday the 19th of November, 1792* as part of their anti-radical propaganda (see *Publications Printed at the Expence of The Society for Preserving Liberty and Property against Republicans and Levellers*, no. 1 [J. Sewell, 1793]). On 15 June 1792, Asshurst was given custody of the Great Seal after Lord Thurlow's dismissal, until Lord Loughborough took over on 28 January 1793.

Contractors. As part of the system of patronage, government officials signed contracts without allowing for competitive bidding. This gave the selected merchandisers a virtual monopoly on trade. A contractor was therefore a *creature of the minister* in being a dependant 'created' by his Government contract. In satirical representations, the London merchant Brook Watson (1735–1807) was satirized as one of those who profiteered from a war with France (*BMC*, 7676). In Cruickshank's caricature of 1791, he toasts to 'Monopoly' as a 'fine Rellish' (*BMC*, 7885). Watson had been Commissary to the British troops in America during the Seven Years War. He was a London ALDERMAN with a seat in Parliament since 1784, where he was a supporter of Pitt (Webster, *Brook Watson*). Government commissioners were by law prevented from sitting in Parliament, so when Watson was appointed Commissary-General to the Duke of York's army in Flanders on 2 March 1793, he had to resign his seat in the Commons. But with a fixed salary of £7 per day, Watson was generously compensated as the highest-paid official in the war administration (chart printed in *PR* 38, p. 233). Rumour had it that Watson made millions by securing deals that benefited the house of merchants in which he was himself involved. However, the painter Joseph Farington acquitted him for such crimes: 'Brook Watson declares he has not gained a shilling by acting as a contractor for the British army on the continent; he was so scrupulous as not to allow the agency of remitting money to be given to the mercantile house in London in which he is concerned by which with the most perfect honour £30 000 was to be gained' (*Diary*, 3, p. 103).

p. 11

Contrast. Pigott contrasts Paine's *Rights of Man* with Burke's *Reflections of the Revolution in France*, to which it was written as a reply. William Murray Mansfield (see 'Cast of Characters') was outspoken in favour of war. Lord Grenville had advocated British neutrality when the French Revolution broke out, but as soon as France declared war on Britain, he supported the Coalition of European powers. Their zeal for armed conflict made the anti-war Whig Earl of Stanhope their political opponent.

Corporation. Many cities and provincial towns were run as corporations, which the Crown, over time, had given much power and influence. They controlled parliamentary elections, regulated trades, markets and urban property, administered charity and levied rates. They acted as governing oligarchies with closed ranks. The London Court of Aldermen (see ALDERMAN) in particular was seen as urban despotism. Corporations were infamous for their maladministration and corruption.

Corruption. Arthur Young (1741–1820) was a prolific agricultural innovator and conservative, who, in his writing on farming, displayed little sympathy for the rustic poor. He was made Secretary of the new Board of Agriculture, which Pitt established in 1793. In *Female Jockey Club*, Pigott commented: 'Mr. Arthur Young, author of the *Farmer's Letters*, who formerly devoted his literary talents to the service of the people, now secretary to the newly appointed board of agriculture, and notoriously, a hireling apostate in the pay of administration' (p. 198n). There, Pigott also quotes 'the oil ... well' (p. 199). In *The Example of France, A Warning to Britain* (W. Richardson, 1793), Young answered the accusations that British Parliaments were not democratic because 'they are corrupt and bribed'. Young argues that this is justified if 'they are bribed in order to act wisely' and thereby 'make a happy people'. 'If the nature of such an assembly demands to be corrupted, in order to pursue the public good, who but a visionary can wish to remove corruption,' he proclaims. 'If corruption and influence have given a century of happiness to this kingdom, and if purity and patriotism can in four years so completely ruin an empire, as they have ruined our neighbour, I beg for one of the vices of England may govern me, and by no means the virtues of France' (pp. 67–8, 70).

Courtier. In *Treachery no Crime*, Pigott wrote: 'Courtiers are hired, bribed by the civil lists of princes, extorted from the *national purse*, to uphold exclusive privileges against *national rights*, to support the useless, scandalous prodigality of sinecures and pensions; draining the substance, the very vitals of kingdom borne down by nearly three hundred million of debt' (p. 3). The Duke of Montrose (1755–1836) was Master of the Horse in the King's Household from November 1790. Pigott criticized him for his meanness in *Jockey Club* II, pp. 14–15. For Lord Chesterfield, see FOOL. Thomas Bruce, Earl of Elgin (1766–1841) was his Majesty's Envoy Extraordinary at the Court of Brussels from 1792. He later became famous for removing the sculpture of the Parthenon from Athens to England (the 'Elgin Marbles'). Thomas Townshend, Viscount Sidney (1733–1800) was Clerk of the Household to the Prince of Wales between 1756 and 1760, first Clerk of the Green Cloth 1761–62, and had been Home Secretary 1782–83. In 1789, he exchanged his place in the Cabinet for a step in the peerage. His daughter was married to Chatham, Pitt's older brother. George Pitt, Baron Rivers (1722?–1803) had represented the King as envoy-extraordinary to Turin and Madrid, but was appointed a Lord of the Bedchamber from 1793. Thomas

Onslow (1754–1827), MP for Guilford, was appointed Out Ranger of Windsor Great Park in 1793. Before 1790, he was one of the Prince of Wales's cronies, but had since acrimoniously fallen out with him (see *Jockey Club* I, pp. 160–63).

Court. In the posthumously published *Political Thoughts and Reflections* (1750), Lord Halifax, George Savile, wrote: 'The Court may be said to be a company of well-bred fashionable beggars' (*Complete Works*, p. 211).

Cowardice. Rev. Vicesimus Knox (1752–1821) was a prolific writer, whose political writings had appeared in the pages of Eaton's *Politics for the People* (see, for example, 'On the Folly and Extravagance of War', 13 [1793], pp. 193–6, and 14 [1794], pp. 209–10). On Sunday 18 August 1793, Knox had preached a sermon at Brighton (at the time known as Brighthelmstone) on 'The Prospect of Perpetual and Universal Peace to be established on the Principles of Christian Philanthropy'. At this occasion, few men from the Surrey regiments quartered near Brighton had been present. When Knox, on the following Tuesday, took his wife and two children to the theatre, he was abused and harassed by several regiment men, who called him 'a democratical scoundrel that deserved to be hanged'. The incident was widely reported and discussed in the press. Many papers printed extracts from the sermon that were found offensive. The loyalist papers *The Sun* and the *True Briton* found his treatment justifiable, whereas many opposition papers printed scores of letters from outraged readers. An account of the incident was given by Knox himself in *A Narrative of Transactions relative to Dr Knox's Sermon* (C. Dilly, 1793).

p. 12

Crown. Paine had drawn attention to the chimerical power of deception that 'the crown' possessed for the people of Britain. The right to govern, he commented, resided 'in a metaphor shown at the Tower for sixpence or a shilling a piece', although this 'inanimate metaphor is no more than a hat or a cap' (*Rights of Man*, p. 128). Paine quotes the figure of £1 million for the King's Civil List several times in his *Letter Addressed to the Addressers* (1792). Due to the way it was granted, the exact figure is hard to estimate, but £1 million is a generous rounding up.

Cruelty. When Lord Alexander Hood (1726–1814) was forced to abandon the siege of Toulon on 18 December 1793, he gave orders that the enemy fleet be destroyed. Fourteen men-of-war were burnt and another eleven were put out of action (see Rose, *Lord Hood*, pp. 69–81). According to those involved, slaves held on the ships were freed first. Yet Hood became the object of a French smear campaign (see *A Letter* to *Admiral Lord Hood, on the cruelties exercised during his command at Toulon* [Paris: 23 brumaire of the second year of the Republic, 1794]).

La Vendee: On 11 March 1793, a riot against the Parisian government and local officials who supported the Republic was launched in the French town of La Vendée. The National Guard was lured into the depths of the Bocage forest and cut down to the last man. However, by the end of the year, the rebellion was quelled. The events at La Vendée marked the real beginning of civil war in France.

criminal laws: In the eighteenth century, there were an estimated 200 to 300 offences for which the death penalty could be imposed. Emanating from the Black Act of 1723, also known as 'the Bloody Code', the extent of capital punishment was continually widened. In *Treachery no Crime*, Pigott had criticized the 'draconian laws, that inflict death for very trivial offences'. These included 'letting fish out of a pond', 'cutting down an apple tree' and 'privately stealing five shillings' and so on, all of which 'have their origin in the vices of our political institutions' (p. 138).

Dagger. During the debate on the Alien Bill on 28 December 1792, news of the radical Dr William Maxwell's plan to export 3000 daggers to France was brought up. Burke shocked the Commons by flinging a dagger on the floor, exclaiming, 'There's French fraternity for you! Such is the weapon which French Jacobins would plunge into the heart of our beloved king' (*PH* 30, col. 189). Satirists joked on the episode a long time afterwards.

Damien. In 1757, Robert François Damiens (1714–57) had attempted to assassinate Louis XV (1710–74). Damiens was punished in a gruesome public spectacle. In *Rights of Man*, Paine asked: 'Who does not remember the execution of Damien, torn to pieces by horses? The effect of those cruel spectacles exhibited to the populace is to destroy tenderness or excite revenge; and by the base and false idea of governing men by terror, instead of reason, they become precedents' (p. 108) The torture had been narrated for an English audience in *A Particular and Authentic Narration of the Life, Examination, Torture and Execution of Robert Francis Damien* [*sic*], trans. Thomas Jones (J. Reason, 1757), see esp. pp. 16–17

p. 13

Death. This is possibly a retort to Burke, who in *Reflections on the Revolution in France* had set the lives of royalty above that of ordinary men, claiming that to the revolutionaries 'a king is but a man, a queen is but a woman; a woman is but an animal, and an animal not of the highest order'. He also thought that the French Revolutionaries were mistaken when they believed that the 'murder of a king, or a queen, or a bishop, or a father' was 'only common homicide' (p. 171). The

'Death-as-Leveller' *topos* from Ecclesiastes was given visual representation in *The Dance of Death*, a series of prints traditionally attributed to Holbein. In these, a personified Death is seen leading everyone – the whole clerical hierarchy, kings, dukes, robbers and peasants – to their common destiny; Death does not care for social position. The radical collector Francis Douce edited these in 1794 with engravings by W. Hollar (on Douce's politicization of the theme, see Butler, 'Antiquarianism', p. 35.) The Dance of Death prints had appeared earlier in a version produced by Thomas Bewick with the title *Emblems of Mortality* (T. Hodgson, 1789).

Debauchery. *Carlton-House* was the Prince of Wales's residence from 1781. After renovations at a cost of £800 000, it was the most palatial mansion of the day. It was the scene of his many parties and drinking binges. The Prince also leased the country residence *Kempshott*, near Basingstoke, as a shooting box from 1788. This became particularly notorious as a place where the Prince caroused with his cronies. The Duke of York, who failed his military mission at Dunkirk, was infamous for his licentiousness. In the press, he was connected to several courtesans, such as Mary Ann Clark, Kitty Fisher and Letty Smith. In this imitation of a stage direction for a pantomime (like the ones the royals enjoyed watching in Covent Garden), the Duke is seen at the brothel of Mother Weston, Berkeley Street. Prostitutes at this time were frequently pickpockets, and made a profit from selling valuables taken from clients who were stupefied with drink or had been beaten up. In *Jockey Club* I, Pigott mentions the Duke of York's 'pretty frequent relaxation amongst the nymphs of Berk[e]ley Row' (p. 15). *Nymph* was a Georgian euphemism for a prostitute, and *Berkeley* denominated the profession (De Barri, *Bucks and Bawds*, pp. 114–15). Berkeley Square is also a place in London, and it was a well-known story that the Duke and the Prince of Wales had been robbed while walking here (White, *Age of Scandal*, pp. 134–5). The Duke of York was particularly unlucky, and in 1788 he had his pocket picked twice within a week (*Morning Chronicle*, 13 March). A double-edged attack on the Duke of York's lack of military ability and his wanton debauchery can be found in the anonymous *The Duke of York: A Letter to His Royal Highness, or A Delicate Inquiry into the Doubt whether He be more Favoured by Mars or Venus* (James Piper, 1807).

p. 14

Debt (National). *Philosopher* was commonly used for a writer on political theory.

Degeneracy. Cf. Paine: '[A]ristocracy has a tendency to degenerate the human species ... it is known ... that the human species has a tendency to degenerate, in any small number of persons, when seperated from the general stock of society, and intermarrying constantly with each other' (*Rights of Man*, p. 135).

Democrat. *The Spirit of the Laws* (1748) by Charles de Secondat, Baron de Montesquieu (1689–1755) was a standard work of reference for reformers in Britain. Chapter 3 begins with the assertion that 'There is no great share of probity necessary to support a monarchical or despotic government'; whereas in a democracy one thing is 'necessary, namely, *virtue*' (2 vols, 6th edn [Dublin: W. McKenzie and J. Moore, 1792], 1, p. 19).

Discontent (popular). The Royal Proclamations against seditious correspondence of May and December 1792 initiated the Government's persecution of radicals. In May 1793, the booksellers H. D. Symonds and James Ridgway had received sentences of two years' imprisonment for publishing the second part of Paine's *Rights of Man*. The same month, the lawyer John Frost was placed in the pillory and sentenced to six months' imprisonment for sedition.

'*When popular* ... *Government*': A citation from Burke's criticism of constitutional corruption *Thoughts on the Cause of Present Discontents* from 1770 (*Works*, 2, p. 224).

p. 15

Disappointment. Only a fortnight after the siege of Dunkirk had begun, the Duke of York was forced to retreat (8 September 1793). Much heavy artillery, including 32 siege guns, was left behind (cf. HASTE and ADVANTAGE).

recovery of King George III: The King's return to mental stability in February 1789 crushed the Opposition's hopes of a change in government. It was a major disappointment for the Foxite Whigs, who had hoped to get into power with the support of the Prince of Wales acting as Regent.

Disinterestedness. The word was used positively of those politicians who acted out a concern for the welfare of the country rather than for personal gains. Pigott is thus wholly ironic here. Lord Grenville was Secretary of State with an earning of £10 000 a year. He was also Remembrancer of the Exchequer in Ireland, a place for life that earned him a salary of £3000 a year (Pasquin, *Legislative Biography*, 1795], p. 16). Lord Loughborough became Chief Justice of the Court of Common Pleas in 1780. He was the first of the Whig grandees to defect to the Pitt Ministry, taking the seal as Lord Chancellor on 19 January 1793. The jurisdiction in bankruptcy cases had passed to the Lord Chancellor by an Act of 1732. Fees for such offices were based on the volume of business that passed through it; so when business skyrocketed, official income rose to preposterous heights. The number of failed businesses in 1793 was a record high (see BANKRUPTCY). Pigott also criticized Loughborough's income from commissions of bankruptcy in *Treachery no Crime* (p. 146n).

Dissimulation. *'a jewel in the crown'*: From the 'Conclusion' of Lord Halifax's (George Savile) defamatory manuscript *A Character of King Charles the Second*, published posthumously in 1750 (*Complete Works*, p. 266).

p. 16

Divinity. In the House of Lords, 26 seats were allocated to the Lords Spiritual (two Archbishops, 24 Diocesan Bishops). As official representatives of the Church of England, they were expected to vote with the Government, and thus, in support of the war with France.

Drunkenness. Pitt was known to take bottles of port with Dundas, and he showed up noticeably drunk in Parliament at least once (Ehrman, *Pitt*, 1, pp. 585–6). The Opposition paper the *Morning Chronicle* published a series of *Epigrammata Bacchanalia* by Richard Porson, an eccentric professor of Greek at Cambridge. In one of these, Pitt and Dundas appear in Parliament: 'In what odd ways we taste misfortune's cup – / While France throws down the gauntlet, Pitt throws up. / Pitt: I can't discern the Speaker, Hal: can you? / Dundas: Not see the Speaker! Damn me, I see two' (quoted in Wardroper, *Kings, Lords and Wicked Libellers*, p. 155). The Prince of Wales's Pavilion in *Brighton* (rented from 1783) was often the place of entertainment. *Holwood* in Kent was Pitt's Country residence, which together with the official London residence in *Downing Street* and *Wimbledon*, where Dundas had his house, the two ministers were believed to carouse. *Gordon House* refers to the residence in Pall Mall of the lively Duchess of Gordon, who was Pitt's hostess and drinking partner on many an occasion (Ehrman, *Pitt*, 1, pp. 454n, 583). Pigott refers to her in *Female Jockey Club* as a 'buxom Caledonian dame' very much like 'Baccahants described by the ancients ... known to thaw the frost off P[it] t' (pp. 49–50). Charles Howard, Duke of Norfolk (1746–1815), was an egalitarian Whig famous for his eating and drinking habits and his numerous sexual escapades. He was nicknamed the 'Royal Duke' perhaps because he was so often 'royally' intoxicated (Hill, *Satirical Etchings*, pp. 102–3). The 'Royal Sovereign' was a courtesan of which he was especially fond. In the print *Le Cochon et set Deux petit – or – rich pickings for a noble appetite* (1792), Gillray represented the Duke with the 'Royal Sovereign ... Nell H—t—n' (*BMC*, 8159). Pigott surmised that the lady received her appellation presumably because she 'has long held this illustrious Peer [the 'royal duke'] in her chains' (*Jockey Club* II, p. 6).

   Common gin: Gin was considered a drink of the lower orders, rarely indulged in by the gentleman.

Dullness. The significance of the theatre as a stage for politics was widely recognized. Theatre managers such as Thomas Harris at the Royal Theatre in Covent Garden maintained close links with the Government, and his theatre was identified as a Tory house. The playwrights were often loyalists, and the plays themselves were at times littered with political commentary (Werkmeister, *London Daily Press*, pp. 70–71). George III, who was known to have a notoriously dull taste, was a frequent visitor to the theatre, which made it an important site for the expression of monarchical authority. The singing of *God Save the King* was a regular part of the ceremony of visiting the Royal Theatre (see Pigott's entry on *Theatre II – Dramatic*). Edward Jerningham (1727–1812) was a poet and dramatist, whose play *The Siege of Berwick, a Tragedy* opened in Covent Garden on 13 December 1793, but only ran five more nights. Eglatine Wallace (d. 1803) had a series of disappointments. Her *The Ton: a Comedy* was produced at Covent Garden on 8 April 1788, and was described as 'very dull' and a dead failure (*DNB*). In *Female Jockey Club*, Pigott tells us that her latest 'comedy … met with a most tragic end' (p. 135). Mary Robinson (1758–1800) was a successful actress, esteemed for her beauty, when the Prince of Wales took her as his mistress in 1779. She portrayed many of Shakespeare's female characters in plays performed at Drury Lane between 1776 and 1780. The Prince knew her as Perdita, having first seen her in *The Winter's Tale*. The subscription list for her collection of *Poems* (1791) was headed by the Prince of Wales, and included many other members of the nobility. She published the bestselling novels *Vancenza, or the Dangers of Credulity* (1792) and *The Widow* (1794). They owed part of their popularity to the rumour that they contained autobiographical elements. Antoine Le Texier entertained society London with his 'readings' of fashionable French plays at his house in Lisle Street. The texts he used were published in *Recueil des Pièces de Théatre lues par Mr. Le Texier, en sa maison Lisle Street, Leicester Fields*, 8 vols (London, T. Hookham, 1785–87). All of the above were, in one way or another, given royal patronage.

fashionable routs: The 'rout' was a popular form of social gathering in high society homes, where a large number of gentlemen and ladies were invited for drinks and refreshments.

Dunce. For Grenville and Steele, see 'Cast of Characters'. John Fenton Cawthorne (1753–1831) was a Colonel in the Westminster Regiment and the Middlesex Militia 1791–96. He deserted Fox in 1784 to support Pitt. In the 1790s, he voted for all the Government's bills to contain radicalism. It was rumoured that it was because of a commercial interest in the slaving port of Lancaster that he became an inflexible opponent of abolition of the slave trade in Parliament.

Effeminacy. The character of French males was often depicted as effeminate for their all-too-keen interest in clothes and grooming. It was a popular belief that the spread of foppish vanity among young men in Britain took its influence from France and degenerated the manly character of the nation. The criticism is here aimed at 'new Whigs' such as Fox and Sheridan, who indulged in the joys of the theatre and society life rather than living up to their duty as political 'descendents' of the seventeenth-century Whigs, who risked their life to resist monarchical encroachments. John Hampden (1653–96) was imprisoned in the Tower in 1685 after the Monmouth rebellion to overthrow the Catholic James II. He was later pardoned. Algernon Sidney (1622–83) was a conspirator in the Rye House Plot of 1681 to assassinate Charles II (in order to prevent the Catholic succession of James II) and was beheaded. Eaton published several of his works. William Russell (1639–83) was also tried for High Treason against Charles II, and was beheaded. These founders of the Whig party were often invoked as heroes for their defence of Parliamentary power and the struggle to limit the King's influence; see, for example, *Speech of the Rt. Hon. C.J. Fox ... Spoken at the Whig Club* (James Ridgway, 1792).

Fop's Alley: The passage between the tiers of benches, right and left in the Royal Opera House in Covent Garden.

p. 17

Emigrant (English). Like many other radicals, the famous dissenting preacher, Joseph Priestley (1733–1804), who led the campaign for the repeal of the Test and Corporations Acts, left Britain on 7 April 1794 to settle in America. The political environment that prompted his departure is described in William Cobbett's *Observations on the Emigration of Dr. Joseph Priestley* (John Stockdale, 1794). His friend, Thomas Cooper (1759–1840), who had affiliated with the Girondist faction in France and publicly criticized Burke and the Pitt's Ministry, followed soon after. However, their plan to set up a community in Susquehanna, Pennsylvania, stranded.

UNTAXED: The American colonies' struggle for independence was sparked by the dissatisfaction with being taxed without having right of representation in the British Parliament. Pigott himself had planned to flee the country for neutral Switzerland with the radical Robert Merry some time in September 1793 (Mee, 'bold and free-spoken').

p. 18

Emigrant (French). Many of noble birth had fled France at the beginning of the Revolution. From June 1791 émigré troops began to be formed, notably under Artois at Coblenz. Émigré forces also participated (albeit feebly and from the rear) in the Allied invasion of France in April 1792. In the autumn of 1792, following the prison massacres, the flow of French emigrants reached England in numbers as many as 4000 (*AR* 1792, Chronicle, p. 39). On 17 April 1794, a bill was passed in the Commons for taking the French royalists who had formed Emigrant Corps into British pay.

p. 19

Enemy (natural). Since the wars with Louis XIV in the late seventeenth century, France had become installed in British political consciousness as a 'natural enemy'. The two nations constantly fought over markets and colonial possession. When Britain was not at war with France (as it was 1702–13, 1740–48, 1756–63 and 1778–83), it was a primary objective to curb French diplomatic supremacy in Europe as well as sustain superiority in the overseas colonies.

gang of plunderers and monopolizers: Cf. *Politics for the People*, in which Eaton included a satirical piece qualifying that rather than the French republicans, 'Our only natural enemies' are the 'allies of the house of Bourbon; fraudulent contractors, useless, placemen, unworthy pensioners' in the British administration. These were 'the fatal troops which have baffled the force of this kingdom' (2 [1794], p. 5).

Enquiry. The *Magna Charta* was imposed by rebellious barons on King John in 1215, and limited the extent to which the king could rule. The Bill of Rights was granted by William III and Mary in 1689, and insisted on the 'the right of subjects to petition the king', and highlighted James II's abuses of the royal prerogative. The Bill received statutory recognition in the Act of Settlement of 1701.

Botany Bay: See ARGUMENT.

p. 20

Enterprize. The 1793–94 campaign against the French on the Continent was a badly managed affair. The many offensives ended in failure. It was only with the victory on the Glorious First of June 1794 that British fortune turned. The Government tried to make the most of the war on the European Continent by employing a large part of its army in the West Indies to take possession of the vulnerable French colonies there. The reallocation of resources to the West Indies was what compromised Earl Moira's planned mission to launch an attack on Brittany in 1793. Moira was persuaded to be content with something over one hundred gunners, which was half of what he had asked for. Furthermore, the guns he was promised never arrived (Fortesque, *History*, 4, pp. 154–5).

Equality. Paine was the leading exponent of the doctrine of *natural rights* as the basis of political rights in civil society. The argument for *natural rights* projected an original, primitive state of nature as an actual historical experience, in which man had enjoyed liberty and equality. It was inspired by John Locke, who received much attention among reformers furthering constitutional change at the end of the eighteenth century.

p. 21

Extermination. The reference here is to the manifesto issued by the Duke of Brunswick (see BRUNSWICK), but Burke had also become associated with the term. In a debate in the Commons of 17 April 1794, Burke had proclaimed that 'The war must be directed to … the entire destruction of the desperate horde that gave it birth' (*PH* 31, col. 427). The radical pamphleteer William Fox wrote in *On Peace* (M. Gurney, 1794): 'Mr. Burke labours with ardour to impress on us the laudable propose of exterminating our enemy' (p. 1). In *Female Jockey Club*, Pigott referred to Pitt as the 'corrupt profligate minister, destitute of merit or humility … swearing never to sheath the sword of war, till France be exterminated or her liberty conquered' (p. 197).

'Ye gods … works!': From Shakespeare's *Julius Caesar*, III, i, 276. These are the words of Antony, Caesar's friend, who stirs the people to react against the conspirators behind the murder of the Emperor.

Faction. Faction was an emotive word. Political theory held that Parliament should serve the well-being of the whole country, and that any party 'interests' were therefore ruinous to the common cause. This is what is behind the staunch Tory Samuel Johnson's rather perfunctory dismissal of the Whigs as 'The name of a faction' in his *Dictionary*.

popular societies: The many reformist groups, including the corresponding societies, which had mushroomed throughout Britain and Ireland from the spring of 1792. The threat of '*STRIKING*' against Pitt seems to refer to intelligence presented in the report delivered by the Committee of Secrecy, and discussed in Parliament on 6 June 1794, that some radical societies were arming for a revolution (see RAPIER).

FREE UNBOUGHT suffrages: See VENDIBLE.

p. 24

Fame. The erection of memorials for British war heroes was suggested to Parliament several times, for instance by Pitt's right-hand man Curtis Lewes on 17 June 1793 (*PR* 25, p. 652). For *Hampden* and *Sidney*, see EFFIMINACY. The poet and republican John

Milton (1608–74) had argued in *The Tenure of Kings and Magistrates* (1649) that people 'free by nature' had a right to depose and punish a tyrant. Milton was appointed Latin secretary to the Council of State established after the beheading of Charles I. Even on the eve of the Restoration, he defended the cause of republicanism in his writing. For this, he had to go into hiding, was arrested, fined and finally released. The words censored in the text are 'Judges', 'Magistrate' and 'downfall'.

p. 28

Famine. *exclusive charters and monopolies*: These were attacked by Paine in *Rights of Man* as instruments perpetuating tyrannical government since the Norman conquest: 'Every chartered town is an aristocratical monopoly in itself.' Granting monopoly of trade to individuals or corporation towns was seen as monarchical bribery used to establish a hierarchical system of rule (pp. 125–6; see also pp. 274–6).

Calcutta: The Bengal Famine of 1769–70 had, according to the impeached Governor of Bengal, Warren Hastings, decimated the population by 'at least one-third' (Letter to the Court of Directors, 3.1.1772, in Hunter [ed.], *Annals of Rural Bengal*, ann. 34, 381, Appendix A). The drought dried up the valley of the Ganges. It was rumoured that the East India Company's servants had created the famine by engrossing all the rice available and selling it for up to twelve times the price at which they had bought it (Sur, *History*, p. 178). Francis William Sykes (1732–1804) joined the East India Company as a writer. He became a close friend to Warren Hastings, and was caught up in the upheaval in Bengal. By successful trading and commission on taxes, he gained great wealth, which he used to establish a dominant interest in the venal borough of Wallingford for which he was elected to Parliament. Sykes was made baronet in 1781.

otium cum dignitate: Usually translated 'ease with dignity'.

heaven-born minister: See HEAVEN-BORN.

just and religious war: See HOLY.

sagacious writer: Paine, who, in *Common Sense* (1776), wrote: 'In the early ages of the world, according to the scripture chronology there were no kings; the consequence of which was, there were no wars; it is the pride of kings which throws mankind into confusion' (p. 11).

p. 31

Fashion. *cant word*: In his *Dictionary*, Samuel Johnson defined *cant* as fashionable diction 'in a great measure casual and mutable' consisting of terms 'formed for some temporary or local convenience'. Johnson disparages *cant* for its flimsiness, 'always in a state of increase or decay', for which reason it 'must be suffered to perish with other things unworthy of preservation' ('Introduction', viii).

excesses of the table: Already as a young man, the increasingly corpulent Prince of Wales (later satirically dubbed 'Prince of Whales') was known for his love of food.

parade of great military talents: The Duke of York had received military training with his uncle, the Duke of Brunswick. He had requested of his father, George III, to be given command of the troops engaged against the French. The Government was against his appointment, but eventually agreed to the King's wishes, and the Duke was assigned command of the land troops on the Continent.

p. 32

Fast (by proclamation). George III proclaimed an annual Day of Fast on which the nation should atone for their sins and thereby appeal to God for help in victory over the French. In 1794, the Fast Day was 28 February.

p. 34

Festival. The revolutionary festivals in France were commissioned to the famous painter Jacques-Louis David (1748–1825).

Jordan's Political State of Europe: A periodical on foreign affairs published by the Fleet Street bookseller Jeremiah S. Jordan, who had attained notoriety for publishing Paine's *Rights of Man*. Cf. TREE OF LIBERTY.

GENIUS: The word is used in the eighteenth-century sense of 'distinctive character or spirit'.

escutcheon: The shield on which a coat of arms is depicted.

PAGOD: A heathen idol.

Joseph Gerrald (1763–1796) was a member of the London Corresponding Society and elected as one of the English delegates to attend the Edinburgh Convention for radical societies in Britain. Spies had infiltrated the meeting, and Gerrald was arrested on 2 December 1793 with Maurice Margarot and William Skirving, and charged with sedition. At his trial on 10 March, Lord Braxfield sentenced Gerrald to fourteen years' transportation.

p. 36

Financier. One of Pitt's ministerial offices was Chancellor of the Exchequer.

frog in the fable: Aesop's 'The Frogs who Wished for a King', about the gods giving the frogs a rock and log to satisfy their want for a king.

confidential and experienced friend: Probably a reference to Pitt's mentor Henry Dundas, who had been in Parliament since 1774 and was often believed to mastermind the Government's economic policies.

p. 37

Flat. *flat*: 'A bubble, gull, or silly fellow' (Grose).

flash: 'Flash Lingo. The canting or slang language' (Grose).

Mr. Montague's speech: On 9 April 1794, the Opposition paper *The Morning Post* reported that John Harrison, the MP for Great Grimsby, who often acted with the Whigs, moved that those who enjoyed sinecures of more than £200 and salaries over £500 a year should resign a fourth of their emoluments while the war lasted, since they were the very men who had 'plunged their country into a War'. Matthew Montague, the MP for Tegony (known as a worshipper of Pitt) 'thought the present motion of a dangerous tendency, as it went to confirm that opinion which had been so much endeavoured to be promulgated in the various seditious publications which had gone forth to the People'. He then 'entered into an eulogium of the talents and great exertions of the Minister (Mr Pitt), for which he thought no sum of money, however great, was an adequate compensation'.

p. 38

Flattery. A citation from Pigott's pamphlet *Treachery no Crime*. Caius Maecenas (d. 8 BC) was a Roman statesman and patron of letters. He became a trusted adviser of Augustus (Octavian, the first Roman emperor), whom he represented on several political missions. His name has come to symbolize a generous patron of the art, as he devoted his later years to the circle around Horace, Virgil and Propertius. Nicolas Boileau (1636–1711) was a French poet and literary critic. His first publications (1660–1666) were satires, but in 1675 he was given a pension by Louis XIV, and two years later he was appointed, along with Racine, official royal historian

p. 39

Fool. George III was fond of the actor John Quick (1748–1831), who played many clowns, comic servants and rustics during his long engagement at the Royal Theatre in Covent Garden. Quick was appreciated by George III so much that he ordered a 'comical pantomime' in which the actor appeared to be 'repeated no less than six times' (*Female Jockey Club*, p. 123). The King also ordered from Zoffany a painting of Quick as Arable in *Speculation*. The Earl of Chesterfield, Philip Stanhope (1755–1815), spent much time with George III at the royal holiday residence in Weymouth. In *Jockey Club* I, Pigott described Chesterfield as a courtier who 'provides food for laughter to the merry facetious humour of the King' (p. 169). It was undoubtedly his connections that secured Chesterfield appointments as Ambassador Extraordinary and Minister Plenipotentiary to Madrid in 1784 (he never went) and a place on the Privy Council. He was appointed master of the Mint (1789–90) and was joint Postmaster-General from 1790.

Fortune. Pitt, Pigott suggests, has taken over the role of Fortuna, the Roman goddess who was believed to determine the fate of men. The joke is that the Prime Minister collects a 'fortune' in state revenue from taxing the people. The idea of speaking of the taxpaying public as votaries of a heathen idol probably takes its cue from Paine's address to the people of Britain against blindly paying for a corrupt monarchical system: 'We can all see the absurdity of worshipping Aaron's molten calf, or Nebuchadnezzar's golden image; but why do men continue to practise themselves the absurdities they despise in others?' (*Rights of Man*, p. 128).

p. 40

Fulsome. A term for causing nausea or exciting aversion or repugnance (*OED*). The expression was used by Burke, who commented on Richard Price's sermon to the Revolution Society on 4 November 1789 (published that year as *Discourse on the Love of Our Country*) that it was spoken in a 'fulsome style' (*Reflections*, 114). It was Price's sermon that made him write *Reflections on the Revolution in France* as an invective against the events in France and reformist ideas in Britain. His dismissive stance on France and reform had meant a break with Fox, his old friend and political ally. The public break took place during a debate in Parliament in May 1791. It was widely reported in the contemporary press as a having been a scene with much pathos. Although Fox saw his close friend defect to support the old arch-enemy Pitt, he maintained a remarkably respectful attitude when their views clashed in Parliament.

p. 41

Gaming. Gambling was generally frowned upon by moral writers and reformers. The great commentator on the laws of Britain, Sir William Blackstone, commented: 'Taken in any light, it is an offence of the most alarming nature; tending by necessary consequence to promote public idleness, theft, and debauchery among those of a lower class; and, among persons of a superior rank, it hath frequently been attended with a sudden ruin and desolation of ancient and opulent families ... and too often had ended in self murder' (*Commentaries*, 4, p. 170). In January of 1794, *The Morning Chronicle* advertised Pigott's edition of Edmond Hoyle's book on various games: *New Hoyle; or the General Repository of Games. To which is added, an Epitome of the Statute Laws on Gaming, with the different cases of Contested Betts, Bonds, and Other Securities, which have been Legally Argued and Determined* (James Ridgway). In this, it was pointed out that common gaming houses were illegal (p. 208); yet, the upper classes gambled openly in clubs. The royals played tennis in St James's Street, whereas *skittle* (bowling for a piece of wood) was the pastime of the common Londoner.

one stroke ... 50,000l: Pitt used the State Lottery, which had been running since 1569, as a means of funding Government expenditure. From selling tickets, the Treasury cashed the money free of interest until the prizes were paid. On 8 April 1794, Pitt could report that the usual profit was estimated at £265000 a year for the last eight years (*PH* 31, 184). The Lottery was discussed in Parliament several times during the early 1790s. The Opposition was against it on social grounds. As the chances of winning were slim, the poor who bet only increased their chance of ending up in the poorhouse. The State Lottery was not abolished before 1826, tellingly, through the efforts of Pitt's close ally William Wilberforce, who turned his attention to it after the abolition of the slave trade. In *Politics for the People*, Eaton included the following lines: 'Trick'd by a million Lottery; / Where for one thousand that get plumbs, / Forty-nine thousand suck their thumbs' (3 [1794], p. 101). Pitt seems not to have had any moral scruples about the State Lottery; at any rate, he promoted it as an efficient way of increasing the State revenue and defeated a bill to stop it in 1792.

adventurer: Name used for one who bought a lottery ticket.

50.000l: This was the prize fund total to be won from the draw that took place on 17 February 1794.

'*On commence ... Fripon*': Lines from the poem *Reflexion sur le Jeu* by the French courtier poet Eustache Deschamps (*c.* 1320–1400), who is known for his condemnations of injustices and wrongs.

p. 42

Garnish. Prisons were privately run, and prisoners had to pay fees to the other inmates and the guards on entrance, before release, and for many privileges while incarcerated. Though gaolers' fees were abolished with the 1774 Gaol Act, gaolers tended to ignore these new measures, and sufficient bribery could ease imprisonment significantly.

courts of law: It was well known, as Pigott makes clear in several places, that many of the juries that found radicals guilty of sedition were 'packed', making the verdict a foregone conclusion. In the case of Muir (see ARGUMENT), for example, the jury was allegedly hand-picked from the loyalist Goldsmith's Hall in Edinburgh (*Morning Chronicle*, 11 March 1794).

polite and immaculate court: The impeached Governor of British India, Warren Hastings, was accused of bribery and there was a rumour that Queen Charlotte had taken a bribe in form of diamonds, by which Hastings should have secured royal protection of the East India Company's dishonest dealings. The allegation was the background for the satirical cartoon entitled *The Queen of Hearts Cover'd with Diamonds* (c. 1786) (*BMC*, 6978). Queen Charlotte was in turn accused of conspiring with Pitt for constitutional power during George III's illness in 1788. Madame Schwellenbergen was the Queen's favourite lady-in-waiting, who was believed also to be vying for influence through Charlotte's increased influence during the King's absence. See, for example, Rowlandson's caricature *The Prospect before Us* (1788) (*BMC*, 7383). Loughborough was the Whig Lord who was seen by some to have accepted a 'bribe' from Pitt in form of the GARTER in 1792. Shortly afterwards, in early 1793, Loughborough took office in the Ministry. This was a turn from having played a role during the Regency crisis of 1788–89, when he was among the faction of 'New Whigs' which was to constitute the Prince of Wales's government to replace that of Pitt had the King not recovered. Dundas is probably included for his role as Home Secretary, preparing the prosecution of the radicals, furnishing the trials with bribed jury members.

p. 43

Garter (order of the). Knight of the Garter was the finest order to be bestowed upon an individual by the King of Britain. There were 26 Knights, including the Sovereign and all his sons. The ceremony took place in St George's Chapel, Windsor Castle, where the insignia of the Order were placed upon the knight by the monarch. These included a garter of blue velvet and a deep-blue riband over the left shoulder.

Government. *'That government ... matter'*: This is not from the source given, but from Burke's *Letter from Mr. Burke to the Sheriffs of Bristol, on the Affairs of America* (1777) (*Works*, 3, p. 183).

GENTRY refusing ... war: See FLAT.

history of our civil list: The reformer John Sinclair published tables of the development in Civil List allotments and other State expenditures from the very earliest time to the present reign of George III in *The History of the Public Revenue of the British Empire* (1785). This became a hugely popular work, and figures were brought up to date in the second edition of 1790 (A. Strahan). It was these figures Paine relied on in the second part of *Rights of Man*, for which he and his publishers were prosecuted. Here we also find reference to the maxim 'kings can do no wrong' (191). Samuel von Pufendorf (1632–94) was a German philosopher of social contract law. The citations given are from his work, *The Law of Nature and Nations: or, a General System of the Most important Principle of the Morality, Jurisprudence, and Politics*, trans. Mr. *Carwe*, 5th edn (J. Bonwicke et al., 1749). The first quote on p. 46 is wrongly referenced and should be Book IV, Ch. ii, art. 13. It is taken from a section entitled 'Of an Oath', on how a promise is 'not always to be interpreted strictly'. The following sentiment, 'Let the good … law', refers to the chapter 'Of the Different Forms of Government' (pp. 665–87).

PRIVY COUNSELLORS: The private advisors selected by the King. In the 1790s, this was the body which undertook the interrogation of radicals suspected of Treason.

Aristides into banishment: Aristides was the statesman with the appellation 'the Just' who was ostracized from Athens by ballot in 482 BC. However, three years later, the Athenians realized their mistake and called Aristides back.

condemned Phocion and Socrates to death: Phocion (402–318 BC), the Athenian general forced by the Athenian democracy to drink hemlock. The same sentence was passed earlier on the philosopher Socrates (469–399 BC) by an Athenian Jury.

p. 49

Gown. *Rook*: 'A cheat: probably from the thievish disposition of the birds of that name' (Grose). In the context of lawyers discussed here, Pigott is probably playing on the name of Judge Giles Rook, who sentenced the dissenting minister William Winterbotham to a large fine and four years imprisonment at Exeter assizes in July 1793. Winterbotham's crime was to have preached two seditious sermons on 5 and 18 November the year before. The prosecutor particularly focused on the statement that there was no divine right of kings. Rook instructed the jury that Winterbotham had conscious intent of provoking revolutionary fervour when delivering his sermons to some of the lowest class of people (*State Trials*, 22, pp. 823–7, 869–76). Rook was knighted the same year.

Grace. The ladies listed here were all ladies known for their vanity. There are Queen Charlotte and her daughters, the six princesses: Charlotte, Augusta, Elizabeth, Mary, Sophia and Amelia (see *Female Jockey Club*, pp. 1–10). There is Elizabeth Farren, a comic actress, whose 'unnatural contortions' may include the alleged lesbian relationship she had with the sculptor Mrs Damer (see STATUE). The Duchess of Rutland (see *Female Jockey Club*, pp. 27–35), took a lover several years younger than herself in the first year of her widowhood. Leeds, who as a Duke should properly be addressed 'His Grace', was an active supporter of old corruption in Parliament. He was invested with Knight of the Garter on 15 December 1790, but as he was fired from his post as Foreign Secretary the year after, it was never installed.

p. 50

Gratis. This word was habitually used to head advertisements in newspapers. Already in September 1793, the British Government was warned that the Prussian troops would be withdrawn from Flanders unless Frederick William II received acknowledgement of his recent Polish acquisitions and an allied subsidy for the 1794 campaigns. Anxious not to lose their military support, a treaty with Prussia was signed by Britain and Holland on 19 April 1794. Prussia had to supply 62 500 mercenary troops to the Coalition. A sum of £300 000 was paid as preparation money, and £100 000 on the return of the troops. In addition, just under £100 000 would be paid for the upkeep of the Prussian army (Ehrman, *Pitt*, 2, p. 337). Prussia signed a separate peace treaty with France in 1795, which meant that the First Coalition was rendered ineffective.

Grave. The campaigns in Flanders resulted in many casualties, not least of which can be attributed to the disease caught by soldiers in the wet and cold trenches during the harsh Continental winter. In the West Indies, the British campaign also cost many lives, totalling somewhere in the region of 40 000, with an equal number of sick.

Greedy. George Rose (1744–1818) was a good friend of George III, and as joint Secretary of the Treasury, he was responsible for the system of patronage. In *Jockey Club* III, Pigott wrote: 'We are told that Mr. R—se is a burthen upon the nation' and, from 'the monopoly of different sinecures and places' collects an 'amount of fourteen thousand pounds annually' (p. 65). Pigott adjusts the amount upwardly here. Rose was regularly attacked in the Commons and the popular press for his multiple sinecures. During a debate on 8 April 1794 on a motion for taxing Placemen and Pensioners during the continuance of the war, Rose was humiliated by being forced to list his sinecures. This included Clerk of the Parliament, Master of the Pleas Office and Surveyor of the Green Wax. Rose, however, had to apologize for the offices he could not mention, as they were not legible in the pencil scribbled on his paper (*PH* 31, col. 178).

Grimace. James Maitland, Earl of Lauderdale (1759–1839), was one of the 16 representative Scottish peers elected to the House of Lords and a co-founder of the Friends of the People with the convicted Thomas Muir (see ARGUMENT). In August

1792, he went to Paris, where he formed an acquaintance with Brissot. He remained in France until December. The journey is referred to in Lauderdale's *Letters to the Peers of Scotland* (London, G. F. and J. Robinson, 1794). The work shows that he had not only come to view the Revolution with scepticism, but that he also felt libelled by suggestions in the *True Briton* that he was a revolutionary. Lauderdale's travelling companion was John More (1729–1802), a medical doctor, who described the trip in *Journal during a Residence in France* (2 vols, G. G. and J. Robinson, 1793). Despite his revolutionary sympathies, More was shocked at the republicans' atrocities (see esp. 2, pp. 450–51).

Groan/Grumble/Grunt. Expressions habitually used in the radicals' ironic adoption of Burke's abuse of the people of the Revolution as a 'swinish multitude' (see MULTITUDE (SWINISH)). In the letters signed by 'Porkulus', 'Gruntum', 'Gregory Grunter', 'A Young Boar', 'Spare-Rib' etc., which appeared in Thomas Spence's journal *Pig's Meat* and Eaton's *Politics for the People*, the terms referred to the people giving expression to political grievances.

Guillotine. Dr Joseph Ignac Guillotin (1738–1814) designed the device used for executions during the Revolution. On 12 March 1794, *The Times* carried a notice of having received a letter from Lyon that Dr Guillotin had been executed by way of his own invention. In fact, his death was many years later, related to the growth of a carbuncle on his shoulder.

unnecessary torture: Pigott's satire recalls John Thelwall in his 'King Chaunticlere' allegory (discussed under COCK (GAME) above): 'I should certainly have guillotined him, being desirous to be merciful even in the stroke of death, and knowing, the instant the brain is separated from his heart … pain and consciousness is at an end, while the lingering torture of the rope may procrastinate the pang for half an hour' (*Politics for the People* 7 [1793], pp. 102–7). The Duke of Monmouth, a.k.a Fitzroy Scott or James Crofts (1649–85) was involved with Russell and Sidney (see EFFIMINACY) in the conspiracies to murder the despotic Charles II. Monmouth launched a protestant rebellion for which he was executed. The executioner did a shoddy job, and one report held that he received five blows and yet his head had to be cut off with a knife (*DNB*).

Mr. P—wis: Thomas Powys, a Pittite MP elected for Northhampton, spoke several times in Parliament during 1792–93, urging the Government to take alarmist precautions. In a parliamentary debate on 10 February 1794, he confessed to feel no shame in referring to himself as an alarmist and proclaimed that he was 'much more afraid of two or three scores of red bonnets, than all the crowns and sceptres in Europe' (*PH* 30, col. 1367).

p. 51

Gun. The Game Laws stipulated that only freeholders of £100 a year could possess an 'engine' for the shooting of animals; cf. LAWS (TRANSGRESSION OF). Under the Game Act, guns might be seized by the lord of the manor, who, with a warrant, had the right to search their tenant's person and his house for guns. This was of more than passing interest to radicals, who saw this as a way of checking insurrection. However, there is little evidence to suggest that the country as a whole was disarmed as an effect of the Act (Munsche, *Gentlemen and Poachers*, pp. 79–81).

p. 52

To guttle. 'To eat voraciously, to gormandize' (*OED*).

Habeas Corpus. Literally, 'you may have the body'. The Habeas Corpus Amendment Act protected the individual against arbitrary imprisonment by requiring that any person arrested be brought before a court for formal charge. The Act was suspended from May 1794 to July 1795 (and again in 1798–1801), which gave the authorities the right to arrest anyone on the suspicion of having committed a crime, and detain them without specifying charges. This was one of the most controversial alarmist measures taken by the Pitt ministry. Yet it was passed in the Commons by 146 to 28 votes (*PR* 28, pp. 237–8). Thomas Hardy, the Secretary of the London Corresponding Society, was arrested on 12 May 1794. John Horne Tooke, John Thelwall, Jeremiah Joyce and John Richter, leading members of the London Corresponding Society and the Society for Constitutional Information, were arrested on 18 May 1794. They were first committed to the Tower, then Newgate, where they were still awaiting trial when Pigott died in late June.

Hag. Catherine II (1729–96), Empress of Russia, had entered into the coalition against France in March 1793. As she progressed in years, the lovers she took were increasingly younger. Pigott provocatively lists her with several well-known society ladies, also advanced in years, such as Mother Hannau, Mrs Montague, Lady Johnston (satirized by Gillray for her gambling) and Madame Schwellenberger (the Queen's Lady of the Bedchamber).

Half-seas-over. The phrase could be used to mean both 'half-way towards a goal' and 'almost drunk' (*OED*). In 1794, the caricaturist Cruickshank made a satirical drawing on the progress of the British troops under the command of the allegedly drunken Duke of York, entitled *Half Seas Over alias the Hopes of the Family* (*BMC*, 8433).

Happiness. Much loyalist rhetoric repeated the wording of the Proclamation against Seditious Correspondence of May 1792, which referred to the 'happy Constitution of Governments, Civil and Religious, established in this kingdom'. In what follows, Pigott adapts a passage from John Locke's *Essays on Human Understanding* (1689), II.xxi.55. Locke here touches on a theme central to Pigott's analysis: why one man chooses 'luxury and debauchery, and another sobriety and riches'.

p. 53

Harlequin. In *Jockey Club* III, Pigott referred to Thomas Killigrew (1612–83), the dramatist who was 'friend and jester' to Charles II, and observes that Lord Chesterfield (see FOOL) now 'fills the place' for George III.

Harlot. Doctors' Commons was the Court of the Bishop of London. Pigott is alluding to the scandal involving the sixth son of George III, Frederick Augustus, Duke of Sussex (1773–1843). He was secretly married to Lady Augusta Murray, second daughter of the fourth Earl of Dunmore (*The Times*, 26 April 1793). A son was born on 13 January 1794. In accordance with the Royal Marriage Act of 1772, which stated that such a marriage required the King's consent, George III set out to declare the marriage void by obtaining a ruling from the Doctors' Commons in early 1794 (*The Times*, 27 January). Receiving much press, the annulment was finally pronounced by the Dean of Arches in the summer the same year.

Harmony. Sir Francis Bacon (1561–1626), philosopher and statesman, was elevated to the peerage, as Pigott indicates. He served in the court of Queen Elizabeth I, and was knighted shortly after the succession of James in 1603. Bacon took a number of important political posts, and prosecuted enemies of the King for treason. For his services, he was first created Baron, then Viscount.

Harmony. *Combined Powers*: See ASSERTION.
    Court of Justiciary in Scotland: See ASSERTION.

p. 54

Harvest. The hated Corn Laws secured a protected market for landowners, and during wars and years of scarcity the landowner's profits usually rose. Eaton published the Sheffield reformer John Harrison's *A Letter of the Right. Hon. Henry Dundas, M.P. or an Appeal to the People of Great Britain* (1794), in which it was stated that the Government's policy on corn 'raises the Price of bread to the Poor, and heightens the Calamities of the People; and was evidently designed to raise the Property of the Landed Lords of the Earth at the expense of the industrious Poor!' (p. 9).

Haste. The Duke of York's retreat from Dunkirk had to be effected with a haste that meant leaving 32 siege cannons and large quantities of stores behind. Satirical references to Frederick's failed 'heroism' abounded; as, for example, the broadside ballad 'Grunting A-la-mode': 'Fred' was a grunting at Dunkirk, mind that! / But he won the race, tho' he lost his lac'd hat' (included in *An Address to William Pitt, with a Lump of Human Hair* [T. Spence, n.d.]). A real sense of flight was seen in the later battle of May 1794 at Tourcoing, on the borders of France and the Netherlands. This was supposed to have been a concerted attack with the Austrians, but before they arrived the Duke had lost 1000 men and 19 out of his 25 guns. Made conspicuous by prominently displaying the Star of the Garter on his breast, the Duke only saved himself by fleeing on horseback.

Haughtiness. *immaculate minister*: Pitt. Mansfield and Loughborough were both Scottish judges, who gave their support to Pitt (see 'Cast of Characters').

Havock. A variation on Shakespeare's *Julius Caesar*, III, i, 274–6, mixed in with an echo of *King John* ('Cry havoc, Kings!'), II, i, 357. Milton's lines from *Paradise Lost* are from Book X, ll. 614–16 (not Book II, as indicated here).

p. 55

Heaven-born. An appellation used of Pitt throughout. In January 1789, the Duke of Chandos, 'parodying what Mr. Pitt's father said of General Wolfe, pronounced the present Chancellor of the Exchequer a heaven-born minister' (Barrell, *Exhibition*, p. 11). Although honestly meant, his compliment became a stock phrase of abuse in radical satire. In Richard Newton's caricature entitled *The General Sentiment* (1797), Pitt is hanged by the neck from a tree. Below him, two characters of obvious plebeian stock express the wish: 'May our heaven born minister be SUPPORTED from ABOVE' (*BMC*, 8999).

p. 56

Hemp. The satire here is heightened by the fact that a select parliamentary committee had been appointed in April 1791 to look into the cultivation of hemp in Britain. Britain imported large quantities of hemp, so growing it domestically was believed to benefit the State revenue.

Hereditary. See DEGENERACY.

Hero (Young). In 1793, on insistence of his father George III, the Duke of York was made Major-General for the British troops on the Continent. At only 29, he had to justify his appointment over seniors in age and rank. Although he had received lengthy military training, public opinion held him to be incompetent. The Government, which fought the King on his decision, assigned three generals to the Duke, with whom he always had to consult. First among them was Sir James Murray (1719?–94), who had served in the Seven Years' War and had distinguished himself in the West Indies during the American War. He was appointed Chief of Staff and joined the Duke of York in Flanders to make good his deficiencies (cf. PERSPICUITY).

Hero. While the Duke campaigned in Flanders, failing to capture Dunkirk and Toulon, rumours quickly reached London from officers on leave in England that the Duke put more effort into feasting with his entourage than in leading the campaign on the battlefield (*Later Correspondence of George III*, 2, p. xxxiv). The situation was satirized in Gillray's print *The Fatigues of the Campaign in Flanders of May 1793* (*BMC*, 8327).

Valenciennes surrendered: 28 July 1793.

magnanimous uncle: The Duke of Brunswick, the army commander of the Prussian army, had married a sister of George III in 1781, which made him an uncle of the Duke of York. Both commanders had hoped to lead their troops into Paris, but the defeat of the Duke of York at Dunkirk and the defeat of the Duke of Brunswick at Valmy put an end to these hopes. In 1794, the Duke of York had to accept that he was now to answer to Austrian orders, whereas Brunswick resigned his command on 6 January. But although the Allied campaign was clearly in trouble, the Pittite MP Robert Jenkinson (see JABBER) would, in an address to the Commons on 3 April 1794, still assert that 'marching to Paris was attainable and practicable', and that such a mission should be undertaken (*PH* 31, col. 249). This declaration of intention was much commented upon in the radical press.

surrender of Landrecies: From 14 to 27 April 1794, the Austrians bombarded the French town of Landrecies. It finally surrendered, but the inhabitants showed remarkable resistance. What Pigott could not know was that Austrian rule would be short-lived, as General Sherer and his revolutionary troops liberated the town in July.

p. 57

Hanover. An electorate of the Holy Roman Empire from 1692 to 1802. George III was both King of England and Elector of Hanover (which he never visited). War was declared between Britain and France in May 1756, which led to the Seven Years' War. Battles were fought over Hanover, as this was Britain's 'Achilles heel'. Prussia and Britain united for its defence against France, Austria, Saxony and Sweden. Peace was secured with the Treaty of Paris in February 1763, but only after a prolonged conflict that proved expensive for the British Treasury.

grave of Britons: In *Treachery no Crime*, Pigott notes: 'twenty battles were fought, and two hundred thousand soldiers were slain' (p. 62).

Hero. For the Duke of York's 'heroism'; see HASTE. Philip Astley (1742–1814) was Sergeant-Major in the British army. He had opened an exhibition of horsemanship in Lambeth called the Royal Grove. Astley fought in Flanders under the Duke of York, who granted him leave from the battlefield in 1794 so he could rebuild his Lambeth entertainment, which had burnt to the ground during his absence. It opened again the same year under the patronage of the Duke of York and the Prince of Wales. Field Marshal William von Freytag (1711–98) was the Austrian Commander-in-Chief whose army collaborated with the Duke of York on the failed attempt to take Dunkirk. Charles Joseph Claifait de Croix (1736–98) was the Austrians' Field-Marshal who suffered defeat with his battalion at Valmy in 1792. In April 1794, he suffered another bad defeat at Mouscron. His folly also meant defeat at Tourcoing in May. Prince Frederick Josias of Saxe-Coburg (1737–1815) led the Austrian Coalition forces in the defence of the Netherlands in 1793. He enjoyed initial success at Neerwinden, but his cautiousness and slow resolve in Flanders was much criticized, not least by Britain. He resigned his command in August 1794. William V, Prince of Orange (1748–1806) was the hereditary stadholder for the independent Netherlands which joined Britain and Prussia in the First Coalition. As the French troops advanced, he was forced to flee to Britain in 1793. He functioned as Major-General in command of the entire Anglo-Allied army until the Duke of Wellington's arrival, after which he remained second-in-command. This was a 'diplomatic' appointment rather than one based on merit, as the 23-year-old prince did certainly not have the competence of more experienced soldiers, who would probably have managed this important job with more skill. The Corsican General Pascale de Paoli (1725–1807) had led the resistance to the French, who conquered Corsica in 1768. He escaped to England, where he was given a pension. In 1789, the Constituent Assembly invited him to return to Corsica, but he overstepped his welcome by declaring the island's independence in 1793. Paoli was accused of reintroducing despotism, persecuting patriots and favouring refractory priests, for which reason the republican party demanded his execution (*AR 1793*, History of Europe, p. 254). He appealed for British protection, which arrived in February 1794 when Lord Hood captured the three towns held by French Republican troops.

p. 58

Hesitation. William Drake (1723–96) was owner of extensive landed property and was reckoned to be among the richest commoners in England. He offered continued support for Pitt, but was notorious for not speaking in the Commons for over forty-four years. When he was re-elected to Parliament in 1790, he appears to have continued his silence, and all the speeches recorded after this date have been attributed to his son, who was his namesake. John Rolle (1756–1842) was also a landowner (hence Pigott's emphasis on the two MPs' titles), an heir to the most extensive landed property in Devon. In the 1790s, he voted for some of Pitt's restrictive measures most despised by reformists. His name gave the title of the serialized satire *The Rolliad*, which was occasioned by his attempt to heckle Burke in Parliament during 1782–83, when he spoke in favour of reformist issues ('When Pitt would drown the eloquence of Burke, / You seem the ROLLE best suited to the work; / His well-train'd band, obedient know their cue, / And cough and groan in unison with you', *Criticism on the Rolliad, Part the First* [J. Ridgway, 1788], p. 30).

Hiccius Doccius. Quote from Samuel Butler's *Hudibras* (1662–78), III.iii.578–82, also cited in Samuel Johnson's *Dictionary*. *Hudibras* was written as a satire on the Cromwellians. 'Fool' here replaces the original (and synonymous) 'sot'. William Mainwaring (1735–1821) was Chairman of Middlesex and Westminster quarter sessions between 1781 and 1794. His charge to the Grand Jury of Middlesex in defence of 'THE ENGLISH CONSTITUTION, reared and perfected by wisdom and experience through ages' was published by the Reeve's Association in no. 2 of the cheap tracts they brought out in 1792. In Parliament, where Mainwaring sat for Middlesex from 1784 to 1802, he introduced a bill backed by the Evangelical William Wilberforce, to promote better observance of the SABBATH. An amended measure, empowering magistrates to pay Government informers to report on lawbreakers, became law on 23 May 1794.

Hierarchy. In the aftermath of the French Revolution, the argument that social hierarchy was part of Divine Providence was emphasized with new vigour. The 'English Freeholder' who authored the alarmist pamphlet *Equality; or, Subordination the Order of God and the Welfare of Man* (n.p., 1792) denounced 'Equality' as that 'which never did exist in the world, which cannot exist in the very nature of things, and (what is more) which God never meant to exist in his whole creation'. It follows that God actually *wills* inequality among men, because 'Providence hath ordered it to be so, for wise and good reasons' (pp. 4–5). A number of religious writers propagated the notion that a class system was beneficial because it made possible the practice of Christian charity. The anonymous author of *Liberty and Equality treated of in a Short History addressed from a Poor Man to his Equals* (n.p., 1792) claimed that without a social hierarchy 'some of the brightest virtues of humanity could not be exercised' (p. 32). Similar arguments can be found in, for example, William Agutter, *Christian Politics; Or, the Origin of Power, and the Grounds of Subordination* (F. & C. Rivington, 1792) and Samuel Bradburn, *Equality: A Sermon* (Bristol: Lancaster & Edwards, 1794).

To hire. See CANDOUR.

p. 59

Hireling. John Reeves, the founder of a network of ultra-loyalist associations (see ASSOCIATION), had held different Government-sponsored posts, such as Commissioner of Bankruptcy, Counsel to the Mint and Law Clerk to the Committee of Trade. He had just returned from Newfoundland in November 1792, where he had acted as Chief Justice of Court, when he issued a prospectus for the Association for the Preservation of Liberty and Property against Republicans and Levellers. The initiative was welcomed by the Government, which subsequently subsidized the Association. Pigott discussed the salaries Reeves earned from his sinecures in *Treachery no Crime*, pp. 96–7n.

History. *Attorney-General*: See BARRISTER.

Historiographer. The Roman historian Cornelius Tacitus (*c.* 56–117) was praised by Edward Gibbon as a 'philosophical historian', whose writings would instruct 'generations of mankind'. Montaigne found that no other author had given 'a more just analysis of particular characters'. Tacitus gave vivid accounts of the cruelty, injustice and corruption of the early emperors in his histories. His *Germania* described the strong belief in justice and liberty among the Germanic tribes, their representative system of government and their invention of a jury system. Hence, radicals and opponents of the Government in the 1790s often referred to this work. Pigott used one of Tacitus' accounts in *Jockey Club* II (p. 73) as an analogy to an example of a contemporary miscarriage of justice. Samuel Johnson gave in his colonialist *Taxation No Tyranny* (1775) and other places an outline of history which favoured the Government against the demands of the Colonists. Johnson was savagely attacked for accepting a pension (installed in 1762) from the hated Lord Bute, George III's First Lord of the Treasury. Cf. PENSION. The Government supporter Arthur Young (see CORRUPTION) made many important observations on British history, as well as the events of his own time. An example of the latter was the hostile account of the Revolution given in *Travels in France* (1792).

p. 60

Holy. John Moore (1730–1805), Archbishop of Canterbury from 1783. He was an outspoken supporter of the war with France and authored the prayers used on the Fast Days declared by George III for victory against the French armies. Moore was also known to dispense his patronage with somewhat generous hand to his own family. Pigott criticized the Bishop's conservative politics in *Female Jockey Club* (193–5). In the House of Lords, the Bishop of Rochester, Samuel Horsley, was noted for speaking warmly in support of the British war efforts.

Honour. *Botany Bay*: See ARGUMENT.

Jockey Club: The association of horse owners who gathered around Newmarket race course and met in the *Thatched Tavern* in St James Street, *The Star and Garter* in Pall Mall and *The Clarendon* in Bond Street. The notorious Brook's Club in St James Street was the place where Fox and the rump of the Whigs dined, drank, gamed and conferred. It was also the haunt of the Prince of Wales and the Duke of York. Fortunes were made or lost here in the Great Subscription Room. The many outrageous bets tendered are recorded in the Club's betting books.

House. In the Government's campaign to clamp down on radicalism, several of the English radicals arrested were woken up at night and had their property searched. On 12 May 1794, at half past six in the morning, a group consisting of two Bow Street Runners, the King's Messenger with his son and the private secretary of Home Secretary Dundas arrested Thomas Hardy of the London Corresponding Society at his house in Piccadilly. The house was ransacked for incriminating documents, and Mrs Hardy was thrown out of her bed and 'obliged to dress herself' in the presence of the intruders (*An Account of the Seizure of Citizen Thomas Hardy* [Printed by order of The London Corresponding Society, 1794], p. 1). Simultaneously, Daniel Adams, the secretary of the Society for Constitutional Information, was also called out of bed and arrested.

Humility. George Nugent-Temple Grenville, Marquis of Buckingham (1753–1813) was a cousin of Pitt. He had been employed as Lord Lieutenant of Ireland 1787–89. He was known for his excessive pride and for taking offence at even quite trivial matters. Horace Walpole said of him that he had 'many disgusting qualities, as pride, obstinacy and want of truth with a natural propensity to avarice' (*DNB*). Nugent-Temple was a demanding cousin, who was offered the marquisate of Buckingham as a substitute when George III refused Pitt's request to grant him a dukedom.

Hypocrisy. For Earl of Moira's hypocrisy, see APOSTATE.

p. 61

Hypothesis. See HERO.

To jabber. Robert Banks Jenkinson (1770–1828) was only 20 when he entered the Commons in 1790 for Rye. Born in the same year, George Canning (1770–1827) was only 23 when he won a seat for the rotten borough of Newtown in 1793. Both were some of Pitt's strongest supporters in Parliament, and seen as youngsters who were nursed under his influence. Thomas Steele's parliamentary duties, apart from acting as teller for the Government, consisted mainly of defending Pitt's policy. Steele never shook off the impression of being a protégé for the Duke of Richmond, as he sat for Chichester on his interest. He was therefore often satirized as a characterless puppet.

Jacobin. Originally, a member of the political club founded in May 1789 among the deputies at Versailles. After the overthrow of the Girondist government in 1793, it became associated with the Terror. In the British debate, conservatives used the term indiscriminately of everyone who did not offer their allegiance to the British constitution.

Idol. See FORTUNE.

Jewel. In *Jockey Club* III, Queen Charlotte was attacked for amassing a huge collection of jewellery, which she is 'indefatigable in her pains, to augment and enrich ... by the addition of every precious magnificent curiosity' (p. 48). Cf. GARNISH.

Jester. Probably a reference to Joseph Jekyll (1754–1837), MP for Calne in Wilshire, who published a number of satires and jests in liberal newspapers during the 1780s and 1790s. In *Jockey Club* II (pp. 79–81), Pigott had commented on Jekyll and his contributions to the celebrated satire *The Rolliad*.

Ignorance. On 13 May 1794, Pitt activated the Committee of Secrecy, with the purpose of monitoring radical activities. Books and papers were inspected, post intercepted and an intricate system of spies put in place. Their first report was submitted to Parliament on 16 May (the day after they had met for the first time). Besides Pitt, the Committee consisted of Dundas, Ellis, Windham, the Attorney General, the Solicitor General, the Lord Advocate of Scotland, Grenville, Steele, Robert Banks Jenkinson, Powys, Earl of Mornington, Lord Mulgrave and Burke, among others,.

To illuminate. To redress the balance of papers that had supported the Opposition in the 1780s, the Government paid regular subsidies to some nine newspapers, as well as to writers for contributions to the press. The total for 1790–91 and 1792–93 came to around £4600 and £4900 respectively (Aspinall, *Politics and the Press*, pp. 163–7; Werkmeister, *London Daily Press*, p. 428). Cf. BRITON (TRUE).

p. 62

Immediately. Bills for reform that it had seemed likely Parliament was warming to pass in the years leading up to the French Revolution fell victim to the new spirit of ALARMISM and were now defeated when put to a vote. An issue Pigott mentions in the *Political Dictionary* is the repeal of the Test and Corporations Acts (see TEST-ACT). When Parliament was partitioned in 1789, before the French example had come to be seen as a dangerous influence, William Windham had supported repeal. In 1791, however, he struck a new note. In a speech, Windham explained that 'one should not repair a house in the hurricane season' (*PR*. 27, p. 208). This reflected a change of heart among many Pittites who had supported innovations but were no longer ready to give way to reform, as any suggestion of constitutional change became tarred with the brush of revolution. Another issue Pigott takes up is the slave trade. In 1788, the Commons had voted to regulate the conditions on slave ships, and Pitt was in favour of the abolition of slavery. Wilberforce and his followers wanted immediate abolition, but in 1792 only a bill for 'gradual' abolition could be passed in the Commons. This was, however, later rejected by the Lords. Abolition would be conferred to 1807.

Impiety. See FAST (BY PROCLAMATION).

Importance. See GARTER.

Impress. Press-gangs roamed the streets to catch 'able-bodied' men between 18 and 45 to serve the King on his vessels in times of war. On the eve of the war, an Impress Service was established with its own gangs and facilities. Eaton published *Reflections on the Pernicious Custom of Recruiting* (1795?), in which it is stated: '[A] legal method of raising Soldiers is by pressing, as 'tis called; that is to say when a poor man, who cannot give a satisfactory account of himself to the magistrate who apprehends him, is liable to be sent to the nearest jail and to be there confined 'till it suits the War-Office to send for him' (p. 7). Already in May 1792, Charles Grey had motioned against pressing as a method of enlisting for the navy, but was voted down in Parliament.

p. 63

Improbable. See HERO.

Incomprehensible. For Horsley, see 'Cast of Characters'. Loughborough's acceptance of office as Lord Chancellor in January 1793 was the culmination of his alienation from his former friends on the Opposition benches (cf. DISINTERESTEDNESS).

Independence. In the political parlance of the day, 'independence' was a badge of honour used to describe the status of an MP who was not dependent on a Lord in the upper chamber or a patron controlling a constituency for his place in the Commons. Theoretically, an Independent therefore had the freedom to vote according to his conscience. Portland and Windham were Whigs who had voted with the opposition but now supported the Government. Pigott suggests that they were now in Pitt's pocket, as the GARTER was bestowed on Portland in July 1793, and Windham was given the office of Secretary at War in January 1794. Burke had also shifted his sympathies from Whig to the Government. Pigott refers to the rumour that Burke had secretly received a pension (see BARGAIN).

Independent. The forty-shilling freeholders of the counties (who had the right to vote) were not entirely their own masters at elections. As most freeholders were tenants too, many electorates were in the pocket of a squire, who would scrutinize the open poll books to ensure that their tenants had voted according to the bribes, promises or threats presented to them. Sometimes an arrangement was made by which tenants would be transported to the polling booth and entertained with beef and beer, so that one member for the Tory gentry and one from the Whig aristocracy could obtain a seat each without the vast expense of a contested election. The Treasury also looked after its convinced supporters by helping them to victory in their constituencies (Plumb, *England in the Eighteenth Century*, pp. 39–40; Pares, *King George III and the Politicians*, pp. 8–11).

Inquiry. See ENQUIRY.

p. 64

Insensibility. *flogged*: See LASH.
    sixpence per diem: The pay received by ordinary soldiers. Cf. the broadside ballad *Sergeant Kite's Invitation to the Swinish Multitude* (Thomas Spence, n.d.): 'For wonderful sums we will promise / Which we possible never will pay, / But of this my brave comrades be certain, / You'll be shot at for sixpence a day.'

To Insnare. Civilians were snared into enlisting for the army by agents known as *crimps*. Men were inveigled into crimp houses by violence, fraud or prostitutes and then effectively kidnapped before being marched in handcuffs to be sworn into the army by a Justice of the Peace. The resistance against these Government-sponsored tactics resulted in the London anti-crimp riots of September 1794. Eaton published *Reflections on the Pernicious Custom of Recruiting by Crimps and on various other Modes now Practiced in the British Army* (1795), in which it is suggested that, as far as the standard of the army goes, it must be a 'great loss to the nation' that the soldiers enlisted are 'the least fit for the fatigues of campaigning' as they are 'generally speaking, debauch'd and unhealthy in the highest degree' since 'it is commonly from the brothels and pot-houses, from Taverns and the other haunts of desperate and unhappy men that these wretched victims are procured' (p. 8). Eaton also published Henry Martin Saunders's closet-drama *The Crimps, or the Death of Poor Howe. A Tragedy in one Act, as lately performed at a house of ill fame, or what is called a Recruiting-Office in London* (1794). This was based on real events that took place 'at a recruiting-office in Johnson's-court, Charing-cross, London, August 15th, 1794'. Howe was 'a young gentleman' who had thrown himself out of a window to avoid enlistment after being kidnapped by recruiting officers.

    shilling: The 'King's Shilling' was the reward originally given to the recruit upon enlistment. However, the crimps often used it to pay a local surgeon to give a cursory health check to their catch.

Insolence. First Lord of the Treasury was William Pitt. The Commons met in the chapel of St Stephen's at Westminster, which had been handed over in the reign of Edward VI

Ireland (the people of). The 1783 Act of Renunciation, which declared 'the exclusive right of Parliament and courts of Ireland in matters of legislation and judicature', had not done away with English appointments and influence. Most of the 300 members of the Dublin Parliament were placemen, and all Irish bills still had to receive royal assent. Pitt's attempt to give Ireland economic freedom was voted down in 1785, and the country was allowed to drift still further into a squalid poverty unparalleled in Europe.

Irony. For Windham, Portland and Burke, see 'Cast of Characters'.

Justice and Impartiality. In the years prior to the declaration of war, the British corps of officer had been weakened by Secretary of War George Younge's use of army commissions as patronage. Younge had sold positions to youngsters of wealthy families, who had absolutely no experience, and even to babies, as the pay provided a regular pension. The situation worsened when the Government was short of troops at the beginning of the war. To alleviate the shortage, independent recruiting companies were authorized. The company director would incur the cost of recruiting – often through *crimping* (see INSNARE), but he was then guaranteed a commissioned rank. If the recruiting director could not be absorbed into the forces, he could enjoy the benefit of half pay for the rest of his life for his services to the State. Those officers who did go to war were often without ability, and displaced the many experienced commanders who would in some cases find themselves assigned to the workhouse (Emsley, *British Society*, pp. 11, 36). The selling of rank in the military was stubbornly supported by the Paymaster General of the forces, Thomas Steele, in a debate of 4 February 1794 (*PR 38*, p. 284).

p. 65

To kidnap. See INSNARE.

King. *a million a year*: See CROWN.

p. 67

Knight. Sir Watkin Lewes, an Alderman of the City of London (see BRAGGADOCIO), 'voted with the Minister [Pitt] upon all great questions' (*City Biography containing Anecdotes and Memoirs of the Rise, Progress, Situation, & Character of the Aldermen and other Conspicuous Personages of the Corporation and City of London* [J. W. Myers, 1800], pp. 19–20). He was knighted in 1773. Lewes was typical of metropolitan reformers, who had followed Pitt in the early 1780s and turned conservative with him in the 1790s. Sir James Sanderson, another City Alderman and regular Government supporter (see ALDERMAN), was knighted in 1786. Jeffrey Dunstan (1759?–97) was pronounced Mayor of Garrett in 1785. This title was given at the famous mock-election at Wandsworth, where the most eccentric characters were brought forward as candidates. Dunstan's knack for vulgar wit secured him three consecutive elections, and he was not ousted before 1796. The jocular proceedings of the election, which included the bestowing of a knighthood on the elected mayor, were described in Samuel Foote's Haymarket comedy *The Mayor of Garret* (1764). Gustavus III of Sweden bestowed on Sidney Smith (see BRAGGADOCIO) the Grand Cross of the Order of the Sword in 1792 for his employment in the Swedish navy against Russia. George III invested him with the knighthood and permitted him to use the title in England.

Lady. Pigott appears to echo Burke, who abhorred the levelling tendencies of the revolutionaries, which meant abandoning all hierarchical orders for a society where the 'king is but a man; a queen is but a woman; a woman is but an animal' (*Reflections*, p. 171).

To lament. In *Reflections on the Revolution in France*, Burke had stressed the importance of holding out a promise to the poor that a reward can be expected in 'the final proportion of eternal justice' as a consolation for their hardships in this world (p. 372). This argument angered the opposition. In *Vindications of the Rights of Men* (1791), Mary Wollstonecraft came out against this particular passage for its 'contemptible hard-hearted sophistry'. 'It is possible to render the poor happier in this world without depriving them of the consolation which you gratuitously grant them in the next,' she writes. Indeed, 'They have a right to more comfort than they at present enjoy' (*Political Writings*, p. 57).

p. 68

Lash. Flogging with the cat-o'-nine-tails had become a regular mode of punishment in the army. As E. P. Thompson has said, next to the press-gangs (see IMPRESS) flogging was 'perhaps the most hated of the institutions of Old England' (*The Making of the English Working Class*, p. 662n). In the satire *Knave's Acre*, published by Eaton in 1794, the members of the fictive loyalist association unanimously agree 'that being strict disciplinarians, we are of opinion, that a few hundred lashes on the naked shoulders ... are a proper reward for a common solider who shall be found asleep on his post' (p. 12). The practice was greatly diminished with the Royal Commission on Military Punishments in 1835, but only abolished completely in 1881. For a list of other radical attacks on flogging, see Dwindiddy, 'Early Nineteenth-Century Campaign', p. 126, n5.

Lavish/Lavishness. The Prince of Wales's increasing debts were discussed in Parliament several times. In 1788, Pitt made special arrangements to finance the Prince's loans by taking £10 000 out of the Civil List (*PH* 26, col. 1207). It was well known that the Prince's younger brothers, the Duke of York and the Duke of Clarence, were also given to betting, gambling and spending well above their means. The Duke of York ran up a debt of £40 000 in less than a year after his return from Brunswick to England in 1787. To cover the losses, he had to sell Allerton house in the West Riding of York, which he had purchased with the revenues of his bishopric of Onasburg, an ecclesiastical designation worth £20 000 a year.

Laureat. James Henry Pye (1745–1813) was granted the laureateship in 1790, not least owing to the support he had given Pitt while he sat in the Commons for

Berkshire between 1784 and 1790. His appointment was widely mocked as a conspicuous example of political patronage.

Lawn. The special kind of fine linen used for sleeves of a bishop, hence denoting the dignity or office of a bishop.

Pudding-sleeve: 'A larger bulging sleeve drawn in at the wrists or above', as worn by bishops and other clergy (*OED*).

Laws (transgression of the). Between 1671 and 1831, 53 principal statutes concerning game, deer stealing and poaching were passed. The statutes were constantly amended, repealed and re-enacted (for example, 5 George III c. 14; 10 George III c. 19; 13 George III c. 80; and 16 George III c. 30), making them, as Blackstone commented, 'many and various, and not a little obscure and intricate' (*Commentaries*, 4, p. 175). The series of statutes defined the classes who were entitled to kill game, and sharpened the laws against persons who killed game without a qualification, who had engines for killing game, or had game in their possession. The basic act of 1651 was biased in making it a prerogative of the landed gentleman to kill game. The legislation that defined the qualifications needed to take out a game certificate was summed up by Blackstone: '1. the having a freehold estate of £100 per annum: there being fifty times the property required to enable a man to kill a partridge, as to vote for a knight of the shire: 2. A leasehold for ninety-nine years of £150 per annum. 3. Being the son and heir apparent of an esquire (a very loose and vague description), a person of superior degree: 4. Being the owner, or keeper of a forest, park, chase, or warren' (*Commentaries*, 4. p. 175). Radicals abhorred the Game Laws for its class-based bias. Mary Wollstonecraft wrote: 'The game laws are almost as oppressive to the peasantry as press-warrants to the mechanic' (*Vindication of the Rights of Men* [J. Johnson, 1790], p. 31). In the 1790s, attacks on the Game Laws became part and parcel of radical agitation. Their abolition in revolutionary France was celebrated in *Rights of Man*, where Paine wrote: 'the farmer on whose lands wild game shall be found (for it is by the produce of his lands they are fed) shall have a right to what he can take; that there shall be no monopolies of any kind' (p. 126). Lord Milton told Lord Kenyon (see CONSTITUTION) that 'The Republican party has made the Game Laws the object of their abuse and detestation; in France the instant they began to overturn the Constitution and level all distinctions, these were the first they pulled down. It therefore seems to me that they should at all times be most respectfully guarded' (Kenyon, *Life*, p. 266).

p. 69

Leveller. Guillaume Thomas François Raynal (1713–96), French writer who published the hugely popular *Histoire philosophiqe et politique des éstablissement et du commerce des Européens dans les deux Indes* (1770), which in the 1780 edition was revised to include an attack on many French institutions of the *ancien régime*.

Liable. *Botany Bay*: See ARGUMENT. Still officially on the statute, the punishment for High Treason was to be hanged by the neck, cut down while still alive, to have one's entrails burnt before one's face, then beheaded and quartered. The full punishment of this medieval ritual was, however, no longer used.

Libation. A drink-offering in honour of a god. The term often appeared in satire to denote DRUNKENNESS.

Liberty and Property. See LAWS (TRANSGRESSION OF THE).

Lie. *'Thou liest … speakest'*: The words spoken to Macbeth by Young Siward in Shakespeare, *Macbeth*, V, vii, 10.

p. 70

Light. Pitt increased the Window Tax, which had been levied since 1697, in 1784. There was also a duty on candles. However, houses with fewer than seven windows became exempt from tax in 1792, and part of the candle tax was relieved the same year. Yet both taxes were featured in radical writings as unreasonable burdens on artisan labour, and were seen as an impediment to acquiring information by reading.

Loaves and Fishes. Jargon for the government subsidies and employment. When Pitt attended a University sermon at Cambridge, his constituency, the gentlemen of the University, showed their dissatisfaction with the decreasing number of bishoprics and deaneries he had to offer by suggesting that the text should be taken from St John 6:9: 'There is a lad here which hath five barley loaves and two small fishes, but what are they among so many?' This, however, was not the text chosen on that day (Leedham-Green, *Concise History*, p. 109). The visual representation of loaves and fishes was a recurrent theme in satirical drawings, especially with the political caricaturist William Dent.

Lord. Cf. Paine: 'Through all the vocabulary of Adam there is not such an animal as a Duke or a Count; neither can we connect any certain ideas with the words … What respect then can be paid to that which describes nothing, and which means nothing? Imagination has given figure and character to centaurs, satyrs, and down to all the fairy tribe; but titles baffle even the powers of fancy, and are a chimerical nondescript' (*Rights of Man*, p. 132). Cf. also BARONET.

Lordling. A lord regarded as immature or insignificant (*OED*). Richard Edgcumbe (1764–1839), a supporter of Pitt in Parliament, was created Viscount Valletort in 1789. On 21 January 1790, he moved for an address against the French Revolution and in praise of the 'the greatest pleasure and satisfaction from a just view of our own happy situation when contrasted with that of other states' (*PR* 27, pp. 2–5). He was described by Fanny Burney in 1789 as 'a most neat little beau' (*Diary and Letters*, 5, p. 49). Probably Thomas Bromley, Baron Montfort, (1733–99) was of a similar small stature. Montfort was High Steward of the borough of Cambridge and managed Government business there for a time. But by the 1790s his influence had declined, and he was forced to advertise parts of his estates for sale, selling off his furniture step by step.

   'To Lordlings … fall': From Alexander Pope's 'Duke upon Duke. An Excellent New Ballad', ll. 1–4

Lords (of the ocean). Britain possessed an impressive naval fleet in comparison with their European counterparts. The navy had 115 ships (39 more than either the French or Spanish navies, albeit only a dozen were in commission on the eve of the war (Emsley, *British Society*, p. 11). The fleet was key in the expanding overseas trade by which British knives, swords and cloth were sailed to West Africa and exchanged for slaves. Africans were shipped to the West Indies, and the ships returned to Britain carrying sugar that had been grown by slaves. There was a policy of protection for the slave traders, who benefited from the continued legality of selling African slaves as part of the profitable trade triangle. In Paris, the National Convention had voted to abolish slavery in all the French colonies on 4 February 1794.

Loyalist. It was custom to give places (that is, administration posts – the holders of which were referred to as *placemen*), pensions (a regular income awarded for life), peerage or a bishopric to those who offered the Government loyalty and support. For Burke's alleged pension, see BARGAIN. For Arthur Young, see CORRUPTION. For John Reeves, see HIRELING.

Loyalty. At the theatre and the opera, which often saw the royal family in attendance, *Te deum* and *God Save the King* were often sung as an expression of popular support for George III – especially after he recovered from his derangement in early 1789.

p. 71

Loyalty (true). Augustus Montague Toplady (1740–78) was a fierce Calvinist and writer of hymns, who in several tracts expressed his political loyalty to the Crown and the present system of government.

Luxury. *Carlton-House*: See DEBAUCHERY.

Madness. *throwing down a dagger*: See DAGGER.
  book full of … false rhetoric: Burke's *Reflections on the Revolution in France* (1790).
  St. Stephen's Hospital: The Commons, which were housed in St Stephen's Chapel. In *Jockey Club* II, Pigott borrowed Philip Dormer Stanhope Chesterfield's term, 'the Hospital of Incurables', to refer to the House of Lords (p. 8). Shakespeare's lines are from *King Lear*, IV, i, 47

p. 72

Magna Charta. See ENQUIRY.

Majesty. Pigott contrasts the deposed despot Louis XVI to Trajan, Emperor of Rome (AD 98–117). Trajan was known for his admirable kindness, and is usually considered one of the ablest of emperors. Another despot, George III, is contrasted with Henri IV (1553–1610), King of France. Paine wrote of Henri that he was 'a man of an enlarged and benevolent heart, that he proposed … a plan for abolishing war in Europe' (*Rights of Man*, p. 195); a reference to the Edict of Nantes (1598), which laid plans for a federation of European States.

Majority. The inactivity of some members of the Commons was notorious. The so-called Independents (many of them country gentlemen who were not placemen but expected some degree of patronage and generally voted with the Government) hardly ever stayed to the end of session. It was thus considered discourteous practice to introduce weighty debates after the Easter recess (Pares, *King George III and the Politicians*, p. 10). Lord William Wellesley-Pole Mornington (1763–1845) had a seat in Parliament for East Loae between 1783 and 1794. He supported Pitt and spoke in the Commons on the 'necessity of war'.

p. 73

Malcontent. See GROAN/GRUMBLE/GRUNT.

Malefactors. Swift, Fielding and Smollett had all popularized a comparison between high politics and the criminal underworld (Thompson, 'Eighteenth-Century Society', p. 142). This was also an analogy used by John Gay in *The Beggars Opera* (1727).

gibbet: A post from which the bodies of executed criminals (especially highwaymen) were exhibited as a warning to others.

p. 74

Man. *homo est duplex animal*: 'man is a two-fold creature'.

the vilest ... earth: Seneca makes the point in *Epistulae Morales ad Lucilium* that man walks upright rather than crawling, a sentiment that is perhaps behind Pigott's depiction of man subjected by monarchy here.

Manage. The reference is to Swift's collaboration with other satirists in *A History of John Bull* (1712–13), which was collected in *Miscellanies* (London: Motte and Bathurst, 1736).

Mangy. *the mange*: A play on the name for the disease infecting furry animals, and its use as a derogatory term for 'mean' and 'lousy' (*OED*).

Manifesto. *lying ministers*: Probably a reference to the manifesto issued by Pitt's Ministry in connection with the capture of Toulon (see ADVANTAGE). It emphasized that the port was only held in trust until 'a stable Government should be established' (the declaration cited in Ehrman, *Pitt*, 2, p. 315). Pigott, like many of the Opposition, believed these words to be a cover for a British claim to the port.

put all Parisians ... sword: See BRUNSWICK.

p. 75

Manifesto. *published by ... Prussia*: See BRUNSWICK.

Manufacturers. Producers of goods suffered from hardship after trade was disrupted in the early war years. Cities such as Manchester, Birmingham and Halifax were particularly hard hit, and there were many disturbances there. Especially many weavers, to whom the term *manufacturer* was applied, ended up in the workhouse. The weavers were behind some of the fiercest rioting throughout the second half of the eighteenth century. Many were shocked at the attitude of Parliamentarians, who held the war as 'necessary' on a matter of principle even if trade and the wealth of the nation suffered. This had been expressed by George Hardinge, the representative for the rotten borough of Old Sarum, in the infamous phrase 'perish our commerce' (*PH* 31, cols 120, 1086). It was since echoed with disgust in the Opposition press, which, however, often ascribed the phrase to William Windham, whom Pitt appointed Secretary at War in January 1794.

March. *long trot*: Jargon for the gait of a horse that moves too fast and hence fails to perfect the steadier pace of the foxtrot.

p. 76

Martyr. The 'prince' is the later Charles I (1600–49), who had accused the Earl of Bristol (1580–1653) of High Treason with the ulterior motive of preventing him from bringing charges again the royal favourite George Villiers, the Duke of Buckingham. In 1626, Charles therefore had Bristol imprisoned. Two years later, the House of Lords obtained Bristol's release. Returning to his seat in the Lords, he helped to pass the Petition of Rights (1628), which condemned arbitrary imprisonment.

Mask (of Religion). Richard Hill (1733–1808), MP for Shropshire, was prominent among the religious revivalists of his time, especially supporting improvements for the poor as a Christian duty. In religion, he was a fervent champion of Calvinist doctrines. Henry Thornton (1760–1815), MP for Southwark, was another religious Commoner. Both these MPs' voting behaviour followed that of the Evangelical faction, whose torchbearer was William Wilberforce. They voted with Pitt on most restrictive measures, but went further than the Ministry on philanthropic issues.

Mercy (of the law). *Muir and Palmer*: See ARGUMENT.
  Young Allen: During a riot for the radical MP John Wilkes in St George's Field, a young man named Allen was followed into a cow-house by a royal guard and shot. No one was charged for the crime.
  Balf and MacQuirk: In a poll at Brentford on 8 December 1768, Sir William Proctor, a Government candidate, stood against the Wilkite John Glynn. Proctor had paid a gang of thugs headed by the experienced election hooligan Edward McQuirk to stir up trouble when he fell behind in the public counting of votes. McQuirk and his companion, Laurence Balfe, were subsequently convicted at the Old Bailey on 9 January 1769 of the murder of a Wilkite lawyer, George Clarke. Controversially, their death sentences were later reprieved.
  Kennedys: In 1770, the brothers Matthew and Patrick Kennedy were accused of killing John Bigby, a watchman on Westminster Bridge, with a poker. One brother was reprieved (for transportation), the other acquitted. It was suspected that the

leniency was because their sister, Polly, was a courtesan who moved in circles of nobility. *The Annual Register* for 1770 mentions that several Lords and 'persons of distinction' who were 'friends' of the accused attended their trial (Chronicle, 109). Pigott also commented on the cases in *Jockey Club* II, p. 45.

p. 77

Metaphysics. Jargon for theoretical reasoning in political speech out of touch with reality. The Catholic radical Francis Plowden accused Windham of speaking 'metaphysics' in his *History ... 1794*, p. 34.

Million. *King of Sardinia*: See BARGAIN.
　　extirpating twenty-five millions: See BRUNSWICK.

Minion. For Dundas, see 'Cast of Characters'. For Jenkinson, see JABBER. The verse lines are from Swift's poem 'On Dreams', ll. 4–5.

Minister. Robert Walpole (1676–1745) is often called the first British Prime Minister. He emerged as the head of Government in 1721, resigning in 1742. He acted with the support of both George I and George II, building a fortune on the profits of office. The Opposition were fierce in their criticism of the way Walpole systematized State patronage. Henry St John, Viscount Bolingbroke (1678–1751), was a Tory politician who served as Secretary at War 1704–08. In opposition to Robert Walpole, he refused to take his seat in the Lords in 1723. He led a literary diatribe against Walpole and the corruption of his government. With Pultney, Swift, Pope and Gay, Bolingbroke savagely attacked Walpole in *The Craftsman* newspaper, arguing for frequent elections and for a limit to placemen and other types of nepotism.

Minister. In 1735, Alexander Pope saw the correspondence he had held with Swift published by the Grub Street bookseller Edmund Curll, a sworn enemy of Pope, in *Dean Swift's Literary Correspondence, for Twenty-four Years, from 1714 to 1738* (E. Curll, 1741). Swift here discussed his acquaintance with the Tory politicians Bolingbroke (see MINISTER above) and Robert Harley, Earl of Oxford (1661–1721), a favourite of Queen Anne, with whom Bolingbroke vied for power. Bolingbroke and Oxford both engaged in correspondence amounting to treason with James Edward (the Old Pretender), the Stuart claimant to the throne. Their character as men and politicians was also assessed in Swift's *An Enquiry into the Behaviour of the Queen's Last Ministry* (1715).

p. 79

Mob (Church and King). The loyalist mobs attacking the property of suspected radicals were often gathered from taverns and promised beer and beef for their participation in the demonstrations. The first mob action against radicalism took place in Birmingham in July 1791. Reformers held a dinner in celebration of the anniversary of the fall of the Bastille. The reformist dissenter Joseph Priestley (see EMIGRANT (ENGLISH)), who had not attended the dinner, had his library and laboratory destroyed and his house and chapel burnt down. The local magistrates were accussed of 'encouraging' the riots rather than preventing them (*AR*, History of Europe, p. 372). In Manchester, December 1792, 'Church and King' crowds attacked the house of Thomas Walker, a reformist member of the Constitutional Society. The offices of the radical newspaper the *Manchester Herald* were also attacked.

Monarch. *Sic transit gloria mundi*: 'So the glory of this world passes away'; a proclamation used at the installation of popes.

p. 80

Monarchy. Citation from Philip Dormer Stanhope Chesterfield (1694–1773), *Letters to his Son ... on the Fine Art of Becoming a Man of the World and a Gentleman* (1774), Letter CXVI. The work was republished twice in 1793. Chesterfield was a courtier and man of letters known for his wit. In Parliament, he acted as a liberal Whig who wasted no time in opposing Robert Walpole.

Multitude/Multitude (Swinish). Criticizing the Revolutionaries as a leaderless mob, Burke had in the *Reflections on the Revolution in France* applied to them the term 'the swinish multitude' (p. 173). More than any other attack, this abuse came to resonate in the political debates in Britain. Burke's allusion was to the Bible story of Christ casting out the demons (St Mark 5:9–13). The demons besought Jesus to 'Send us into the swine' after which 'the herd ran violently down a steep place into the sea ... and were choked in the sea'. In response to Burke's provocation, a wealth of satirical pamphlets and magazine verse appeared mocking this metaphor. It is also what provided the titles of the two most influential radical magazines of the 1790s, Thomas Spence's *Pig's Meat* (1793–96) and Eaton's *Hog's Wash*, re-named *Politics for the People, or a Salmagundy for Swine* (1793–95).

My (pronoun). Cf. Paine on monarchical tyranny: 'A king in France does not, in addressing himself to the National Assembly, say, "My Assembly", similar to the phrase used in England of my "Parliament;" neither can he use it consistently with the constitution, nor could it be admitted' (*Rights of Man*, p. 141).

p. 81

Nab. 'To seize or catch unawares' (Grose).
   Cull: 'A man' (Grose).
   well-policed metropolis: Probably a reference to the militia brought into London after the Royal Proclamation of 1 December 1792 (*PR.* 34, pp. 31–2; cf. Pigott's entry on *Police*). He may also have in mind the Middlesex Justices Act of March 1792, which made it possible to take into custody, and for a justice to sentence to a term of imprisonment, a person *suspected* of an evil intention. This had great effect on the policing of the metropolis in an age of riots. Section 17 (referred to as Section D) created the possibility of a 'preventive police', and, when brought into Parliament, the bill had been criticized fiercely by the Opposition.

Nadir (of Adversity). *1760*: The year of George III's ascension to the throne.

Nænia. Roman God of funerals.

Naissant. A critique of the central position the King had in the political life of the nation. *Naissant* is a term for a figure issuing out of the middle rather than at the bottom of the shield or charge.
   G.R.: The initials of George Rex (George III).

Nakedness of the Land. Phrase from Genesis 42:9 used of the famine-plagued land of Canaan, when Jacob's sons see the abundant crops of Egypt.

p. 82

Name. The notoriously dull and dreary George III, whose court frowned upon balls as dissipations and kept a strict observance of etiquette, is contrasted with Dionysus, the Greek god of revelry and wine. The politics of Burke and Paine are contrasted, as is Pitt and the revolutionary leader of the French Jacobins, Maximillien Robespierre (1758–94). The arch-loyalist Bishop Horsley, who spoke warmly in favour of the war and vehemently objected to granting dissenters relief, is paralleled (rather than contrasted) with the notorious Bishop Bonner (1500?–69), who was responsible for numerous burnings of heretics on the stake.

Nameless. George III, Pitt and Henry Dundas.

National Debt. The passage here is copied from page two of the pamphlet *Explanation of the Word Equality*, which was printed by subscription among members of the London Corresponding Society in 1793 (see Davis [ed.], *London Corresponding Society*, 1, p. 117). Pigott adjusts the calculations upwards from the original £270 million. The official figures given for the national debt in 1793 and 1784 were £242.9 million and £249.6 million respectively (Gregory and Stevenson, *Britain in the Eighteenth Century*, p. 272).

p. 83

Natural Enemies (to England). See ENEMIES.

Navy. *torn by force*: See IMPRESS.

Nebuchadnezzar. In the Old Testament book of Daniel, God punishes the Babylonian king Nebuchadnezzar because he would not 'break off' his 'sins' and 'iniquities'. God takes away both Nebuchadnezzar's kingdom and reason, driving him into the fields to wander the wilderness for seven years (4:27). He would 'eat grass as oxen, and his body was wet with the dew of heaven, till his hairs were grown like eagles' feathers, and his nails like birds' claws' (4:33). The story of Nebuchadnezzar's madness became a conventionalized reference to the 'mad' George III in radical satires. For comparisons in caricature drawings, see Carretta, *George III*, pp. 162–9, and for broadsides, see Barrell, *Exhibition*, pp. 6–8. During George III's mental derangement (1788–89), his physicians prescribed that the King be removed from Windsor to the White House of Kew so he could spend time in the gardens for fresh air without being watched by the public. The land of Georgia (named after George II) was the last of the 13 American colonies to be added. During the War of Independence, Georgia was recaptured in December 1778. Pigott suggests that George's lust for land may be tempered by letting him out to roam his own gardens.

vide Lemon: A reference to George William Lemon's *English Etymology; or, a Derivative Dictionary of the English Language* (G. Robinson, 1783). 'Potentate' does not appear, but in *The History of the Civil Wars between York and Lancaster* (Lynn, W. Whittingham, 1792), Lemon set out to correct Horace Walpole's earlier attempt to 'exculpate' Richard III for the murder of his brother Clarence (p. xvi) and show him as a potentate.

p. 84

Necessary War. For the supporters of war, the phrase 'just and necessary' became a catch-phrase. It had appeared in the 'King's Message Respecting the Declaration of War with France', which was read to Parliament on 11 February 1793 (*PH* 30, col. 344). When Dundas, in March 1794, proposed to include the phrase in an address of thanks to the King, the Foxite Whigs asked for its omission because, although they supported a defensive war with France, they were against launching offensive military action as the Government preferred. The Whigs complained that the phrase was introduced deliberately to force a debate that would make them appear unpatriotic (*PH* 32, col. 92; *Morning Chronicle*, 17 March 1794).

Neck. Charles I of England was beheaded by axe in 1649; Louis XVI of France was guillotined on 21 January 1793.

  solution of continuity: Pigott reapplies the phrase originally used by Burke to describe the hereditary succession of monarchs (*Reflections*, p. 102). Pigott had begun the third part of *The Jockey Club* with a comparison between Louis XVI and George III, suggesting that the latter may meet the same fate as the former. See also Pigott's entry on *Scaffold*.

  '*Hear it … hell*': From Shakespeare's *Macbeth*, II, i, 62–3.

Necromancer. A term for one who claims to communicate with the spirits of the dead. Paine had thundered against Burke for adhering to laws made by legislators long dead: 'Mr. Burke is contending for the authority of the dead over the rights and freedom of the living' (*Rights of Man*, p. 92). Pigott similarly spoke of the authoritarian Church and State as 'Necromantic founds' (*Jockey Club* III, p. 10). Pigott's representation of Pitt as a magician with a magic wand recalls Paine's critique of how the people are deluded to accept a divided class society: 'Titles are like circles drawn by the magician's wand, to contract the sphere of man's felicity' (*Rights of Man*, p. 131). The spirit of Liberty, which had resided in Britain and flared out against monarchical tyranny several times in history, seems now to have left Britain for France. The fugitive spirit of liberty is well illustrated by Windham, who had defected from the Whigs to the Government ranks in January 1794 to become Pitt's Secretary at War.

p. 85

Ne exeat regno. 'Let him not go out of the kingdom', a writ to restrain a person from leaving the country or jurisdiction of a court. In *Treachery no Crime*, Pigott had criticized the Government's alarmist measures preventing citizens 'to leave the kingdom without the licence in due form of his Majesty and the privy seal'. This, he noted, was a 'violent encroachment on the Magna Charta', in which it was stated 'that it shall be lawful for every one to go out of this kingdom, and safely return by land and by water' (pp. 138–9). The Traitorous Correspondence Bill, passed by one vote on 9 April 1793, made it necessary for a British subject to obtain a passport or leave before travelling out of Britain, or else deliver himself to the next magistrate upon his arrival to undergo an inquisitorial examination, and faithfully disclose where he had been, where he was going, the reason for his journey and so on (Plowden, *History ... 1793*, p. 233). Pigott had attempted to flee England for Switzerland via Harwich in 1793 (Mee, 'bold and free-spoken man'). It is possible that a problem with obtaining a permit was the reason why Pigott had to turn around.

Nefati dies. Days on which judgment should not be pronounced nor public assemblies held – that is, 'unlucky days'. Lord Kenyon (cf. CONSTITUTION), who had been made President of the Court of the King's Bench in 1788, was responsible for outlawing Paine in the trial of December 1792.

Negociation. Pigott may be thinking of the arrangement reached after the NOOTKA SOUND crisis of 1789, which brought Britain and Spain to the brink of war. It was solved when the King of Spain and George III signed a Declaration in July 1790 negotiating the conditions for peace. Less than three years later, the two kings were united in the Coalition against France.

Negro. *The flesh ... fricasseed*: Pigott may draw inspiration here from Swift's satirical suggestion in *A Modest Proposal* (1729) that cannibalism could solve the poverty problems of Ireland, another former English colony. Slaves were used in the West Indies to cultivate sugar cane, and Pigott is possibly alluding to an incident brought to the attention of Parliament on 8 April 1791 during a motion for the abolition of the slave trade. William Wilberforce had on this occasion given an account of an overseer in the West Indies who 'threw a slave into the boiling cane juice' as a punishment, causing his death four days later (*PH* 29, col. 289). The incident became notorious, and Gillray caricatured it in the print *Barbarities in the West Indies* (BMC, 7848).

p. 86

Neighbourly. Pigott suggests that Britain's interpretation of the Biblical Commandment 'love thy neighbour' was to pay enormous subsidies to its Coalition partners in the war with France (see BARGAIN).

slavery to the Poles: See PARTITION.

exterminate the French: See BRUNSWICK.

Nem. Con. From *nemine contradicent* '(with) no one contradicting', used in parliamentary reporting to describe a motion agreed upon unanimously.

Nero. This may refer to an engraving entitled 'Nero' in the 1773 edition of the satire *The New Foundling Hospital for Wit, being a Collection of Curious Pieces in Verse and Prose* (J. Almon).

Nest-egg. A sum of money serving as a nucleus for the acquisition of more. The Cinque Ports were a number of important seaports administered by the same Warden. Pitt was awarded the Wardenship in 1792, which gave him an official residence at Walmer-Castle, gazing out over the Kentish cliffs. In *Jockey Club* III, Pigott describes the administrative post as 'a comfortable little sinecure, between four and five thousand a year, that Mr. P—tt has lately conferred on himself as a corroborating testimony of his patriotic disinterestedness' (p. 62n). In *Letter Addressed to the Addressers*, Paine had called the sinecure of the £1372 paid to Master of the Hawks ludicrous, because 'there are no hawks kept, and if there were, it is no reason the people should pay the expense of feeding them, many of whom are put to it to get bread for their children' (pp. 373–4).

p. 87

Neutral Powers. Before 1793, Britain's official line had been to keep neutral in regards to France. However, His Majesty's Ministers, the ambassadors, worked to secure advantages against the French by helping and supporting loyalist parties and so on. A British embargo on supplies to France was in effect in 1792, before war was declared. In France, where people were starving after a failed harvest, the embargo was seen as a plot to destroy democracy, and Pitt became the focus of much hatred by supporters of the Revolution on both sides of the Channel.

George the Last: Just as Louis XVI came to be 'the Last' in the line of French kings (see NECK), George III was to be the last of British monarchs.

'Villain! Villain!': The exclamation is spoken by St Pol in Act Two of *The Siege of Meaux: A Tragedy* by Henry James Pye (see LAUREAT), which was performed at the Theatre Royal in 1794.

Newgate. *Foot-pads*: The lowest kind of highwaymen, who robbed their victims on foot.

'Clausi in … exigent': Slight misquotation of 14.15.18 from *de Bello Iugurthino* (On

the War with Iugurtha) by the Roman historian Sallust (*c.* 86–34 BC). The passage from which this quote comes is a speech to the Roman senate by Adherbal, son of the tyrant Iugurtha, appealing for help against his father, and is rendered in a modern translation as: 'Of those taken by Iugurtha, some were crucified, others thrown to wild beasts; a few, whose lives were spared, *in gloomy dungeons amid sorrow and lamentation drag out an existence worse than death*' (trans. J. C. Rolfe, *Sallust* [Cambridge, MA.: Harvard University Press, 1965]).

'*Yet think … inflame*': John Gay's 'The Wild Boar and the Ram', ll. 12–13 in *Fables* (1727). Gay (1685–1732) was a political satirist, who collaborated with Pope and Swift in the author collective of the Scriblerus Club.

Newspapers. Several London and regional newspapers were subsidized by the Government to secure positive press (see TO ILLUMINATE).

p. 88

Nick (Old). The Chancellor of the Exchequer was the Scottish Lord Loughborough, who from supporting the Opposition had taken office in Pitt's Ministry.

'*pert prim pleader of the Northern race*': The poet Charles Churchill's description of Loughborough in *The Rosciad* (1761), l. 73. Churchill (1731–64) was a supporter of the radical John Wilkes.

Nick-name. *probi*: 'probity, honesty, uprightness' (*OED*).

Niggard. *Guelph*: George III's family name.

Nim the Cits. '*Nim*. To steal or pilfer: from the German *nemen*: to take' (Grose). '*Ci*. A citizen of London' (Grose).

p. 89

Nobility. Honoré Gabriel Riquitti, Comte de Mirabeau (1749–91). French revolutionary and political leader, who fell out with the Jacobins. During his sojourn in England in 1785, he associated with the English Whigs. His revelations of scandal and intrigue at the Prussian Court in *The Secret History of the Court of Berlin, or the Character of the Potentates of Europe* (Eng. trans., Dublin: P. Burne, 1789) caused concern in the French Government. This was just one example of Mirabeau's persistent denunciations of the abuses under the *ancien régime*. He later published *Gallery of Portraits of the National Assembly* (Dublin: B. Chamberlain et al., 1790), which can be seen as a model for Pigott's vignettes of leading politicians in *The Jockey Club* I–III and *The Whig Club*.

Nobility (privileges of). THE CORINTHIAN … SOCIETY: Burke uses this metaphor in *Reflections on the Revolution in France* to praise nobility as grace to the civil order (p. 245). Paine picked out the phrase for criticism in *Rights of Man*, p. 279.

p. 90

Noli me tangere. Jesus's words to Maria upon his resurrection: 'Touch me not; for I am not yet ascended to my Father' (John 20:17). The general election of 1790 returned a safe majority to the Government, which made Pitt seem untouchable as the political leader of the country. In Parliament, he also enjoyed the benefit of some devoted followers who voted with him on every issue.

Nominative Case. James Harris (1709–81) was author of *Hermes, or a Philosophical Inquiry concerning Universal Grammar* (1751), which was one of the most influential grammars of the century.

Non-Conformists. See TEST-ACT.
   '*Costoro hanno … Palzzo*': 'Such men have one mind in the public square and another in the palace', the Romans' criticism of hypocritical politicians, as quoted in Book I, Ch. 47 of Nicollò di Bernado Machiavelli's *Discorsi supra la prima deca di tito liva* (1531). This work reveals Machiavelli's preference for a republican state.

Nonjurors. Originally, a term used of those members of the Church of England unable to take oaths of allegiance and supremacy to the Protestant William III and Mary for fear of breaking their oath to the Catholic James II. At the end of the eighteenth century, Blackstone wrote that 'Every person refusing the same [oaths of allegiance and supremacy] … is properly called a non-juror, [and] shall be adjudged a popish recusant convict' (*Commentaries*, 4, p. 124). Although some relief was granted on taking an oath of allegiance in June 1791 (31 George III c. 32), the Test and Corporations Acts still barred Catholics from practising at the Bar and from holding anything higher than 'local' government offices.

Nonplus. Cf. DRUNKENNESS.

Nootka Sound. The scarcely populated area of western Canada, which is now Vancouver Island. In July 1789, a Spanish warship took possession of the small British fur station there in order to assert Spanish dominion of this part of the continent. The British response was a full mobilization of the army – an armament which cost £4 million. As Spain received no support from its ally, France, which was in the throes of revolution, they had to back down and pay compensation.

Incidet … Charybdim: 'He falls in Scylla's jaws who would escape Charybdis', a well-known hexameter often ascribed to Virgil, though the exact formulation actually comes from the thirteenth-century poet Walter of Châtillon's *Alexandreid*.

p. 91

Notes (Bank). As a response to the credit crisis of the spring of 1793, when State bankruptcy seemed imminent, Pitt would in March 1793 set into effect a scheme of public credit to help businesses cope with hardships. The Bank of England issued notes of £5 (previously less than £10 had been forbidden). Also bills worth £2 200 000 were issued to increase the money supply. The scheme alleviated the situation but also created a surplus for the Government (Ehrman, *Pitt*, 2, pp. 386–7). In *Treachery no Crime*, Pigott calls this a 'specious, but eventually ruinous circulation of paper' (p. 154). Counterfeiting banknotes, bank bills or any other form of money was a capital offence (Blackstone, *Commentaries*, 4, pp. 88–91).

Novitiate. For Jenkinson and Canning, see JABBER.

Numskulls. '*Numbskull*. A stupid fellow' (Grose). For Ashhurst, see CONSTITUTION. For Rook, see GOWN. For Garrow, see BARRISTER. For *Dunkirk Hero*, see HASTE.

Nuncio. A term originally used by the Roman Imperial forces in their campaigns for colonies.

p. 92

Obedience. Paul Le Mesurier (1755–1805) was born in Guernsey from a family that traced its roots back to Normandy. He was appointed director in the East India Company after his opposition to Fox's India Bill. As a London Alderman from 1784, he also had a seat in Parliament, where he was attached to Pitt's administration. Le Mesurier was elected Lord Mayor of London for the period 1793–94, during which time he became famous for his persecution of radical activities in the metropolis. He defended his alarmist measures in a Parliamentary debate on 4 May 1793 (*PR* 35, pp. 24–7). Pigott may here refer to the fact that Thomas Hardy, the Secretary of the London Corresponding Society, was ordered to be held in custody in the house of John Gurnel, the King's Messenger, from his arrest on 12 May 1794 until he was committed to the Tower on the 29th of the same month. Hardy later said that he was 'civilly treated' by Gurnel and his family (Hardy, *Memoir ... written by Himself* [James Ridgway, 1832], p. 32).

Oeconomy. Cf. Paine: 'As to the Civil List, of a million a year, it is not to be supposed that any one man can eat, drink, or consume the whole upon himself. The case is, that above half this sum is annually apportioned among Courtiers, and Court Members of both Houses, in places and offices, altogether insignificant and perfectly useless, as to every purpose of civil, rational, and manly government' (*Letter Addressed to the Addressers*, p. 373).

One. William Paley (1743–1805) was known for his *Reasons for Contentment Addressed to the Labouring Part of the British Public* (1793), in which he explained that the poor should be content with their station in life, and that they should thank the divine spirit for providing the possibility of dependence. It was published in a number of cheap pamphlet editions during 1792–93, among others by order of the Society for Preserving Liberty and Property against Republicans and Levellers.

p. 93

Opposition. 'The Lark and her Young Ones' is one of Aesop's fables, which was versified in Eaton's *Politics for the People* (7 [1793], pp. 92–5).

Orator. Marcus Tullius Cicero (106–43 BC) was a writer, orator and Roman statesman. His name was often used to denote an eloquent speaker in Parliament. Hence both Burke and Pitt were depicted as the great Roman orator in contemporary prints (see, for example, *BMC*, 6784, 6925, 7138 and 7670).
  by inch of a candle: Expression used to advertise an auction in which bids were received so long as a small piece of candle was burning. The Commons, which met in the Chapel of St Stephens, is here compared to a market place, where dubious bartering takes place.
  '*Happy the man ... them*': Psalm 127:4.

Orgies. See DRUNKENNESS.

Orthodoxy. As part of the system of patronage, many men of influence had a relation, chaplain or former tutor whom he wanted to reward at public expense. Peers, politicians and others thus often took clerical preferment for a friend as payment for their own services to King and Government (Pares, *King George III and the Politicians*, p. 25). For clergymen, appointments depended not only on orthodoxy to the doctrines of the Church of England, but also to the Government. Bishop Horsley (see 'Cast of Characters') is a good illustration of this. On 30 January 1793, he preached a remarkable sermon before the House of Lords outlining the dangers of a revolutionary spirit. In November of the same year, he was translated to the important see of Rochester. Pitt himself notoriously pressured George III to promote his former tutor, George Pretyman, to Dean of St Paul's and Bishop of Lincoln in 1787

p. 94

Ostentation. *blue ribbands, embroidered garters*: See GARTER.

journeys ... excursions: After his recovery in 1789, George III's thanksgiving procession to St Paul's on 23 April was cause for public celebration. The festivities were a triumph for Pitt, with the crowds in London uttering shouts of 'Death of Fox' (Rogers, *Crowds*, pp. 184–8). The royal family owned Gloucester House and four other houses in Weymouth on the English south coast, which they used as summer residences. When the King was seen here for the first time after his recovery, he was carried around the town to a finely decorated esplanade, to much applause and cheering from the crowd.

Oversight. See HASTE.

Overtures of Peace. See NECK.

Outcast. For Dumourier, see APOSTATE. For Cobourg and Clairfayt, see HERO (entry for p. 57).

p. 95

Pageant. *Spanish armament*: see NOOTKA SOUND.

Russian armament: In 1791, Pitt requested extra funds from Parliament to arm against Russia in favour of the Turks, which was the underdog in the war between the two. The dispute was over Oczakow, a fortress on the northern shore of the Black Sea, which Russia had annexed after a siege in 1788. In order to prevent Russia's imperial ambition and maintain the BALANCE OF POWER, Pitt set as an ultimatum the return of the Oczakow to the Turks. This was debated in the Commons in April 1791 (*PH* 29, cols 217, 29). However, there was strong opposition to dragging Britain into an unnecessary war, and Pitt had to retract as his plans were voted down in the House of Lords.

Painite. An adherent to the principles of Thomas Paine.

Mr. Reeves's Association: See ASSOCIATION.

p. 96

Palace. *elegant author*: Paine, who had criticized George III for holding the nation's liberties in 'contempt' (*Rights of Man*, p. 132).

in Spain! ! !: Spain was ruled by the inept and despotic Charles IV (1748–1819), who from 1788 acted as an absolute monarch. The opulence, luxury and corruption of Spanish royalty were notorious throughout Europe.

Pannic. Cf. ALARMISM. The Duke of Richmond was Master-General of the Ordnance and, in January 1786, he had twice brought forward the unsuccessful proposal to enforce the coasts ports of Plymouth and Portsmouth. The fortification projects became a theme of public derision and was memorably ridiculed in the popular satire *The Rolliad*. With the outbreak of war, Richmond did, however, post defensive vessels along the Kent and Sussex coasts; two floating batteries and over fifty gun boats were provided by the end of 1794 (Ehrman, *Pitt*, 2, p. 328).

Pantheon. The Pantheon in Paris was formerly known as the church of St Genevieve. The revolutionary Government changed it to a mausoleum in 1791. It became the resting place for many of the heroes of the Revolution, such as Rousseau, Voltaire, Mirabeau and Marat.

Papacy. In 1789 over 400 monasteries were closed in France. Some 8000 Roman Catholic priests and nuns were given sanctuary in Britain in 1794. Around 1000 of them were welcomed at Winchester by Anglicans, and Catholic institutions were established across the country. For the Pope's interest in the Coalition against France, see ALLY (NEW).

p. 97

Pardon. On the front benches in the House of Commons, the Treasury Bench is seated to the right of the Prime Minister. The reference is probably to Burke, who had taken his seat here in 1792, and whom Pigott believes had accepted a secret pension (see BARGAIN).

'mercy endureth forever': Biblical phrase used numerous times in reference to God in the Old Testament.

Parliament. *Prussia ... not accountable*: See GRATIS.
armaments: See NOOTKA SOUND and PAGEANT.

Parson. *Defender of our faith*: The King of England.
Archbishop of Canterbury: John Moore, Archbishop of Canterbury, supported the
Government's war with France. He was author of the prayers to be read on the Fast
Days declared for victory against the French.

p. 98

Partition. *Royal Gaoler*: Frederick William II of Prussia.
Northern Bear: Catherine of Russia. Both the two royals had annexed large parts
of Poland in the partitions in 1772 and 1793. The Polish constitution of 1791 was
unacceptable to both William and Catherine, who believed that a strong Poland
would reclaim the lost land. Acting as a guarantor of the old Polish regime,
Catherine ordered an invasion in 1792, which was followed early in the following
year by an invading force of Prussian troops. The second partition marked the real
end of Poland as an independent state. Prussia obtained Great Poland, Kujavia,
Torun and Gdansk (Danzig), and Russia took possession of all the eastern provinces
from Livonia to Moldavia. This reduced Poland to less than one-third of its original
size. It was rumoured that that there were similar conspiracies to divide France after
what the Coalition forces believed would be a swift war.

Partition. The Duke of Brunswick was the Prussian Commander-in-Chief, whose
troops were defeated by the French at the Battle of Valmy on 20 September 1792.

Partnership. Roger L'Estrange (1616–1704) was a prolific English Tory journalist and
pamphleteer, who narrowly escaped hanging as a Royalist spy. He was pardoned by
Cromwell in 1653, but, after the Restoration, he continued his service for the
monarchy.
Quere ... bankruptcy: The other European partners in the Coalition against France
received heavy subsidies from Pitt: a total of £833 273 in 1793, and £2 550 245 in 1794
(Gregory and Stevenson, *Britain in the Eighteenth Century*, p. 200)

p. 99

Party Jury. Originally a *jury de mediate linguae*, where half the jury were of foreign
origin. The dissenting minister William Winterbotham was prosecuted for sedition
on 25 and 26 July 1793 at the Exeter Assizes and sentenced to four years'

imprisonment and a fine. An anonymous gift of £1000 reached him afterwards, as conscience money from one of the jurymen (*DNB*).

Patriot. *justum & propositi tenax*: 'just and firm of purpose'.

Patriotism. In December 1792, the Government introduced a bill 'for establishing Regulations respecting Aliens arriving in this Kingdom, or resident therein in certain places', and it passed into law on 8 January 1794. This was one of the alarmist measures against fears of republicans infiltrating Britain and fermenting a revolution. The Bill provided for the registration, deportation and restrictions of the movements of any foreigner who had arrived after 1 January 1792. The Association for Preserving Liberty and Property against Republicans and Levellers published Lord Loughborough's speech for the bill, given in the House of Lords on 26 December 1792, in no. 6 of their publications of cheap tracts aimed at the lower orders (J. Downes, 1793).

p. 101

Peculator. Lines from Shakespeare's *Othello*, III, iii, 162–6.

Peerage. *nomina rerum*: Lit. 'the names of things'. Given the context of the quote, the implication may be that peers are names only with no merit or dignity.
  '******** ... lord': From the satirist Peter Pindar's 'On a New Lord,' l. 399. The poem appeared in *Expostulatory Addresses to a Great Duke, and a Little Lord* (G. Kearsley, 1789).

p. 102

Peers. Adaptation of Burke from *Thoughts on the Cause of Present Discontents of 1770* (*Works*, 2, p. 246).

Pension. In Johnson's *Dictionary*, 'Pension' is defined as 'An allowance made to anyone without an equivalent. In England it is generally understood to mean pay given to a state hireling for treason to his country.' It was ironic, as often noted, that Johnson himself accepted a pension (see HISTORIOGRAPHER).
  Bedlam: The Hospital of St Mary of Bethlehem, specializing in insanity.

Pension. Joseph Addison (1672–1719) was an essayist, poet and statesman, who defended the Whigs in several magazines.

p. 103

Pensioner. In his *Dictionary*, Johnson describes a Pensioner as 'A slave of state hired by a stipend to obey his master'. Alexander Pope's lines are from 'To the Right Hon. Allen, Lord Bathhurst', Epistle III, v, 357–8.

People. Jean Jacques Rousseau (1712–78), French deist philosopher, whose *Social Contract* (1762) became the text-book of the French Revolution. Rousseau projected a republic in which all people are born free and equal. The State should be formed on the basis of a 'contract' in which the people as a whole form the governing body of the democratic State without sacrificing their natural rights. This is accomplished by the dual role every individual plays as both citizen and governing body. Rousseau's text was published as part of Eaton's 'Political Classics' programme (see 'Introduction').

People. *swinish multitude*: See MULTITUDE (SWINISH).

Permit. The entry here may reflect the fact that Pigott had tried to flee to Switzerland via Harwich in September 1793, but had turned around possibly out of difficulties with obtaining a permit (see EMIGRANT (ENGLISH) and NE EXEAT REGNO).

twenty-four electors: John Robinson, MP for Harwich from 1774 to 1803, had, in order to ensure that he was returned for Harwich at the general election in 1790, made changes among the electors of the municipal corporation. This led to a quarrel in the Commons with MP Richard Rigby, who denounced such tactics, declaring that the independent interest in the borough had been overthrown.

Persecution. Eaton, Winterbotham, Muir and Palmer had all been sentenced for spreading seditious propaganda.

p. 104

Perspicuity. General of the British Forces, James Murray (see HERO (YOUNG)), had his letters to Home Secretary Henry Dundas on the progress of the Flanders campaign printed in '*Extraordinary*' editions of the *London Gazette* (an official Government journal) in August and September (see *Jordan*, 4, pp. 529–56).

Petition. Parliament was petitioned by several reform organizations in the early 1790s; none of their demands were met.

Pillory. An ancient instrument of punishment, traditionally used for those who libelled the Government. The most famous pillory in London was located at Charing

Cross. The lawyer John Frost, who was charged with uttering seditious words in May 1793, was placed in the pillory before he was struck off the roll and sentenced to six months' imprisonment.

Placeman. It was integral to the system of Government patronage that positions in the administration were given as a reward for political loyalty to a deserving individual or, on his request, to his family or friends. A 'place' provided a steady income. In *Legislative Biography*, the political commentator Anthony Pasquin provided a long list some of Pitt's own offices and the salaries they yielded as well as those enjoyed by his family connections (p. 16).

Pluralist. Ecclesiastical term for the system or practice of a cleric holding more than one benefice at the same time. As clerical life still attracted young men of the nobility, plurality was encouraged in order to secure them an income equal to their standing.

Poet Laureat: See LAUREAT.

p. 105

Police. See ALARM.

Popularity. *hanging thief*: In 1783, executions in London had moved from Tyburn to Newgate Prison, largely because the vast numbers of people lining the processional route disrupted traffic. The spectacle of executions often attracted up to 10 000 people. When the case had received a lot of publicity, numbers could reach 50 000. Pigott is suggesting that Pitt's popularity, in the context of the bloody war with France, is similarly based on the spectacle of death under the pretence of serving nation and society in a good cause.

p. 106

Precedent. See CONSTITUTION.

Press (the). *'O tempora, O mores!'*: 'Alas for the times and the manners,' from Cicero's *In Catilinam*, I.i.2. This work describes the Cataline conspiracy of 63 BC; see TALE-BEARER.

Press (licentiousness of the). Conservatives abhorred the liberties taken by the radical press, and with the Government's measures of restriction introduced in

1792–93, these were increasingly clamped down on through prosecutions. Pigott was a member of an association called the Friends of the Liberty of the Press, which had been established on 3 June 1791. On 15 June 1792, the Friends held a celebration dinner in honour of the passing of Fox's Libel Act, which took the power to convict accused libellers away from the judges and gave it to the jury. On 13 June, Opposition papers advertised 'reservations' to be made for the dinner with one of the 'Stewards', of which Pigott was mentioned alongside other famous reformers, such as the Earl of Lauderdale (see GRIMACE), Sheridan and James Mackintosh (Werkmeister, *London Daily Press*, p. 358).

p. 107

Princes. Citation from Swift's 'Thoughts on Various Subjects', collected in *Battle of the Books and other Short Pieces*.

Prisoner. In January 1793, the reformist MP Charles Grey had moved for a committee to look into the laws on imprisonment for debt. Debtors who were imprisoned for forfeiting payments petitioned Parliament several times in 1794. A Bill for the Relief of Debtors was passed on 28 May 1794 (*PR* 38, p. 343).

Proclamation. See ADDRESS.

Prudence and Oeconomy. The end of the war with France in 1763 had increased the national debt from £70 million to £130 million (Plumb, *England in the Eighteenth Century*, p. 126). The struggle with the American colonies made it necessary to introduce new taxes and duties, which were responsible for much popular unrest. The taxation levied on the populace is here seen in connection with consistent criticism of Pitt for making allowances for many new sinecure positions.

p. 108

Qualification. All Members of Parliament were men of property unless they were Scottish burgh members or an English member who was not obliged by the provisions of an Act of 1710. To stand as a borough member, one needed an assured income of £300, and a county member twice that.

Queen. George III's economy in the royal household – especially in the kitchen – was to the brink of avarice, and often the subject of mockery, especially since it contrasted with the draining of the public funds which his system of patronage and military aggressions required. Queen Charlotte was seen as even more miserly than her husband, and became the butt for some of the caricaturist Gillray's most malicious satires.

Quorum. That a poor man could be subject to removal from a parish if he was seen to be a burden or did not belong there was much criticized. Cf. Paine: 'In these chartered monopolies, a man coming from another part of the country is hunted from them as if he were a foreign enemy. An Englishman is not free of his own country; every one of those places presents a barrier in his way, and tells him he is not a freeman – that he has no rights ... A man even of the same town, whose parents were not in circumstances to give him an occupation, is debarred, in many cases, from the natural right of acquiring one, be his genius or industry what it may' (*Rights of Man*, p. 126). In an attempt to improve the situation described here, a Poor Removal Bill was brought into Parliament in the spring of 1794.

> *to sentence ... inability of payment*: See PRISONER.
> *knocked down a hare*: See ASSOCIATION.
> *not being worth ... licence*: See GUN.

p. 109

Rabble. See MULTITUDE (SWINISH). In the widely reported summing-up in Muir's trial for sedition on 30 and 31 August 1793, Judge Lord Braxfield had referred to the common people as 'the rabble, who have nothing but personal property'. He also uttered the opinion that 'no attention could be paid to such a rabble' when they petitioned Parliament for reform, for 'What right had they to representation?' (*State Trials*, 33, pp. 229–31).

> *'Sincere, plain-hearted ... groan'*: James Thomson description of the British People in *The Seasons* (1726–30), 'Summer,' ll. 1467–76.

p. 110

Rain. After the good harvests of 1789–92, the yield in 1793 (the most recent harvest Pigott can be referring to) was catastrophic. August and September of 1792 had heavy rainfall, resulting in blackened crops. There was an insufficient produce, and the price of wheat rose. Several counties called for an embargo on export of grain, and bread riots ensued up and down the country. The inches of rain are recorded in *AR* 1793, Chronicle, p. 103.

Rank. Lines from Shakespeare's *Hamlet* III, iii, 36.

p. 111

Ransom. In wars, a fixed rate for exchanging one prisoner of war for another was often settled. A senior officer was therefore normally worth several non-ranking soldiers. Pigott here gives his evaluation of the Duke of York, who was the highest-ranking British commander in the Flanders campaign.

Rapier. The second report of 6 June 1794 from Pitt's Committee of Secrecy stated that the 'London Corresponding Society admit that some of their members have applied themselves to the knowledge of arms', which included firelocks and pikes (a simple wooden staff). The use of pikes in Sheffield was also discussed on the same occasion (*PH* 31, cols 688–97, 743, 891). See 'The Arming of the LCS,' in Barrell, *Imagining the King's Death*, pp. 210–30.

Rara-avis. A person of a type seldom encountered; an exceptional person.

Rascal. Alexander Wedderburn was Lord Chancellor. There is no separate entry on him, as Pigott indicates he had intended. Wedderburn is, however, referred to several times in the present work under his title as Lord Loughborough.

p. 112

Rebellion. *rights of nature*: See EQUALITY.

Recess of Parliament. Parliamentary sessions were remarkably short. When the Commons reassembled on 21 January 1794, it was after an interval of exactly seven months.

Recruit. See INSNARE, CRIMP and NAB.

Reform in Parliament. The Commons received several petitions for relief from trade organizations, debtors and others in need of economic aid in the early 1790s. Pigott implies that a French-style revolution would make petitioning unnecessary.

p. 113

Reeves. A pun on the profession, which was an office with local jurisdiction, and John Reeves, who had acted as Chief Justice of Court in Newfoundland before he undertook to persecute radicals in Britain. Lord Loughborough had given up his place as Chief Justice of the Court of Common Pleas in January 1793 (see DISINTERESTEDNESS). The Scottish Justice Clerk was Lord Robert Macqueen Braxfield, who was responsible for sentencing Muir and Palmer to transportation.

Refugees. See EMIGRANT (ENGLISH).

Regent. A reference to the regency crisis of 1788–89. During George III's illness, the Whigs took measures to install the Prince of Wales as Regent. The Foxites supported his accession to the throne, because his support of the Opposition would mean a change of government. Pitt introduced a bill that would restrict the Prince's constitutional powers (a veto on creating peers and granting places for life, and placing the Royal Household and the King's property in the hands of the Queen). In the Opposition press, Pitt was accused of conspiring with the Queen to rule the country in the King's stead. George III's recovery was announced on 20 February 1789, and the bill was subsequently dropped in the House of Lords only a few days before it would have finally passed.

Refugium. *Brutus*: See ANKERSTROM.

p. 114

Regiment. Pigott cites the Bishop of London, Beilby Porteus (1731–1808), who was an avid writer of prose and verse. His proverb is from *Death*, l. 154

Religion. The verse lines are from Daniel Defoe's hugely popular *True Born Englishman* (1701) I.i.1.

p. 115

Representative. A criticism of the apostasy of the Duke of Richmond and Pitt (see ASSOCIATION).

Representatives of the People. The passage adapts Burke's *Thoughts on the Cause of Present Discontents* (*Works*, 2, p. 288).

p. 116

Requiem. *Berwick upon Tweed*: English town on the border to Scotland. It had status of an independent 'burgh' and had to be mentioned separately in all parliamentary legislation.

Retrograde. See HASTE.

p. 117

Resignation. This could refer to the Duke of Leeds, Secretary of State for Foreign Affairs, who was forced to resign on 21 April 1791 (though allowed to stay until the end of the session in June). He had increasingly come to disagree with Pitt on important issues, not least in the much-criticized armament against Russia (see PAGEANT). The whole Oczakow affair had been engineered by Pitt, who had no choice but to back-pedal when a parliamentary majority came out against the prospect of a war with Russia.

Revolution. The invitation to Mary and William of Orange to rule England in 1688 was given by a faction of Whigs to disrupt Catholic ascendancy (James II) to the English throne.

p. 118

Riot Act. The 1715 Riot Act strengthened the power of the civil authorities when faced with mob riots. It was made illegal for crowds of twelve or more people not to disperse within an hour of a magistrate reading them the Act.

Rival Nation. Britain had armed against Russia in 1791 (see PAGEANT). Catherine, the Empress of Russia, appears on the title-page of the present work as the 'Tigress of Russia' to emphasize her cruelty.

Robbery. See MALEFACTORS.

p. 119

Rope. *Canaille*: In *Strictures*, Pigott explained this word: 'An Aristocratic Epithet used in France, to describe the inferior order of citizens' (p. 74n).
   Swinish Multitude: See MULTITUDE (SWINISH).

Rose. *deluged this country … thirty years*: War of the Roses, 1455–85. Cf. Paine, who criticized the spoils of these monarchical wars, which he recorded as lasting from 1422 to 1489 (*Common Sense*, p. 18). Richard was deposed by his cousin Henry IV because of his arbitrary and factional rule. Richard died in prison.

p. 120

Royalty. *the curse of God Almighty*: Cf. Paine's discussion in *Common Sense* of how 'Monarchy is ranked in scripture as one of the sins of the Jews for which a curse in reserve is denounced against them' (12–15). Stanhope had recently given a speech in the Lords of 4 April 1794, in which he condemned intervention in the affairs of France and read to a bench of bishops a passage from 1 Samuel 8 to prove that kings were a curse to mankind. (*PH* 31, cols 141–7, 198–205).

p. 121

Sabbath. See HICCIUS DOCIUS.
    pay their tribute … Dog and Duck: A reference to notorious haunts where one could find prostitutes.

p. 122

Sacerdotal. Louis de la Vicomterie's *Les crimes des papes depuis S. Pierre jusqu'a Pie VI* (Paris: Au Bureau des Révolutions de Paris, 1792) was a 568-page attack on the crimes committed by the popes throughout history, sponsored by the new Republican administration.

Sack. *Toulon*: See ADVANTAGE.

Sack-cloth. *Pickling*: 'To pickle' was a term for rubbing salt or vinegar on the back after whipping.

p. 123

Sacrament. Gustavus Katterfelto, Highman Palantine and Henry Breslaw were popular healers and mountebanks trading in London. They were accused of charlatanism and luring money out of the pockets of gullible society ladies. Their cures were based on occultist lore, and they all had deep connections with Freemasonry.

Sacrifice. Bernard Mandeville (1670–1733) was a Dutch doctor who practised in London. The authorities denounced his *Fable of the Bees* (1714; rev. edn 1723) as a public nuisance. The citation here is quite in line with the theory that became attached to his name: private vices and luxury are the origin of all public benefits. He set out to describe the true causes of social welfare and progress as based on human self-interest, and thus hypocrisy. Mandeville argued that defenders of classical virtue were hypocrites and led the nation to poverty.

p. 124

Sacrilege. *tenth of produce*: see TENTH.

they toil ... spin: Matthew 6:28, on seeing the kingdom of God rather than occupying oneself with the necessities of life, such as food and clothing.

Sailor. See IMPRESS.

Salute. Henry Beaufoy (1750–95) was MP for Yarmouth, and a friend rather than just a follower of Pitt. The exact nature of the event referred to here is unclear, but it may relate to the fate of the attempts to repeal the Test and Corporations Acts in Parliament (see TEST-ACT). Beaufoy, a Church of England man with dissenting connections, was chosen in 1787 and 1789 to speak the dissenters' case. Pitt allowed him to bring in the motions for repeal, though he himself voted against it. They were twice defeated by a small majority. However, when Fox motioned repeal again on 2 March 1790, the tide had changed; the spread of revolutionary fervour was now more acutely felt. This time, Pitt made an inveterate, alarmist speech in which he warned against weakening the Anglican Church. Beaufoy, who spoke after him, clearly saw his old friend's harshness, on a matter with which he had been so closely associated, as a personal attack (*PR* 27, pp. 155–74).

p. 125

Sans. Unidentified verse lines.

Sans-Culottes. Literally, 'without knee-breeches', denoting the wearer of workman's trousers rather than the genteel breeches. The term was originally used pejoratively to describe those supporting the revolution in Paris. In the British debate, it was often applied to all supporters of egalitarian and radical politics. In *Jockey Club* III, Pigott writes: 'it was an aristocratic term of brutal reproach, applied in derision to the wants and miseries of our fellow creatures. [...] Sansculottes may be literally applied, with equal propriety, to the lower classes of the inhabitant of North Britain [Scotland], where these symbols of slavery (breeches) are dispensed with' (p. 21). After the Scottish rebellion led by Bonnie Prince Charlie was crushed in 1746, the fear of insurrection was so great that a law was passed forbidding Highlanders to wear their traditional kilt, and the bagpipe was banned. Those who did not obey were shot.

Satellites. This plays with the original sense of the word 'revolution', which was from astronomy and meant a return to the point of origin.

518/558: From the end of 1792, Fox and Grey rarely mustered more than 50 members behind them in the Commons. One example of this magic limit was the debate on the King's Speech (13 December 1792). On this occasion, Fox told the Commons that 'We are come to the moment, when the question is, whether we shall give to the King, that is, of the Executive Government, complete power over our thoughts' (*PR* 34, p. 24). In this debate aiming to put Pitt's emergency measures into the context of the whole reign of George III, Fox was defeated by 290 votes to 50. For Dundas, Jenkinson and Windham, see 'Cast of Characters'.

p. 126

Scabbard. See Luke 22:49–50 and Matthew 10:34.

Sceptre. Allegations were made during the Regency Crisis of 1788–89 that Pitt was attempting to usurp royal authority and misuse the Queen's influence to give extended powers to the Cabinet. The lines are an adaptation of Lady Macbeth's words in Shakespeare's *Macbeth*, II, i, 33–5.

p. 127

Scots. The Government ministers Henry Dundas, George Rose and Lord Loughborough hailed from Scotland and are all objects of Pigott's fierce sallies throughout the present work.

whited sepulchres: Jesus's accusation of Jewish scribes and Pharisees of hypocrisy in Matthew 23:27: 'For ye are like unto whited sepulchres, which indeed appear beautiful outwards, but are within full of dead men's bones, and of all uncleanness.'

Scoundrels. *London Coffee-House*: This was the establishment in Ludgate Hill where Pigott was arrested on 30 September 1793 with William Hodgson, also a member of the London Corresponding Society, after they had been overheard speaking seditious words against the King.

Leach: The name of the master of the London Coffee House who 'directly sent for and gave us in charge to a constable' (*Persecution*, p. 7).

Scramble. A play on 'a dish composed of hastily-mixed ingredients,' and the meaning 'a struggle with others for something, or a share of something', often rapaciously or unscrupulously (*OED*).

p. 128

Scrawl. George III signed himself with the initials 'G.R.' (George Rex).

Seamen. Judge Michael Foster (1689–1763) made his mark in legal history with the case of Alexander Broadfoot, who was indicted in 1743 for the murder of Cornelius Callahan, who was a Press-officer (see IMPRESS). Broadfoot had killed Callahan in an attempt to avoid being pressed for the navy. Foster judged that it had been manslaughter, but, more significantly, that pressing was legal, thereby creating an important precedent (*State Trials* 17, p. 1003, and 18, p. 1323).

Season for Reform. See IMMEDIATELY.

p. 129

Seat in Parliament. See FACTION.
 A little ...lump: Corinthians 5:6.

Second-Sight. See BANKRUPTCY.

Secretary of State. Henry Dundas, who as Home Secretary, engineered the persecution of the radicals.

Sedition. *Dreams may be seditious*: This refers to the English statute of Treason of 1351; 25 Edward III has the wording: 'when a man doth compass or imagine the death of our lord the king'. Treason needed therefore not be an open or overt act. The interpretations of this in the Treason trials of 1784 are discussed by Barrell in *Imagining the Kings Death* ('Introduction').

See. See ORTHODOXY.

Senate. 'Honourable', the conventional form of address to a fellow MP in the House of Commons.

p. 130

Sepulchre. See SCOTS.

Sermon. On the insincerity and hypocrisy of priests.

   Black-legs: 'gambler or sharper on the turf or in the cockpit: so called perhaps, from their appearing generally in boots; or else from game-cocks whose legs are always black' (Grose). The implication of a dishonest character is here conferred to priests, also recognized by their black dress.

   'such things … again': An adaptation of William Cowper's lines from *The Task* (1784), on the dreariness of Anglican preaching, Book Two, ll. 407–8.

Shuttle. See MANUFACTURERS.

   to weave … war: From Thomas Gray's 'The Fatal Sisters. An Ode', l. 36.

Sickle. *name of a gentleman*: Anyone entering into a volunteer corps, infantry company in the towns or Yeomanry Cavalry Squadrons in the countryside was addressed by the name of 'gentleman'. In the pamphlet *Reflections on the Pernicious Custom of Recruiting*, published by Eaton, the question is posed: 'Can we help wondering that … so many unhappy wretches should be so silly as to be proud of being called Gentlemen Soldiers?' (p. 6).

p. 131

Simony. The practice of buying or selling a religious post, benefice or other privilege.

Sine-cure. Any job or post that carries a salary but has either very little or no work attached to it.

Slave. A reference to Miguel de Cervantes's *Don Quixote* (1605), in which Don Quixote's 'Trufty Squire' is given governorship of the 'Island' of Barataria.

p. 132

Slavery. Henry Lawes Luttrell, Earl of Carhampton (1737–1821), was Lieutenant-

General of the Ordnance in Ireland. He had inherited a Jamaican plantation and vigorously opposed the abolition of the slave trade whenever it was raised by Wilberforce in Parliament. On 27 April 1792, he asserted that negroes only wanted 'to murder their masters, ravish their women, and drink all their rum' (*PR* 32, pp. 431–7). He vacated his seat in February 1794 – according to his own account, to take up the sinecure office of patent customer at Bristol, which was incompatible with a seat in the Commons.

Sleep. *'Methought … sleep'*: An adaptation of Shakespeare's *Macbeth*, II, ii, 35–6, substituting 'King George' for 'Macbeth'.

p. 133

Soldier. *a distinct order, kept apart*: Cf. the anonymous satirical pamphlet *The Knave Society*, published by Eaton in 1794, which pretended to be the minutes of a fictitious loyalist association, in which it was 'resolved' that soldiers 'be kept a distinct body from the people: that being the surest way of preventing the citizen and the solider from being more intimately connected together; and of preventing the army from possessing the same spirit with the people' (p. 12).

Sovereign. *'clothed … every day'*: From the parable of the Rich Man and Lazarus, Luke 16:19.

p. 134

Sponge. *son of Chatham*: William Pitt, the younger, was son of William Pitt, the elder (1708–78), who had been Prime Minister 1766–68, after which he sat in the House of Lords as Earl of Chatham.

'A sponge … nothing': Unidentified, but there may be an echo of Charles Churchill (who is quoted under NICK (OLD) above) in his political satire *The Candidate* (1765): 'When all men fear'd a bankruptcy of state; / When, certain death to honour and to trade, / A sponge was talk'd of as our only aid; / That to be saved we must be more undone / and Pay off all our debts, by paying none', Book. 4, ll. 493–7.

Spy. Robert Watt (?–1794) was arrested in March 1794 for having concocted a plot, under the auspices of the Edinburgh Friends of the People, to seize the Edinburgh Post Office and Bank and set up a provisional government. He had previously been an informer to the Government, and the charges may have been a ploy to prevent him from revealing national secrets (Barrell, *Exhibition*, p. 45). Watt was hanged on 16 October 1794 for High Treason.

Santon Barsisa: A Persian tale with a Faustian theme.

p. 135

Squire. Swift refers to William Conolly, who was selected ten times for the office of Lord Justice of Ireland and was speaker of the Irish House of Commons from 1715 to 1729. He was a titled gentleman who 'has sixteen thousand pounds a year' (Swift, *Drapier's Letters*, pp. 8, 197). Joseph Damer (or Demar) was born in England in 1630. He bought land in Ireland and set himself up as usurer in Dublin.

Stage. Cf. DULLNESS and LOYALTY.

Standing Army. See ARMY (STANDING).

p. 136

Staple-commodity. The stock phrase used to describe British wool. The troops in Flanders were so poorly equipped in the campaigns of 1793–94 that women across the country sent them flannel garments as an act of charity.

Star-Chamber. A court made up of judges and privy councillors, which was successfully installed under Henry VII. It centralized the judicial system and enforced the law where other courts were unable to do so because of corruption. Charles I, however, took advantage of its privileges to enforce unpopular political and ecclesiastical policies. The Star Chamber was used to persecute dissenters, sentencing them to the pillory and corporal punishment. It became a symbol of conspicuous oppression and was abolished by the Long Parliament in 1641. Pigott draws parallels between the Star Chamber and Pitt's Committee of Secrecy, which was constituted in May 1794 to monitor the correspondence and publications of radical organizations in order to prosecute them.

p. 137

Statue. Anne Seymour Damer (1749–1828) was a classical sculptor who had studied under Giuseppe Ceracchi and John Bacon. She exhibited in the Royal Academy from 1784, and specialized in portrait busts. In 1794, she had finished the commission for the over life-size sculpture of George III, now in Edinburgh Register House.

Statutes. *lex scripta*: The written law.

Stiletto. *St. Edmund, the Jesuit*: Burke (see BARGAIN).
  convenient instruments ... on the floor: See DAGGER.
  'Hic crazy ... cavetto': An adaptation of a line from the Greek poet Horace's *Satires* (35 BC), which originally began 'hic niger est ...' (1.4.85) and translated 'that man is black of heart; of him beware good Roman'.

p. 138

Suborn Witnesses. In *Treachery no Treason*, Pigott writes: 'On Eaton's trial, for publishing Paine's Letter to the Addressers, the evidence on which the prosecution was founded was on the information of a man suborned by the Chief Magistrate ... to buy the pamphlet. The informer with visible reluctance gave his evidence; but he was bound to obey the instructions of his master' (p. 119n).

Substitute. Recruitment of men to the militia was by ballot. Every able-bodied man was obliged to serve, though there were several exceptions. Once balloted, a man could, however, avoid service by paying a fine or providing a substitute. In England, Roman Catholics were by law prohibited to serve in a military capacity. Yet several Catholics were admitted into the militia and volunteer corps (Plowden, *History ... 1794*, p. 140). An Act passed in Ireland in 1793 allowed Catholics to become lower-ranking officers in the Irish division of His Majesty's Army. The absurdity of the situation was discussed in Parliament on 26 May 1794, with contributions by Sheridan and Fox, who denounced the Government's hypocritical stance.

Successor. Pigott sets up a comparison between the popular George III and his successor, the Prince of Wales, who was so unpopular that he was often hissed at in the street.

p. 139

Sugar and Coffee. The increasing consumption in Britain (and Europe) of these goods, which were becoming household staples, entailed the transportation to America of millions of African slaves.

p. 140

Surplice. A large-sleeved tunic of half-length made of fine linen or cotton, which can be worn by all clergy.

Swinish Multitude. See MULTITUDE (SWINISH).
    Jesuit of St. Omer: See BARGAIN.

Sword. *massacre of Glencoe*: William III's victory over the rebel Scottish clan army on 13 February 1692.
    Lexington: The battle of 19 April 1775 at Lexington Green, which marked the beginning of the American War of Independence. English troops were ordered to seize colonist gunpowder stores at Concord. No gunpowder was found, but as a result there were many dead on both sides.
    six-pence a day!: See INSENSIBILITY.

p. 141

Sycophants. Loughborough and Windham both took offices under Pitt in 1794.

System of Courts. Pigott takes up an observation close to that of William Godwin in Book Five, Chapter Five of *Political Justice* (1793) on 'the ill consequences attendant upon this species of government [monarchy], the existence and corruption of courts'. Pigott had quoted Godwin on monarchy and courts in *Treachery no Crime*, pp. 39, 40, 56, 156.
    '*Othello's occupation's gone*': Othello's words on himself after having lost all that is dear to him in Shakespeare's *Othello*, III, iii, 362.

Tale-bearer. 'Mischief makers' (Grose). On 13 December 1792, Windham informed the Commons that there were 'serious and well-founded alarms from the conduct of ... those who had sworn an enmity to all Government'. He informed the House that there had been a 'constant communication between persons in Paris, and persons in London,' and that there 'in every town, in every village, nay almost in every house, these worthy gentlemen had their agents, who regularly disseminated certain pamphlets,' all being part of 'a well-arraigned, methodized plan, for gradually undermining the principle of the British Constitution' (*PR* 34, 45–8).
    Cataline: Lucius Sergius Catalina (*c.* 106–62 BC) headed a group of conspirators, plotting to kill Caesar. His plans were prevented by Marcus Tullius Cicero, to whom the plans had leaked.

p. 142

Tally. A stick or rod of wood marked on one side with notches representing a debt.
  The little boy ... bean: Reference to the folk-tale of Jack and the Beanstalk.
  Dr. Pangloss: The clownish master of 'metaphysico-theologo-cosmolonigology' in Voltaire's *Candide* (1759). Dr Pangloss preaches that the effects of causes are necessarily for the best, thus rendering everything for the best 'in this best of all possible worlds'.

Tartarus. In Greek mythology, the lowest region of the world, as far below earth as earth is from heaven. In some versions, Tartarus was a place of punishment for sinners.

Taxes. *Taxing the light of heaven*: A reference to Pitt's measure of taxing the population according to the number of windows their houses had.

p. 143

Tear. St Hegesippus was a writer of the second century, who Eusebius tells us wrote in the style of apostolic preaching. Eusebius included a list of heresies against which Hegesippus wrote.

Te Deum. *bloody banners*: Military banners carried by the British troops were consecrated.
  Auto-de-fe: [*auto-de-fé*] A public ceremony at which sentences of those brought before the Spanish Inquisition were read, later to be effected by secular authorities.

p. 144

Temper of the Times. *Tempora ...in illis*: 'The times are changing, and we are changing with them', a maxim usually attributed (but wrongly) to Ovid. The pro-slavery MP Earl of Carhampton (see SLAVERY) quoted this line, as what he called a 'little schoolboy Latin', in a Commons debate on the abolition of slavery on 27 April 1792 (*PR* 32, p. 434).

Temple. *residence of legal monsters*: The Temple Law Courts in the City of London.

p. 145

Temporal. *Lay-lords*: Those peers in the House of Lords who were not bishops. Cf. DIVINITY.

Temporize. The quote is from the first of Paine's series of pamphlets entitled *American Crisis*, p. 63.

Tenth. A reference to the hated *tithes*, which was the old feudal right of the clergy to claim one-tenth of all produce and animals within the parish. At the time this right had changed to the payment of monies. The system was not abolished before 1836.

p. 146

Test-Act. Charles II had enacted the Corporation Act in 1661 to purge local government of potential puritan rebels, and Parliament had passed the Test Acts of 1673 and 1678 to halt the creeping Catholicism. They prevented Dissenters from public office unless they agreed to subscribe to a sacramental test. This included the proclamation in a belief of the Holy Trinity. The Unitarians, fronted by the radical preacher Joseph Priestley, petitioned Parliament specifically on this issue

Tetrachy. *Demoberos Basileus!*: 'The king, devourer of the people!' The phrase is from Achilles' enraged speech to king Agamemnon in the *Iliad*, 1.231.

Theatre I – of War. The classificatory list that follows imitates the manner of eighteenth-century natural philosophy. As a satire, it compares with other popular opposition satires, such as the *Cabinet of Curiosities* printed in the *Morning Chronicle* on 10 March 1794. This also parodied scientific discourse, and both satires refer to Carolus Linnaeus (1707–78), the Swedish botanist whose *Species plantarum* (1753) introduced a whole new classification system of plants. Linnaeus's works were brought to England, and by 1788 a Linnean Society was established in London. What follows is a translation of the playful pseudo-Latin:

Class and Order. Men only. No women. [Greek]
Genus and Species. Soldier. Bloodthirsty.
Generic character. He fights and slaughters in return for gold.
Figura ('shape'). Human, and he has a human voice.
Calyx ('outer covering of a flower'). Helmeted, decorated with plumes of a blood-red colour.
Corolla ('the inner set of petals within the calyx'). Oval; with nose, and mouth, and tongue, and mind, and with hair on the chin just like a human being, adorned with two ears, and two eyes.
Cortex ('bark'). Red.
Caudex ('stem and root of a plant'). Legs, arms, and *wearing trousers*.
Stamina ('the pollen producing parts of a flower'). Generally debilitated by cold or humid breezes, as well as by the destructive exhalations of the earth [a play on the English sense of *stamina* as endurance and the Latin plural of the botanical *stamen*].

Pistilla ('the gynaecea of a flower'). Two, loaded with gun-powder and balls [*pistilla* is interpreted playfully as 'pistols'; *cum pulvere* means 'dust' or 'ash', obviously not gun-powder].

Pericarpium ('the wall of a fruit if derived from that of an ovary'). A small bag, filled with cartridges.

Fulcra ('accessory organs or appendages of a plant'). Weapons. Bayonet-fitted muskets; and the dangerous (double-edged) sword out of its sheath [*sine vagina*: Also 'without a vagina' – there is a play on the sexual connotations of the Latin words throughout the sentence].

Habitat. Variable: in the most squalid barracks, and in damp fields.

This shrub [*frutex*: In reference to Latin comedy, also 'blockhead'] is perennial, parasitical [*parasitus*: The 'parasite', is a common role in Latin comedy]; and it is very often found mutilated, e.g. without head, without legs, without arms, &c. It flourishes best in the Christian World.

p. 148

Theatre II – Dramatic. Cf. DULLNESS.

Theologian. At Cambridge and Oxford, it was obligatory for most fellowships and heads of colleges that their holders take Holy Orders after a fixed term of years.

Thousand. An imitation of George III's hurried and abrupt speech, which was worsened by the compulsive speaking which was one of the symptoms of porphyria. The King was an avid hunter, and this is what is on his mind here. He was also interested in agriculture, hence satirists often referred to him as 'Farmer George'. His favourite son, the Duke of York, is seen as a fly-dog, who leads the troops in Flanders like sheep (to the slaughter).

p. 149

Thraldom. 1760 was the year of George III's coronation.

Throne. *Wooden god of Otaheite*: The island of Otaheite (Tahiti) had a profound impact on European imagination at the time. The religion of the Polynesians was described by Captain James Cook in the account of his second voyage in the South Pacific (1785).

p. 150

Thrum. See MANUFACTURERS.

Tick. 'buying on credit'. In 1794, Pitt raised loans worth £11 million (Newmarch, *Loans*, pp. 10–11).

Tomb. *'Come unto … rest'*: Adaptation of Jesus's words in Matthew 11:28.

p. 151

Torture. *Auto-de-Fe*: See TE DEUM.

Tower. The Tower of London, where those accused of High Treason had been imprisoned since medieval times. In early 1794, Thomas Hardy and other radicals accused of treason were interred there for a short period (see HABEAS CORPUS).

Trade. See MANUFACTURERS.

Train-bands. The name for a company of trained militia in England, here applied to ageing society ladies who frequented Georgian parties and other entertainments.

Treason. *Tresilians, Empsons, Dudleys, Jefferies and Scroggs*: Names of judges infamous for their cruelty and harsh sentences. During the reign of Charles II, these men of the law were responsible for sending several of the Whigs fighting against monarchical tyranny to the scaffold on charges of treason (see EFFIMINACY).

p. 152

Treasury. *newspapers under the pay of the Minister*: See TO ILLUMINATE.
   Bench: In 1794, Lords of the Treasury were Earl of Mornington, Viscount Bayham (who was replaced by John Smyth in May that year), Richard Hopkins and John Thomas Townshend. Secretaries were George Rose and Charles Long. Burke had taken his seat on the Treasury Bench in 1792.
   Dominus respondens!: 'the master replying'. The phrase is used several times in the Latin Vulgate Bible.
   Habeas Corpus Act: See HABEAS CORPUS.
   Lottery tickets: See GAMING.
   'nemo omnium gratuito malus est': 'nobody absolutely wants to make the evil without profit'. This is another reference to Sallust (see NEWGATE) – or rather pseudo-Sallust, taken from the second letter to Caesar concerning the Republic (Epist. II, *ad Caesarum de re publica*, 8.3.15).

p. 154

Tree of Liberty – Habitat. Cf. the account of a 'Fete in Honour of Liberty' in *Jordan's Political State of Europe* (1792) of the planting of liberty trees outside the French Parliament: 'The officers of the National Guards and battalion of St. André-des-Arts … requested and obtained leave to march through the House, and after to plant the tree of liberty at the door … The tree we set up brings grateful remembrance: It is an Italian poplar, it comes from the country the Gracchi – from the land of Valerius Publicola – from the spot on which Cato inhaled his first breath. This tree is sacred to Liberty; it is its fate to flourish from one pole to the other, may our sons one day, under the shade of the tree we planted, relate with enthusiastic joy the exploits of the fathers, and the grand era of the Revolution' (1, pp. 183–4).

Trial. *Argus*: In Greek mythology, the beast-son of Arestor, with a hundred eyes, of which he could only close two at a time.

p. 155

Trinity. The holiness of the Trinity was a key issue in barring dissenters from influence (see TEST-ACT). In the wake of the abolishment of church privileges in France as an effect of the revolution, the repeal of the discriminatory Acts became a reformist issue. On 7 March 1792, Fox presented a Petition against the Thirty-nine Articles, 'Where any Person shall deny the Doctrine of the Holy Trinity, in Speech or in Writing' (*PR* 32, pp. 347–8).

Truce. Deliberately faulty etymology; the Latin *trucido* means 'slaughter' or 'killing'. The English word comes from the Middle English *trewes*, *treowes*, pl. of *trewe*, a truce.

Trumpet. Clotho, Lachesis and Altropos were the three Greek Fates who determined human destinies, and their misery and suffering. They were often represented as old women who spun the thread of human destiny, Clotho being its spinner, Lachesis its allotter, and Altropos the one who eventually cuts it.

p. 158

Unction Extreme. A Catholic sacrament for spiritual and bodily health given to the seriously ill.

Uncultivated. There may be a reference here to the loyalist 'Song to the *Tune of Hearts* *of Oak'* with its haunting chorus 'To defend our Old England, Huzza, boys, Huzza', in *One Penny-Worth of Truth* (J. Sewell, 1792), pp. 14–15, which was the first of the series of tracts published by the Association for the Preservation of Liberty and Property against Republicans and Levellers. The tract was discussed by Charles Grey in Parliament on 17 December 1792 for its harsh invectives against the dissenters (*PR* 34, pp. 154–62).

Unenvied. *generosity of the Queen*: See QUEEN.
   economy of … Duke of York: See HASTE.
   economy of the Prince of Wales: See LAVISH.
   'Honi soit … pense': The royal motto 'Evil be to him that evil thinks.'

p. 159

Unhanged. *'vrai gibier du potence'*: The French expression for a 'gallows bird'.

University. The universities of Cambridge and Oxford continued to be the main suppliers of ministers for the established Church, and a majority of their graduates were destined for holy orders. The greatest number of the fellows, as well as almost all the heads of houses, were in priests' orders (Greaves).
   heu! meminisse dolor!: 'Alas! It is sorrowful to have remembered!' Although this is not a direct quote, it seems to play on one of the most famous and much-imitated passages of the *Aeneid*. After the great storm in Book 1, Aeneas cheers his crew with a speech that reminds them that although things may look grim, they will one day arrive at their destined homeland and achieve peaceful rest. At *Aeneid* 1.200, he says *'forsan et haec olim meminisse iuvabit'* ('perhaps one day you will enjoy looking back even on what now you endure'). So Pigott may eruditely appropriate the language but not the sentiments of Virgil.

Unking. See NECK.

p. 160

Unthrone: See NECK.

Uproar. *tempus erit quando &c*: 'there will be a time when …'. Probably another half-remembered allusion to a quote from the *Aeneid*, the rest of which Pigott implies the reader will be able to complete mentally. After Turnus has slain the young friend of Aeneas, Pallas, the victor, despoils his victim of his sword-belt, at which point the narrator laments that this action will come back to haunt him: '*tempus erit, … cum optaverit …*' (10.501): 'there will be a time when he [Turnus] will wish that he could pay a great price for Pallas to be restored unharmed, and will hate this day and its spoils'.

Usurping Power. See PARTITION.

p. 161

Vacation. *Temple*: The Temple Law Courts of London.

Gotham: Village in Nottinghamshire that proverbially was inhabited by fools. In the eighteenth century, the name was often applied to London.

p. 162

Vendible. In concordance with many reformist attacks, *Jordan's Political State of Europe* printed a list in 1792 showing 'the imperfect state of Representation in Parliament' to demonstrate 'the necessity of an amendment'. The list was arranged under the following descriptive heads 'Boroughs which are private property, with the names of the proprietors; Boroughs under particular influence with the names of those who posses that influence [and] … those Borough, whose electors usually dispose of their suffrages to the highest bidder.' Afterwards followed a list of 'the independent Boroughs, Cities, and Counties' (1, pp. 105–10). Before an election, seats could be seen offered for sale in newspapers.

Drake: See HESITATION.

Vice Chancellor. For Lord Kenyon, see CONSTITUTION.

contra bonos mores: 'Contrary to good morals'.

Vice-gerent. 'One acting in place of a superior'. The hyphenation also activates the Latin pun 'vice-doers', playing on *vice* in the sense of 'blemish, fault', and *gerent* for 'it is' (*gerentes* means 'doers', from the verb *gero*, 'to do').

p. 163

Vice-Roy. The Marquis of Buckingham (see HUMILITY) had held the office of Viceroy of Ireland till 1790, when the Earl of Westmoreland replaced him.

Violet. From Shakespeare's *Henry V*, IV, i, 106.
  Jure Divino: 'By divine right'.

p. 164

Volunteer. See ALARM.

War. *'Cry havoc … War'*: From Shakespeare's *Julius Caesar*, III, i, 274–6.

p. 168

Weaver. Cf. BEGGARS. In Opposition satire and other representations, Windham was generally attributed with a resolve to pursue the war with France at the cost of the disruptions of the trade it caused for supply and demand of fabrics and other goods (see MANUFACTURERS). This impression was reinforced when he was made Secretary at War in January 1794.

p. 170

Whigs. The party that came into being in the struggle of 1679–81 to exclude the Stuart Duke of York (later James II) from the throne. In the crisis of 1688–89, which resulted in the Glorious Revolution, they favoured limited monarchy against absolutism. The royal veto was used for the last time by Queen Anne in 1707, thereafter the King only acted officially on the advice of his ministers, who in turn needed the support of Parliament. With the accession of George I in 1714, the House of Hanover came to the British throne and chose a policy of exerting 'influence' on Parliament rather than limiting its powers. The HABEAS CORPUS Act was suspended from May 1794 to July 1795.

p. 171

Woolsack. The name given to the large square cushion of wool, without back or arms, and covered with red cloth in the House of Lords, known as the seat of the Lord Chancellor. Pigott makes irony of the fact that it is said to have been placed in the Lords during the reign of Edward III to remind the peers of the significance and prosperity of the English wool trade. Cf. STAPLE-COMMODITY.

p. 172

World. *Proteus*: In Greek mythology, a prophetic old man of the sea, known as a shape-shifter.

'*O lord thy slippery turns*': From Shakespeare's *Coriolanus*, IV, iv, 12.

p. 173

Wrongs, Public. '*would not … written*': John 31:25; on Jesus's many good deeds.

Cast of Characters

Burke, Edmund (1729–97). Irish statesman and man of letters. Born in Dublin. Entered Parliament at the end of 1765, where he acted as a spokesman for the Whigs. In 1770, he published *Thoughts on the Cause of Present Discontents*, which was an attack on the unreformed Commons, royal patronage and corruption. He criticized the Government's policy during the American War of Independence. He denounced the misuse of power in India by the East India Company, and took a leading role in the impeachment trial of the Governor General of British India, Warren Hastings. By the end of the 1780s, he increasingly disagreed with his old friend Fox and the reformist faction of the Whigs. His *Reflections on the Revolution in France* (1790) was the most influential of the criticisms on the French Revolution. It sold an estimated 19 000 copies and sparked at least 100 pamphlet replies.

Canning, George (1770–1827). Educated at Eton and Oxford before becoming a lawyer in 1790. Canning's uncle was a reformer who brought him into contact with Fox and other reformist Whigs. After a period under their influence, Canning made friends with Pitt in 1793, and as a result was given a place in the Commons for the rotten borough of Newtown. He was appointed Secretary of State for Foreign Affairs in 1796. He later became Prime Minister for a short period in 1827.

Duke of Leeds, Francis Godolophin Osborne (1751–99). Appointed Secretary of State for the Foreign Department by Pitt in 1783. In consequence of the disagreement with his colleagues on the question of the Russian armament, Leeds was forced to resign his post in 1791. He was a fierce opponent of the French Revolution. While speaking in support of the second reading of the Alien Bill in 1792, Leeds proclaimed that he 'would always be so much an Englishman as to believe it unlikely that a Frenchman should be a friend to England' (*PH* 30, 160). Pigott gave vent to his intense dislike of Leeds in *Jockey Club* II, 20–22.

Duke of Portland, William Henry Cavendish Bentinck (1738–1809). Succeeded Marquis of Rockingham as nominal leader of the Whig party. During the Regency crisis of 1788–89, he was suggested as the Whig candidate to the post of Prime Minister. However, he later accepted Pitt honouring him with the Order of the Blue Ribbon of the Order of the Garter. Pitt also helped him in his candidature to the post as Chancellor to the University of Oxford, which he won in 1792. He joined Pitt's Ministry in 1794.

Duke of Richmond, Charles Lennox (1735–1806). Served in the British army and distinguished himself in the Battle of Minden. He entered the Commons in 1756. Richmond criticized Lord North's American policy and supported the colonists. He moved for a reduction in the Civil List spending of the monarchy in 1779. At this time, Richmond supported both annual Parliaments and manhood suffrage. On 3 June 1780, his radical proposals for the reform of Parliament were thrown out of the Commons without a vote. In April 1783, Richmond was invited to join Pitt's Ministry, after which he became an opponent of parliamentary reform. His turncoat policies came under fire from the Opposition after the Government began prosecuting radical reformers from 1792.

Duke of York, Frederick Augustus Hanover (1763–1827). The second son of George III, and the favourite of his father. He was elected as Bishop of Onasburg, Westphalia, when only seven months old, which was often ridiculed in the press. While the Duke campaigned in Flanders, failing to capture Dunkirk and Toulon, rumours quickly reached London that far from enduring the hardships of the field, the Duke put more effort into feasting with his entourage. This was captured in a cartoon by James Gillray, *The Fatigues of the Campaign in Flanders* of May 1793 (*BMC* 8327). The stories of his hasty retreat from the battlefields of Flanders after his defeat also had great currency. He was known for his gambling and was constantly in debt.

Dumouriez, Charles-François (1739–1823) ['Dumurier' was the spelling often used in the British press]. A career soldier who joined the Jacobins in 1789 and was appointed Minister of Foreign Affairs for France under the Girondists in March 1792. In August 1792, he was appointed army Commander of the North and won important victories for France between 1792 and 1793. He deserted to the Austrian side in late March 1793 after defeat at Neerwinden. Plotting with the Austrian Colonel Mack, he attempted to march to Paris with his army intending a military coup against the Girondists, which he had to give up. His defection discredited the Girondists, and their leaders were subsequently expelled from the Convention by the Jacobins. He later fled to Britain, where he was granted a pension in the early 1800s.

Dundas, Henry (1742–1811). Scottish lawyer, who entered Parliament in 1774 and became one of Pitt's closest supporters throughout the 1790s. He was Treasurer of the Navy from 1783, and was a Commissioner of the Board of Control after 1786. He was in effect minister for Scotland, and as First Commissioner for India he controlled the political patronage and military operations of the East India Company. He was made Secretary of State for Home Affairs (1791–94), which also made him responsible for the colonies. As Home Secretary, he co-ordinated the attack on the radical societies, organizing a network of spies and informers for the Government. He was appointed Secretary for War 1794–1801.

Earl Mansfield, William Murray (1705–93). Scottish peer and judge known for his hostility to radicalism. He presided against Wilkes, and was active in the exclusion of this rebel MP from the Commons. In 1777 he passed verdict on the radical Horne Tooke for a seditious libel. He also presided against Lord Gordon after the riots, exhibiting much judicial impartiality. His definition on the law of libel was used until Fox introduced the Libel Act of 20 May 1792, which transferred the decision of conviction from judge to jury. He was an outspoken supporter of war. For this and his 'hereditary and acquired wealth, together with other sinecures', making him 'perhaps the richest individual in his Majesty's dominion', he was criticized in *Treachery no Crime* (115n). Mansfield was in the eyes of many a symbol of the corruption of court.

Earl of Moira, Francis Rawdon-Hastings (1754–1826). Elevated to peerage in 1783 and created Earl in 1793. As a soldier, he had fought bravely at Bunker Hill in 1775. Moira quarrelled with Pitt, and would from 1787 associate himself with the Opposition. He became a close intimate of the Prince of Wales and moved for the amendment of the Regency Bill (1789) in favour of the Prince, which would have brought the Whigs into government. However, he apparently overcame his difficulties with the administration when he accepted appointment as Major-General on 12 October 1793. He was to lead an expeditionary force, which in December was sent to aid the insurrection of the royalists in Brittany.

Earl Stanhope, Charles (1753–1816). He was nicknamed 'Citizen' for his pro-revolutionary stance. He was chairman of the Revolution Society (1788). Having originally supported Pitt's suggestion for parliamentary reform, and having married Pitt's sister in 1774, Stanhope fell out with the Prime Minister after the outbreak of the French Revolution and the Government's instigation of their repressive policies. He was also opposed to the British policy of intervention against France, because 'war is a state so unnatural, so barbarous in itself, so calamitous in its effects so immoral when unnecessary, and so atrocious when unjust' (*PH* 30, 336–8). On 23 January 1794, Stanford also protested in Parliament against the transportation of Muir and Palmer and put forward a motion to prevent their sentences from being carried out.

Eaton, Daniel Isaac (1751?–1814). In 1792, Eaton had moved to London from Hoxton and, like Pigott, joined the London Corresponding Society. He began to sell radical pamphlets and, by mid-1793 he had acquired his own printing press. He became the self-styled 'Printer and Bookseller to the Supreme Majesty of the People', and sustained no less than eight prosecutions between 1793 and 1812 for publishing seditious material. He was apparently also willing to gamble his freedom with the publication of Pigott's highly incendiary *Political Dictionary*. He began the radical journal *Hog's Wash; or, A Salmagundy for Swine*, which was later renamed *Politics for the People*, on 21 September. During its lifetime (1793–94), this was to become a popular vehicle for radical theory and satire.

Fox, Charles James (1747–1806). Known for his skills as and orator and his magnetic personality. During the American crisis, he favoured the independence of the thirteen colonies. He was in opposition to Pitt after 1783, where he was one of the leading Whigs. From the late 1780s, he became the leader of the reformist faction of the Whigs. In the 1790s, he remained opposed to the Government, whereas other Whigs followed the nominal leader, the Duke of Portland, to vote with, and finally join, Pitt's Ministry. Fox was an active supporter of economic and parliamentary reform. He was sympathetic to the events in France of 1789, and throughout the war with France he argued for a negotiated peace. He was also known as a gambler and drunkard often in debt. In *The Jockey Club*, Pigott slated him for his 'aristocratic connections'.

George III (1738–1820). King of Great Britain and Ireland (1760–1820). Detesting the Whig Charles James Fox, he used the India Bill crisis of 1783 to install the younger Pitt as premier. From 1788, he suffered several attacks of porphyria, which led to the regency crisis. He was a staunch opponent of the French Revolution, and became a focus for loyalist sentiments in Britain.

Grenville, William Wyndham (1759–1834). First cousin of Pitt, who entered the Commons in 1782 for Buckinghamshire. In 1784 he was appointed Postmaster-General. He moved with Burke for the Alien Bill, and strongly condemned republicanism. Grenville was a supporter of the war with France, and after he was elevated to peerage in November 1790, he became the leading spokesman for the Government in the House of Lords. He was appointed Home Secretary 1789–90, and promoted to Foreign Secretary in 1791 after the forced resignation of the Duke of Leeds. On 11 July 1794, he took office as Secretary for War.

Grey, Charles (1764–1845). Took a seat in Parliament for Northumberland at the age of 22. A follower of Fox and consistent critic of Pitt. In April 1792, Grey joined with a group of pro-reform Whigs to form the Friends of the People. On 30 April 1792, he brought in a petition in Parliament for constitutional reform, but, on the backdrop of rising alarmism, it was defeated by 256 to 91 votes. He was also unsuccessful with his second attempt on 6 May 1793, when he was defeated by 282 to 41 votes. He was responsible for passing the great Reform Act in 1832.

Hastings, Warren (1732–1818). Administrator in the East India Company, who was impeached in the longest political trial in British history (1788–95). Burke, Fox and

Sheridan moved to impeach him for purely political reasons, making him the symbol of British abuse in India. The trial ended in acquittal.

Hood, Samuel, First Viscount (1724–1816). Having made himself noticed in the West Indies, George III entrusted to him the naval education of his son William. In 1782 he became Peer for Ireland. In 1793, he was appointed Commander-in-Chief of the Mediterranean. When, in August 1793, French royalists offered Toulon to the British, Hood attempted a capture, and continued his mission despite suffering serious blows dealt by the revolutionaries. Eventually he had to withdraw, but only after capturing or destroying 13 battleships, the greatest number before Trafalgar. The following year, Hood displayed similarly aggressive tactics when Corsican nationalists asked him to aid them in ousting the French from their dominion.

Horsley, Samuel (1733–1806), Bishop of Rochester. Horsley was an arch-loyalist who ferociously opposed the repeal of the Test and Corporations Acts. In his *Sermon preached before the Lords Spiritual and Temporal ... January 30, 1793* (J. Robson, 1793), he had made the notorious assertion that the dissenters were more dangerous to the British constitution than French émigré clergy. In the House of Lords, he also spoke in favour of the war with France.

Lord Loughborough, Alexander Wedderburn (1733–1805). Edinburgh-born and educated. A close associate of the hated Lord Bute, but also a supporter of Wilkes. Solicitor-General under the North Government from 1771. He became Attorney-General in 1778. On 28 January 1793, he obtained the great seal as Lord Chancellor. The appointment made him a symbol for politicians who barter principles for position. The ministry also supported his candidature for the Chancellorship of Oxford University, to which he was elected in August 1792.

Muir, Thomas (1765–99). A pupil of John Millar, the republican sociologist, Muir became interested in parliamentary reform. Trained as a lawyer, he often appeared in court on behalf of poor clients unable to pay legal fees. On 26 July 1792, he co-founded the Scottish Association of the Friends of the People. Muir organized a General Convention of pro-reform societies. On the evidence of a Government spy, Muir was arrested on 2 January 1793, charged with sedition, but released on bail. He joined Paine in France to save Louis XVI from execution. Returning to Scotland on 23 August, Muir was arrested the next day and tried before Lord Braxfield and a 'packed' jury. He was sentenced to fourteen years' transportation.

Paine, Thomas (1737–1809). Early in life, Paine was a staymaker, then an excise man, but was dismissed for writing a pamphlet demanding better pay. Crossed to America in 1774, where he wrote the pamphlet *Common Sense* (1776), which with its

500 000 copies sold had an eminent influence on the Declaration of Independence of the same year. Paine returned to England in 1787 to promote an iron bridge he had designed. He made history when he published the most important tract in favour of the French Revolution and against old corruption, *Rights of Man* (1791–92), which was written as a reply to Burke's *Reflections on the Revolution in France* (1791). He had fled to France when he was outlawed *in absentia* at the Old Bailey on 18 December 1792 for the second part of *Rights of Man*, in which he proposed a radical reorganization of society. He became the major inspiration to many radicals in Britain, but his ideas were disliked by many of the more moderate reformist Whigs, and he was burnt in effigy by Church and King mobs on the streets.

Palmer, Thomas Fyshe (1747–1802). An Anglican minister who, influenced by Joseph Priestley, moved to Montrose in Scotland, where he joined a group of Unitarians. He wrote several pamphlets in favour of parliamentary reform and universal suffrage. On the model of the London Friends of the People, Palmer formed a similar organization called Friends of Liberty in April 1792. Its meetings in Dundee were infiltrated by Government spies, and on 12 September 1793 Palmer was arrested and charged with writing a seditious pamphlet, *Dundee Address to the Friends of Liberty*. Palmer was sentenced to seven years' transportation.

Pitt, William, the younger (1759–1806). Entered Parliament in 1781. He was made Prime Minister of Britain and Ireland by George III from December 1783 (when he was only 23). He maintained this position until his resignation in 1801, then held it again from 1804 to 1806. A long-postponed general election of 1784 gave him a majority. He advocated parliamentary reform in 1782–83, and again as Prime Minister in 1785, but failed to secure approval.

Powys, Thomas (1743–1800). From supporting the Opposition, Powys became enthusiastic about Burke's *Reflections* and embarked on a determined battle against sedition. He criticized the Friends of the People and seconded the Royal Proclamation against Seditious Publications in 1792. He also seconded the address in favour of 'a just and necessary war' on 12 February 1793, and opposed Grey's motion for parliamentary reform on 6 May of the same year.

Prince of Wales (1762–1830). Ruled as George IV (1820–30). Incessantly quarrelling with his father, who supported Pitt, the Prince of Wales became the centre of Opposition intrigue. Fox attempted to install him as Regent during George III's illness in 1788–89. The Prince of Wales's debauched lifestyle and luxurious living was a constant embarrassment for the monarchy. Through gambling and other pastimes, he worked up significant debts. In 1787, the King would ask Parliament for permission to make a special provision in the Civil List for £10 000 a year and a capital sum to cover the Prince of Wales's debts. The questions of the ever-mounting debts arose again in 1792 and led to new discussions, but no new provision was made.

Reeves, John (1752?–1829). Lawyer who founded the association for 'Protecting Liberty and Property against Republicans and Levellers', commonly known as the Crown and Anchor Association, from the tavern where it occupied a room. The Association issued an address for the reporting of seditious activities, which it then sought to prosecute. It also undertook an aggressive publication programme of loyalist propaganda.

Savile, George, Marquess of Halifax (1633–95). A favourite in the court of Charles II, who became privy counsellor in 1672. Falling out of favour with the Catholic James II, he came to head the faction of patriots who invited William and Anne of Orange to take the throne in 1688. He was made Lord Privy Seal immediately after William's ascension to the throne. Halifax is seen as a figure of moderation, who stood by James as long as any man reasonably could, and only brought William to the throne when this was the only chance of securing peace in the country.

Sheridan, Richard Brinsley (1751–1816). Born in Dublin, but moved to London as a young boy. Sheridan wrote several plays. His *The Rivals*, first performed at Covent Garden in 1775, became a very popular comedy. In 1776, he entered into a partnership of buyers who purchased the Drury Lane Theatre for £35 000, where he produced his most popular comedy, *The School for Scandal*, in 1776. Having made friends with Fox, Sheridan became MP for Stafford in 1780. He was appointed Under Secretary for Foreign Affairs in 1782 under the Marquis of Rockingham. Throughout the 1780s and 1790s, Sheridan supported reform and spoke against the war with France and the Government's alarmist policies. In *The Jockey Club*, he was, despite his 'pursuit of voluptuous enjoyments ... and frequent bacchanalian sacrifices', held in high regard by Pigott, who wrote that 'he will be adored while living, and his name enrolled on the register of immortality, amongst the most distinguished patriots and benefactors of mankind' (I, 59–63).

Steele, Thomas (1753–1823). Privy Councillor and member of the Board of Control. He had shared the Treasury along with George Rose until 1791, when he was forced to resign due to an election scandal. He became joint Paymaster General of the forces in 1791, and was a steady supporter of old corruption.

Wilberforce, William (1759–1833). A friend of Pitt from his time at the University of Cambridge, and one of his staunchest supporters in Parliament. In 1784 Wilberforce was converted to Evangelical Christianity, and joined the Clapham Sect, a group of evangelical Anglicans who gathered at the Clapham Church in London. As a result of this conversion, Wilberforce procured a royal proclamation against vice in 1787 and became a social reformer. On 12 May 1789, he made his first speech against the slave trade, which he fought hard against for the rest of his life. Wilberforce had an equal hatred of the French Revolution and the lapse he saw in British morals, which typified the voting behaviour of the Evangelicals.

Windham, William (1750–1810). Elected to Parliament in 1784, he was a Whig and friend of Edmund Burke, whom he assisted in the impeachment of Warren Hastings. In the 1790s, he took the side of Burke against Fox on matters of the war and domestic radicalism. He was made Pitt's Secretary at War in January 1794. His apostasy earned him the nickname 'Weathercock Windham'.

Winterbotham, William (1763–1829). Dissenting minister, who had preached two sermons for which he was prosecuted for sedition on 25 and 26 July 1793 at the Exeter assizes court. He was found guilty and sentenced to 'four years imprisonment' and '£100 fine' (*State Trials*, 22:848). On 27 November, he was sentenced to four years' imprisonment and a fine. His trial, as well as the two sermons for which he was charged, were published in 1794.

Bibliography

Works of Reference

Baylen, Joseph O. (ed.) (1979), *Biographical Dictionary of Modern Radicals*, vol. 1, Sussex: Harvester Press.

Blackstone, William (1793–95), *Commentaries on the Laws of England*, London: T. Cadell.

Foss, E. (1870), *A Biographical Dictionary of the Judges of England … 1066–1870*, London: J. Murray.

Mitchell, B. R. and Deane, P. (eds) (1976), *Abstract of British Historical Statistics*, Cambridge: Cambridge University Press.

Namier, L. and Brook, J. (eds) (1985), *The House of Commons 1754–1790*, 3 vols, London: Secker & Warburg.

Scott, S. F. and Rothaus, B. (eds) (1985), *Historical Dictionary of the French Revolution, 1789–1799*, Westpoint, CT: Greenwood Press.

Thorne, R. G. (ed.) (1986), *The House of Commons 1790–1820*, 5 vols, London: Secker & Warburg.

Venn, J. A., (ed.) (1953) *Alumni Cantabrigienses: A Biographical List*, Part 2, Cambridge: Cambridge University Press.

Editions and Anthologies of Eighteenth-Century Material

Aspinall, Arthur (ed.) (1962–70), *The Later Correspondence of George III*, 5 vols, Cambridge: Cambridge University Press.

——— (1963–71), *The Correspondence of George Prince of Wales 1770–1812*, 8 vols, London: Cassell.

Burke, Edmund (1986) *Reflections on the Revolutions in France, and on the Proceedings in Certain Societies in London Relative to that Event* (1790), C. C. O'Brien (ed.), London: Penguin Books.

——— (1803) *Works*, London: F. C. and J. Rivington.

Davis, Michael (ed.) (2002), *London Corresponding Society 1792–1799*, 6 vols, London: Pickering and Chatto.

Dobson, H. A. (ed.) (1904), *Diary and Letters of Madame d'Arblay*, 6 vols, Macmillan.

Farington, Joseph (1979), *The Diary of Joseph Farington*, K. Garlick and A. MacIntyre (eds), vol. 3, New Haven, CT: Paul Mellon.

Halifax, George Savile (1969), *Complete Works*, J. P. Kenyon (ed.), London: Penguin.

Hill, Draper (ed.) (1976), *The Satirical Etchings of James Gillray*, New York: Dover Publications.

Hunter, W. W. (ed.) (1868), *Annals of Rural Bengal*, 7th edn, London: Broomhill House.

Johnson, Samuel (1990), *Johnson's Dictionary of the English Language*, facsimile of 1775 edn, 2 vols, Harlow: Longman.

Paine, Thomas (1995), *Common Sense* (1776), *American Crisis I* (1776), *Rights of Man* (1791–92), *Letter Addressed to the Addressers on the Late Proclamation* (1792), in M. Philp (ed.), *Rights of Man, Common Sense and Other Political Writings*, Oxford: Oxford University Press.

—— (1945), *The Complete Writings of Thomas Paine*, Philip S. Foner (ed.), 2 vols, New York: Citadel Press.

Pitt, William (1806), *The Speeches of the Rt. Hon. William Pitt*, W. S. Hathway (ed.), 4 vols, London: n.p.

Sainty, J. C and Bucholz, R. O. (eds) (1997), *Officials of the Royal Household 1660–1837*, London: University of London.

Swift, Jonathan (1941), *Drapier's Letters and other Works*, H. Davis (ed.), Oxford: Blackwell.

Thale, Mary (ed.) (1983), *Selections from the Papers of the London Corresponding Society 1792–1799*, Cambridge: Cambridge University Press.

Wollstonecraft, Mary (1994), *Political Writings*, Janet Todd (ed.), Oxford: Oxford University Press.

Secondary Literature

Alger, John G. (1889), *Englishmen in the French Revolution*, London: Sampson Low.

Aspinall, Arthur (1949) *Politics and the Press, c. 1780–1850*, London: Home and Van Thal.

Ayling, Stanley (1972), *George III*, London: Collins.

Barrell, John (2000), *Imagining the King's Death: Figurative Treason, Fantasies of Regicide 1793–1796*, Oxford: Oxford University Press.

—— (ed.) (2001), *'Exhibition Extraordinary!!' Radical Broadsides of the Mid 1790s*, Nottingham: Trent Editions.

Bewley, Christina and Bewley, David (1998), *Gentleman Radical: A Life of John Horne Tooke, 1736–1812*, London: Tauris Academic Studies.

Black, Jeremy (2001), *British Diplomats and Diplomacy 1688–1800*, Exeter: University of Exeter Press.

Black, Robert (1891), *The Jockey Club and its Founders*, London: Smith et al.

Burtt, Shelley (1992). *Virtue Transformed: Political Argument in England 1688–1740*, Cambridge: Cambridge University Press.

Butler, Marilyn (1999) 'Antiquarianism (Popular)', in McCalman, I. et al. (eds), *Romantic Age: British Culture since 1776–1832*, Oxford: Oxford University Press.

Cameron, David Kerr (2001) *London's Pleasures: From Restoration to Regency*, Gloucestershire: Sutton Publishing.

Caretta, Vincent (1990), *George III and the Satirists from Hogarth to Byron*, Athens, GA, and London: University of Georgia Press.

Davis, Michael (1999), '"Good for the Public Example": Daniel Isaac Eaton and Prosecution, Punishment and Recognition, 1793–1812', in Davis, M. (ed.), *Radicalism and Revolution in Britain 1775–1848, Essays in Honour of Malcolm I. Thomis*, Basingstoke: Macmillan, pp. 110–32.

De Barri, Kinsman (1974), *The Bucks and Bawds of London Town*, London: Leslie Frewin.

DeMaria, Robert Jr (1986), *Johnson's Dictionary and the Language of Learning*, Chapel Hill, NC, and London: University of North Carolina Press.

Duffy, Michael (1996), 'William Pitt and the Origins of the Loyalist Association Movement of 1792', *Historical Journal* **39**, pp. 943–62.

—— (2000), *The Younger Pitt*, Harlow: Longman.

Dwindiddy, J. R. (1992), 'The Early Nineteenth-Century Campaign against Flogging in the

Army', in Dwindiddy, J. R. (ed.), *Radicalism and Reform 1780–1850*, London: Hambledon Press, pp. 125–48.

Ehrman, John (1983–84), *The Younger Pitt*, London: Constable, vols 1–2.

Emsley, Clive (1979), *British Society and the French Wars 1793–1815*, London: Macmillan.

—— (1983), 'The Military and Popular Disorder in England 1790–1801', *Journal of the Society for Army Historical Research* **61**, pp. 10–21 and 97–112.

Ewen, L'Estrange (1932), *Lotteries and Sweepstakes: An Historical, Legal, and Ethical Survey of Their Introduction, Suppression and Re-Establishment in the British Isles*, London: Heath Cranton.

Ford, John (1971), *Prizefighting, the Age of Regency Boximania*, Newton Abbot: David and Charles.

Fortescue, J. W. (1906), *A History of the British Army*, vol. 4, London: Macmillan.

Frow, Edmund and Frow, Ruth (1981), 'Charles Pigott and Richard Lee: Radical Propagandists', *Bulletin of the Society for Studies in Labour History* **42**, pp. 32–5.

Fry, Michael (1992), *The Dundas Despotism*, Edinburgh: Edinburgh University Press.

Greaves, R. (1986), 'Religion in the University, 1715–1800', in Sutherland, L. S. and Mitchell, L. G. (eds), *The History of the University of Oxford*, Vol. 5, Oxford: Clarendon Press, pp. 401–24.

Gregory, Jeremy and Stevenson, John (2000), *Britain in the Eighteenth Century, 1688–1820*, London and New York: Longman.

Harling, Philip (1996) *The Waning of 'Old Corruption': The Politics of Economical Reform in Britain 1779–1846*, Oxford: Clarendon Press.

Hay, Douglas (1977), 'Property, Authority and the Criminal Law', in Hay, D. et al., *Albion's Fatal Tree: Crime and Society in Eighteenth-Century England*, London: Penguin.

Heaney, Peter (ed.) (1995) 'Introduction', in *An Anthology of Eighteenth-Century Satire*, Lewiston: Edwin Mellen Press.

Kenyon, George T. (1873), *The Life of Lloyd, the first Lord Kenyon, Lord Chief Justice of England*, London: n.p.

Leedham-Green, Elisabeth (1996), *A Concise History of the University of Cambridge*, Cambridge: Cambridge University Press.

Levi, Leon (1880), *History of British Commerce*, 2nd edn, London: J. Murray.

Lucas, John. (1996), *Writing and Radicalism*, London: Longman.

Mee, Jon (forthcoming), '"A bold and free-spoken man": The Strange Case of Charles Pigott', in Wormersley, D. (ed.), *The Culture of Radicalism*, University of Delaware Press.

—— (forthcoming), 'Libertines and Radicals in the 1790s: The Strange Case of Charles Pigott', in O'Connel, L. and Cryle, P. (eds), *Libertine Enlightenment, Sex, Liberty, and Licence in the Eighteenth Century*, Basingstoke: Palgrave.

Mitchell, Linda C. (2001), *Grammar Wars: Language as Cultural Battlefield in Seventeenth and Eighteenth-Century England*, London: Ashgate.

Munsche, P. B. (1981), *Gentlemen and Poachers: The English Game Laws 1671–1831*, Cambridge: Cambridge University Press.

Murray, Venetia (1999), *High Society in the Regency Period 1788–1830*, London: Penguin.

Newmarch, William (1855), *The Loans raised by Mr. Pitt during the First French War 1793–1801*, London: Effingham Wilson.

Pares, Richard (1967), *King George III and the Politicians*, London: Oxford University Press.

Pickering, Samuel F. (1981), *John Locke and Children's Books in Eighteenth-Century England*, Knoxville, TN: University of Tennessee Press.

Pigott, Harriet (1832), *The Private Correspondence of a Woman of Fashion*, 2 vols, London: H. Colburn and R. Bentley.

Plowden, Francis (1794), *A Short History of the British Empire during the Last Twenty Months; viz From May 1792 to the Close or the Year 1793*, London: J. Robinson.

—— (1795), *A Short History of the British Empire during the Year 1794*, London: J. Robinson.

Plumb, John Harold (1950), *England in the Eighteenth Century*, Harmondsworth: Penguin Books.

Pocock, Tom (1996), *A Thirst for Glory: The Life of Admiral Sir Sidney Smith*, London: Aurum Press.

Reddick, Allen (1996), *The Making of Johnson's Dictionary 1746–1773*, Cambridge: Cambridge University Press.

Rogers, Nicholas (1993), 'Pigott's Private Eye: Radicalism and Sexual Scandal in Eighteenth-Century England', *Journal of the Canadian Historical Association*, new series, **4**, pp. 247–59.

—— (1998), *Crowds, Culture, and Politics in Georgian Britain*, Oxford: Clarendon Press.

Rose, J. Holland (1922), *Lord Hood and the Defence of Toulon*, Cambridge: Cambridge University Press.

Rosenberg, Daniel, (1991), '"A New Sort of Logick and Critick": Etymological Interpretation in Horne Tooke's *The Diversions of Purley*', in Burke, P. and Porter, R. (eds), *Language, Self and Society: A Social History of Language*, Cambridge: Polity Press, pp. 300–327.

Smith, Olivia (1984), *The Politics of Language 1791–1819*, Oxford: Clarendon Press.

Sur, A. K. (1963), *History and Culture of Bengal*, Calcutta: Chuckervetti and Chatterjee.

Thompson, E. P. (1980), *The Making of the English Working Class*, London: Gollancz.

—— (1978), 'Eighteenth-Century Society: Class Struggle without Class', *Social History* **3**, pp. 133–65.

Thompson, Laura (2000), *Newmarket from James I to the Present Day*, London: Virgin.

Urstadt, Tone Sundt (1999), *Sir Robert Walpole's Poets: The Use of Literature as Pro-Government Propaganda, 1721–42*, Newark and London: Associated University Presses.

Wardroper, John (1973), *Kings, Lords and Wicked Libellers: Satire and Protest 1760–1837*, London: John Murray, 1973.

Webster, J. Clarence (1924), *Brook Watson, Friend of the Loyalists: First Agent of New Brunswick in London*, Sackville, New Brunswick: Mount Allison University.

Werkmeister, Lucyle (1963), *London Daily Press, 1772–1792*, Lincoln, NE: University of Nebraska Press.

White, T. H. (2000), *The Age of Scandal*, London: Penguin.